DATE DUE

MAY 1 3 2012	
SEP 2 2 2015	
DEC 0 1 2015	

BRODART, CO.   Cat. No. 23-221

WHITE BREAD

WHITE BREAD

A Social History of the Store-Bought Loaf

Aaron Bobrow-Strain

BEACON PRESS, BOSTON

Beacon Press
25 Beacon Street
Boston, Massachusetts 02108-2892
www.beacon.org

Beacon Press books
are published under the auspices of
the Unitarian Universalist Association of Congregations.

15   14   13   12   8   7   6   5   4   3   2   1

This book is printed on acid-free paper that meets the uncoated paper
ANSI/NISO specifications for permanence as revised in 1992.

Text design by Wilsted & Taylor Publishing Services

Portions of chapter 5 originally appeared as "Making White Bread by
the Bomb's Early Light: Anxiety, Abundance, and Industrial Food Power
in the Early Cold War," *Food and Foodways* 19, nos. 1–2 (February 2011):
74–97 (a Taylor & Francis publication).

Lyrics from "White Trash Manifesto" by Crimson Spectre reprinted courtesy of
Magic Bullet Records.

Library of Congress Cataloging-in-Publication Data
Bobrow-Strain, Aaron.
White bread : a social history of the store-bought loaf / Aaron Bobrow-Strain.
p. cm.
Includes bibliographical references and index.
ISBN 978-0-8070-4467-4 (hardcover : alk. paper)
1. Bread—Social aspects 2. Bread—United States—History. 3. Bread industry—
United States—History. I. Title.
GT2868.2.B63 2012
641.81'509—dc23   2011032529

*'Tis a little wonderful . . .
the strange multitude of
little Things required in . . .
Providing [and] Producing . . .
this one Article of Bread.*

Daniel Defoe, *Robinson Crusoe*

CONTENTS

PREFACE

*And which side does an object turn toward dreams? . . . It is the
side worn through by habit and patched with cheap maxims.*

—Walter Benjamin

IS THIS STUFF EVEN FOOD?

Supermarket white bread can pick up difficult bits of broken glass,
clean typewriter keys, and absorb motor oil spills. Squeezed into a
ball, it bounces on the counter. Pressed into my palate and revealed
in a big gummy grin, it gets giggles from my kids, who can also use it
to sculpt animal shapes. But should they eat it? Among its two dozen
ingredients, the loaf on my desk contains diammonium phosphate,
a yeast nutrient and flame retardant produced when ammonia and
phosphoric acid react. Is this stuff even food?

Be careful how you answer that question. Perhaps more than any
other food in the United States, what you think of sliced white bread
says a lot about who you are. Over the past hundred years, it has
served as a touchstone for the fears and aspirations of racial eugenicists, military strategists, social reformers, food gurus, and gourmet
tastemakers. The 1960s counterculture made white bread an icon
of all that was wrong with *Amerika*, and 1970s style arbiter Diana
Vreeland famously proclaimed, "People who eat white bread have
no dreams"—by which she meant that they don't dream the right
dreams, the up-to-date, hip dreams. Because, through its long history,
few foods have embodied so *many* dreams as industrial white bread,
particularly during times of recession, war, and social upheaval.

In writing this book, I set out to uncover the social dreams (and
nightmares) played out in battles over industrial white bread. I wanted

to understand how one food could inspire so much affection and so much animosity; how something so ordinary could come to symbolize both the apex of modern progress and the specter of physical decay, the promise of a better future to come *and* America's fall from small-town agrarian virtue. And I wanted to know how those battles over bread shaped America and its fraught relationship with food.

This turned out to be quite difficult. As important as it has been—both as sustenance and symbol—bread is not something that typically gets written about in diaries, described in letters, or remembered in oral histories. As social reformer Eleanor Bang reflected in 1951: "Bread? Of course. There it is for breakfast, for lunch, for dinner in a rhythm as regular as the ticking of our electric clocks—so regular we'd notice it only if it stopped."[1] Unlike other bewitching icons of industrial eating that mark the past century and a half—unlike Twinkies, TV dinners, Jell-O, and Jet-Puffed anything—bread was, and is, just bread. Of course. Industrial white bread may have been as much a marvel of modern industry and space age food chemistry as any other product, but it was also the ultimate background food, rarely discussed—except when it went wrong.

As a result, uncovering bread's place in American society required wide-ranging and creative detective work. My sources range from the letters of early twentieth-century food reformers to the records of Allied occupation forces in postwar Japan (detailing how teaching Japanese schoolchildren to eat white bread would improve their "democratic spirit"). Finding this material took me to far-flung libraries and archives where I read the personal papers of social reformers, advertising executives, food scientists, and industrial designers as well as the records of numerous government agencies. I traced the early history of industrial baking at the Brooklyn and New York historical societies, and spent a week in Manhattan (Kansas) immersed in the archives of the country's oldest baking science school. I visited Chillicothe, Missouri (the "Home of Sliced Bread"), and Mexico City (the home of Grupo Bimbo, one of the world's most powerful industrial baking conglomerates). Then I pored over more than a hundred years of bread advertisements and women's magazine advice columns. Perhaps most importantly, small-town newspapers, consumer marketing studies, oral histories, and community cookbooks provided invaluable insight into the silent space between expert advice and daily diet. And, through all this, I began to understand that dreams of good bread and fears of bad bread are not innocent. They channel much bigger social concerns.

This is a book about one commodity—industrial white bread—that has played an incredibly important, and largely unnoticed, role in American politics, diet, culture, and food reform movements, but it is not another story of how one food "saved the world." Rather, it's a history of the countless social reformers, food experts, industry executives, government officials, diet gurus, and ordinary eaters who have thought that getting Americans to eat the right bread (or avoid the wrong bread) could save the world—or at least restore the country's moral, physical, and social fabric. Sadly, this turned out to be the difficult story of how, time and time again, well-meaning efforts to change the country through its bread ended up reinforcing forms of race, class, and gender exclusion—even when they also achieved much-needed improvements in America's food system.

Anyone paying attention to the rising cries for slow, local, organic, and healthy food today—the growing demands for food justice and restored community that mark our own exciting moment—will find the trials and tribulations of 150 years of battles over bread surprisingly contemporary. In them, you will see all the contradictory expressions of our own food concerns: uplifting visions of the connection between good food and healthy communities, insightful critiques of unsustainable status quos, great generosity of spirit, and earnest desires to make the world a better place—but also rampant elitism, smug paternalism, misdirected anxieties, sometimes neurotic obsessions with health, narrow visions of what counts as "good food," and open discrimination against people who choose "bad food." Fluffy white industrial bread may be about as far from the ideals of slow, local, organic, and health food reformers as you can get today. But, in many ways, we owe its very existence to a string of just as well-meaning efforts to improve the way America ate. Perhaps learning this history can help us avoid the pitfalls of the past.

INTRODUCTION: BREAD AND POWER

THE BREAD QUESTION

I don't remember exactly when my bread baking crossed the line from hobby to obsession. The time I nearly destroyed my oven by lining it with construction bricks might have been a warning sign. Maybe it was when bubbling, microbe-oozing jars of sourdough starter crowded out the food in my fridge. I'm not sure. But I do remember exactly when I first thought about the political life of bread.

Twenty-five and living in Tucson, I had agreed in a fit of hubris to bake twenty large loaves of French country bread for a friend's wedding. I had one cheap oven and no electric mixer. This was the mid-1990s and my friends and I were working as activists and community volunteers. "Low-paid" wouldn't quite do justice to our income bracket—the wedding dinner would be soup and bread. Lots of bread. I was making the soup too, but, in my mind, everything depended on the bread. The bread would turn a soup course into a meal. A kind of leavened alchemy would complete the table; simplicity would become celebration.

The bride and groom were devout Christians, and bread radiated spiritual connection for them. For me, it evoked community and sharing. The word "companion" itself came into English from the Latin roots *com* and *pan*—"with bread." To share bread, I thought, was to tap some ancient chord of togetherness. I wanted to knead all that sweet, golden emotion into my dough, and got myself up at three a.m. to do it.

By afternoon my thoughts had darkened. With only soup and

bread on the wedding menu, I could not let the bread supply fail. The clock was ticking on twenty loaves, and, as finishing on time seemed less and less possible, visions of fellowship turned to cold calculation. If one emotion has defined humans' relation to food over the millennia, I thought as the dinner hour loomed, it's not pleasure or companionship. It's anxiety. And if there is one food that has crystallized anxiety about food, across much of the world and in many different eras, it is bread.

I had only a slim grasp on world food history back then, but it was enough to know that unpopular bakers—maybe even ones who didn't finish bread on time for important weddings—were wont to find themselves the subject of mob violence, late-night beatings, and unexpected ambushes. When the groom poked his head into my apartment "just to see how things are going," I could only think of an old English engraving I had seen somewhere. It pictured a pair of bakers confined in wooden stocks surrounded by townspeople, jeering and brandishing hooks. The complete inscription escaped me, but there was definitely something in it about preparing a hemp noose for "the Jolly Oven-Rakers."

I wondered how many loaves short on their wedding order those bakers had been to deserve such treatment. Do they hang bakers in Tucson?

My brick-lined oven fit only two loaves at a time and it had been cranking on high for six hours. Rick, my upstairs neighbor, lurked outside my open apartment door, dropping casual comments along the lines of "Boy, is it hot upstairs," "I can't figure out why my air-conditioner can't keep up today," and "My floor sure seems hot to the touch today." "By the sweat of your brow you will eat your bread until you return to the ground," I may or may not have quoted back at him.

In the end, however, I had twenty loaves ready just in time for dinner. They weren't cool enough to develop a full flavor, but they were crisp-crusted and filled with bright holes. Time, temperature, and the sugar magic of *Saccharomyces cerevisiae* had turned pallid lumps of flour, water, and salt into something transcendent.

The soup, on the other hand, was terrible. If I didn't get stoned or clapped in irons, it was thanks only to the bread.

• • •

These may sound like the ravings of a sleep-deprived baker, but as I would learn years later, the details bore me out. There is a reason why the word "bread" means "food in general" in so many languages and why it has carried so much weight for so many people. "The bread question"—how to make bread, whether there is enough, how much it costs, and whether it is good enough—has haunted social and political life for millennia.[1]

Despite the appeal of meat-centered "caveman diets" among denizens of the twenty-first century, even our late Paleolithic ancestors made something like bread. Since then, the lives of large swathes of the world's population have depended on it. The world's first class structures formed around bread distribution. Armies marched with it and formal religious ritual revolved around it. If I was desperately scrambling because I thought bread was important for a wedding celebration in Tucson, at least I had very good company.

Archeological evidence from Italy, Russia, and the Czech Republic suggests that people were grinding plants into flour to make crude flat breads as early as 28,000 BCE. By 11,000 BCE, emmer and einkorn wheat along with barley were cultivated across Mesopotamia, Anatolia, and the Levant (modern-day Iraq, Turkey, Syria, Lebanon, Jordan, and Israel). There, Neolithic groups in the gray zone between hunter-gathering and settled agriculture subsisted largely on gritty bread cakes baked on hearthstones or in hot ashes.[2]

Although the degree to which bread formed the central component of human diet varied greatly by region, epoch, and social hierarchy, the biblical proverb simply didn't hold up even in the time and place of its writing: man *did* subsist on bread alone, or at least fairly close to it in the ancient Middle East. Around 2500 BCE, Gilgamesh, god-king of the Sumerians and hero of the world's first great epic literature, was described sitting down to what was probably one of the most common meals for kings and serfs alike for the better part of four millennia from North Africa to the steppes of Russia, from Egypt to the Indus River: bread and beer, both made from the same base of fermented barley dough.[3]

Not surprisingly, the bread supply has long been a crucial concern of states and rulers. Subjects of the Assyrian Empire ate a mixed diet of legumes, onions, greens, and meat from sheep and goats, but social order revolved around a centrally controlled bread ration. In Pharaonic Egypt, state workers received wages in bread and bread grains, and soldiers were known for eating so much bread—a ration of four pounds per day—that Greeks called Egyptians *artophagoi*, "the bread eaters." Rome was no different, building its vast imperial reach on a foundation of sophisticated bakeries and highly developed bread distribution systems.[4]

During the European Middle Ages, bread remained central to culture, religion, and survival. In thirteenth-century Britain, for example, workers on feudal manors ate 70–80 percent of their daily calories in the form of bread and cheese. Beer, essentially liquid bread, made up much of the remaining 20–30 percent, with meat, fruit, and vegetables appearing as rare seasonal treats. During periods when labor was scarce and wages higher, such as after the great population decline caused by the Black Death, Europeans ate significantly more meat, but bread still anchored the diet in most places and vegetables were sparse.[5]

The advent of modernity didn't do much to change Europeans' reliance on bread. Residents of seventeenth-century Sienna consumed between two and three pounds of bread per person every day. Under Louis XIV, Parisian workers subsisted on three and a half pounds of bread a day, and not much else. Speaking very broadly, we can say that from the 1600s to as late as the 1950s, Europeans received between 40 to 60 percent of their daily calories in the form of bread.[6]

Even in the United States, a country big enough to grow almost anything, bread remained central. As one observer of the early Republic wrote, American "wage-earners . . . were probably better fed than laborers in Europe." Still, "they rarely tasted fresh meat more than once a week. . . . They ate bread, one of the cheapest sources of energy."[7]

From the mid-nineteenth century to the mid-twentieth century, Americans got, on average, 25–30 percent of their daily calories from bread, a figure that began to dip significantly only in the late 1960s. During times of war or recession (or in the ranks of the poor), the percentage rose even higher.[8]

Under conditions like these, governments perceived as neglecting the bread supply faced mob violence, bread riots, and worse. Marie Antoinette may never have actually said, "Let them eat cake" in response to her subjects' demand for bread, but the French monarchy's neglect of the bread supply did pave the path to Madame Guillotine.

In October 1789, it was French women's outrage over, among other things, the monarchy's lavish dining during a time of high bread prices that tipped the balance in favor of the masses. The Revolution had begun several months earlier with the storming of the Bastille and the Declaration of the Rights of Man and the Citizen, but the king and queen, lying low in Versailles, had remained largely insulated from the upheavals. Then, on October 5, six thousand women, marching on the monarchs' summer residence armed with lances, pitchforks, and muskets, changed that. A number of different offenses triggered the march, but when the women reached Versailles, their anger shifted to bread. Chanting, "Bread! Bread! Bread!" and facing little resistance from sympathetic National Guardsmen, the women ransacked the palace. They seized and distributed the royal bread stores and forced the king and queen to return to Paris, where they lived under virtual house arrest until their executions three years later. As the royal carriage left Versailles for the last time, thousands of women surrounded it, triumphantly brandishing loaves of bread speared on the tips of bayonets. [9]

Across the channel, English peasants and workers also demanded bread, but where French officials' efforts to maintain a moral economy of bread had collapsed, with disastrous results, British rulers maintained firmer control. From 1266 to 1863, the English Assize of Bread strictly regulated bread sales and bakery profits. But even that system wasn't perfect, and bread riots regularly erupted during moments of waning faith in the benevolence of government. [10]

The modern English word "lord" still carries this political history in its bones. Lord derives from the Old English title "hláford"— "keeper of the bread"—a privileged status, but also a perpetually anxious one. Ruling has always meant a tense dance between the power of bread keepers and the demands of bread eaters.

The dance was even harder for bakers. Throughout history, the village baker was not the jolly, romantic figure we picture today. Not only was the baker the target of intense government regulation, but his almost absolute control over people's sustenance made him so-cially suspect. Accused—often with good reason—of false weights, grain hoarding, hunger profiteering, and cutting flour with cheap whiteners like chalk, alum, or borax, bakers earned dubious reputations over the centuries. When things went wrong in town—even things unrelated to bread—the baker often got the blame.

• • •

Today, of course, the bread supply is not so central to the physical survival of most nations, nor to the politics of life and death. My two breadaholic kids have been known to chant, "We demand baguettes!" like some Parisian mob, but even they don't get 30 percent of their calories from bread. On average, Americans today get less than a quarter of their calories from grain, and much of that takes the form of breakfast cereals and snacks. No single item accounts for anything close to a third of the U.S. diet anymore—not even high fructose corn syrup.[11]

Nevertheless, the history of bread has a lot to teach us. Good bread is more than just the stuff of sepia-toned sentimentality, of hearth and home, of wholesome life. It has a more worldly and disquieting side; a side where bread and power intertwine. The story of bread is the story of how social structures shape what we eat, and how what we eat shapes social structures.

The same could be said about many staple foods. Milk, meat, rice, tortillas, and sugar will all appear briefly in this book, and are the subject of other excellent books on the intertwining of food and power.[12] But there's something about bread—it's so basic. No other food has been so central to so many regional diets, nor has any other food borne the weight of so much symbolism and cultural connotation, at least in the West and despite its unnoticed background nature. In this sense, bread provides an especially good lens through which to understand the larger relationship between food and politics.

The word "companion" isn't so simple after all. Yes, it speaks to bread's role in forging bonds and connecting groups, but eating also divides. A companion isn't just someone you share bread with; it is someone you are willing and permitted to share bread with.

Bread consumption has long marked hierarchies of social status. From the very first city-states, bread sustained serfs, merchants, slaves, kings, and gods alike—but they did not all eat the same bread. They ate loaves assigned to their specific segment of society, either by formal decree, as in imperial Rome and Assyria, or by implicit custom, as in late twentieth-century America. For bread-eating peoples, the very act of eating bread defined boundaries between "civilized" and "savage."

In most times and places throughout history, the social order of bread arrayed itself in a spectrum from the lightest, whitest, and most wheaten for elites to darker, chewier, and more admixed loaves for the rest. In early twentieth-century America, for example, it would have been almost impossible to escape the message, conveyed by food advertising, scientific studies, political cartoons, foreign correspondents, and even church sermons, that only savage peoples and unwashed immigrants ate dense, dark bread. Eating white bread was said to "Americanize" undesirable immigrants, and a few social commentators even claimed that eating white bread literally changed newcomers' complexions.[13]

And yet, in many places and times, food experts, philosophers, and ordinary eaters contested that ancient order. Whether white or dark bread constituted the best foundation for a vigorous, moral society was quite possibly the first great food fight. Plato debates this question in *The Republic,* concluding that the ideal *polis* must be built on dark, hearty rural loaves, not soft, citified white ones.[14] So too some ancient food writer probably waxed lyrical about Gilgamesh's decision to eat "authentic" peasant barley cakes instead of overcivilized einkorn wheat.

This points to something else important about status and the staff of life. While the type of bread one eats has long marked one's social position, more abstract ideas about what counts as "good bread" shape the very ground on which social groups interact. When we define what counts as "good bread," we are talking about a lot more than food. Dreams of "good bread" are statements about the nature of "good society." Such dreams come with unspoken elaborations of who counts as a responsible citizen and how society should be organized.

When, for example, Americans debate, as they have periodically since the 1800s, whether "Mother's bread" or store-bought loaves are more virtuous and authentically "American," they are also making claims about the proper place of women in society. When robber barons of the late 1800s Gilded Age lauded abundant and inexpensive white bread churned out by factories as the foundation for social harmony, they were also arguing against a society of labor organizing and government regulation. And when back-to-the-land movements of the 1840s and 1960s contended that hearty whole wheat bread baked on independent family farms was a bedrock of democratic society, they rarely stopped to ask themselves who got left out of this invariably white and propertied vision. Yet these abstract dreams of good bread and good society had real consequences for real people.

For these reasons and more, this isn't really a book about the history of bread. It's a book about what happens when dreams of good society and fears of social decay get tangled up in campaigns for "good food."

More specifically, it traces six different deeply felt notions that have defined America's relationship to bread at different moments: dreams of purity and contagion; control and abundance; health and discipline; strength and defense; peace and security; resistance and status. In doing this, the book's scope is limited to the era of standardized, mass-produced industrial bread, from about 1840 to the present. Although a relatively small piece of world bread history, the story of American industrial loaves and their political lives offers a unique vantage on a question that concerns growing numbers of people in the early twenty-first century: What's behind our fraught relationship with industrial food and, by extension, how does our relation with industrial food reflect our messy relations with one another?

By "industrial food," I'm referring to the products of capital-intensive agriculture, processed into homogeneous, standardized edibles designed to maximize efficiency and profit over other values such as taste or sustainability. And industrial food has, for the better part of two centuries, stood at the center of Americans' fears and aspirations about eating and its relation to good society. Mass-produced white bread, in turn, has long epitomized our contradictory relationship to industrial food, simultaneously embodying the promise of industrial abundance and the dangerous hubris of science.

Not surprisingly, then, nearly every diet guru, health expert, food activist, gourmet tastemaker, government official, and social reformer concerned with how the country ate had something—often *a lot*—to say about industrial bread. Scratch the surface of any public figure, government official, or social movement interested in changing how the country ate during the past 150 years, and you will almost certainly find a powerful vision of good bread standing in for a larger vision of good society.

So what can we learn from this history? Or, more urgently, how can reflecting on what now seem like strange and outdated efforts to change America through its bread inform the way we think about food today? Concern about the country's food—where it comes from, how it is grown, what it contains, and how it affects our bodies, environment, and society—mounts every day. Stories about obesity, food safety, carbon footprints, and conditions on farms and in food factories appear daily in the media, heightening the growing sense that something is wrong with the U.S. food system. In the face of this, an energetic new social movement—often called the "alternative food movement"—has exploded onto the scene. A diverse assemblage of locavores, farmers' market lovers, community-supported agriculture subscribers, fair trade coffee sippers, New Agrarian back-to-the-landers, artisanal food enthusiasts, home cheese makers, backyard chicken raisers, community garden organizers, neo-traditionalist advocates for "eating like Great-Grandma," hardcore and occasional organic food purchasers, co-op shoppers, and Slow Food gourmets, the alternative food movement is hard to pin down.[15] But one thing is clear: millions of Americans are, once again, setting out to change the way the country eats.

Thanks to an explosion of politically charged food writing and reporting that began in the late 1990s, members of the alternative food movement have access to a great deal of information about *why* and *how* the food system needs to change. Much less is known about the successes and failures of such efforts in the past. Even less is known about the rich world of attachments, desires, aspirations, and anxieties that define American's relations to the food system as it is.

This book tackles both of those lacunae, and regardless of what your own vision of good food and good society may be, I hope that the story of industrial bread and its discontents will unsettle it a little. This is a critical book, but my hope is not to naysay social change, or belittle the efforts of food reformers in any era. Indeed, I hope that my affection for people concerned about the politics of food in the past and present shines through, even as I dwell on the limits and dangers of their efforts. That sympathy is the product of my own experiences trying to change the world through food—and a hard-learned awareness of the limits and dangers of my own actions.

The idea for this book took form in three very different places that I've called home over the past few decades—a cattle ranch in southeastern Arizona, the "Gourmet Ghetto" of Berkeley, California, and the upstart wine tourism town of Walla Walla, Washington. In each of these three places I encountered people working to change the American food system in different ways. I participated in many different manifestations of the alternative food movement and I absorbed elements of remarkably different visions of the relationship between good food and good society. As much as I've grown critical of all those dreams, each one deeply shaped the way I think about the history of industrial bread and what that history can teach present-day foodies.

CHANGING THE WORLD THROUGH FOOD?

A few months after my stint as village baker, my wife and I left Tucson to apprentice on a humane-sustainable cattle ranch in southeastern Arizona. There, we lived in a trailer with rattlesnakes under the front steps. Under the tutelage of Jim Corbett—a Quaker rancher from Wyoming with a Harvard philosophy degree, a history of political activism, and a deeper appreciation of the spiritual connections between human community and the natural world than anyone I've ever met—we learned to gently move cattle through the range on foot. We practiced an ethic of compassion for animals and the land, protected riparian areas, cared for pasture, and sold what may have been the first meat advertised as "local grass-fed beef" in Tucson. My wife started an informal raw milk collective and I baked a lot of bread. It was the one thing on this list of jobs that I was actually qualified to do. It also gave me a way to connect with folks on the ranch, and over many fresh, crusty loaves of *pain au levain,* we talked endlessly about the politics of food.

During that time, I set myself to understand global food politics and history. Books like *Fast Food Nation* and its heirs were still years away, so I read what I could find: dry agricultural economics textbooks, even drier treatises on trade policy, and their colorful antithesis, counterculture food manifestos of the 1960s and 1970s. For fun, I soaked up food histories—accounts of grain traders, sugar merchants, and, yes, old English bakers. Books by feminist food historians, like Laura Shapiro's *Perfection Salad,* taught me that food politics wasn't just about big business and government policy. It included more intimate struggles over gender, race, and class.

Even then it was clear that labels like "organic" and "sustainable" could easily be co-opted by big companies with almost oligopolistic control over markets. What really mattered was not *what* we ate as much as the distribution of power that brought us that food. Seen from that light, raising humane-sustainable cattle on the Saguaro-Juniper Ranch seemed like a small way of redistributing power and resetting the terms of the food system. By avoiding the oligopolistic middle, we were forging a true alternative based on direct connections between land, animals, and people. What happened in a small community of ranchers, livestock, and grasses in southeast Arizona could have global ramifications.

The North American Free Trade Agreement (NAFTA) had just passed and a specter loomed just south of the ranch. Cheap U.S. corn, exported by multinational grain traders subsidized by the U.S. government, threatened to displace a million or more small farmers in Mexico. This would leave them few options other than picking crops and working construction in *el Norte.* Breaking the cycle of corn and beef oligopoly in Arizona seemed part of a larger struggle to give the world's food producers, farm workers, and consumers more options—not just the illusion of choice offered by big agribusiness.[16]

Eventually, my wife and I left the ranch and Arizona altogether so I could go back to graduate school in the Bay Area. In that milieu, I encountered a kind and intensity of desire to change the way the world eats that I couldn't have imagined in Arizona. We lived in a

Berkeley grad student ghetto of WWII-era barracks and decommissioned public housing blocks that made our ranch trailer seem luxurious. Luckily, we were too busy eating to notice. We couldn't afford to eat at Chez Panisse, the culinary epicenter of California's alternative food movement, but we could revel in local organic produce from the Berkeley farmers' market and subscribe to a weekly box of food from a farm in Yolo County. When we had a daughter a few years later, we could take her to milk her first goat at the open house of one of America's best artisanal cheese makers. Like other folks then forging what David Kamp called "the United States of Arugula," we discovered artisanal olives and practically took out student loans to buy artisan cheese.[17] With Acme Bakery, one of the world's best bread makers, only a few blocks from our apartment, I stopped baking. And I began to notice what an affluent white project alternative food was.

It wasn't just the high price tags, pale skin tones, or collective sensibility of the comfortably liberal, comfortably professional populace. In many ways, the thing that made me realize how affluent and how white the alternative food movement could be was the strenuous, back-bending-Berkeley-yoga-studio effort it made to insist that it wasn't (or didn't have to be). For, if there was one thing besides sheer hedonistic pleasure that marked Berkeley food politics, it was the mantra "We need to make this more inclusive." If only "we" could bring the virtuous spirit of good food to "them," everything would be okay.

It's a seductive attitude, buttressed by the language of nutrition science and America's intuitive belief in the moral virtue of small farms, but I slowly came to realize that it often reinforced injustices as much as it challenged them. While increasing dietary options for less fortunate others isn't bad per se, it can bolster social hierarchies and strengthen inequality—particularly when expressed as an enlightened "Us" helping "Them" to sit at our preset table. As Julie Guthman, a keen observer of the Berkeley food scene, has noted, there is a difference between inviting others to sit at the table you've laid and engaging with people about how the table got made in the first place. The latter requires tackling tough questions about how power is distributed in society, often obscured even in the most well-meaning efforts to make "good food" accessible.[18]

In Berkeley I learned that my own dreams of changing the world through good food were complicit in an elitism that I didn't support. This has been a difficult realization, and it's tempting to hide from its implications. The mantra "It might not be perfect, but at least I'm doing *something*" provides a partial rejoinder—but glosses over the real consequences of acting without critical self-reflection. Critique is important. At the same time, I wouldn't want my critiques of the alternative food movement to align me with conservative voices ranging from right-wing cable TV pundits like Glenn Beck to chemical company lobbyists lining up to defend America's industrial food against the threat of "liberal elites." How can I critique a movement that I care about deeply without undermining its efforts?

DREAMWORLDS AND FOOD POLITICS

History—a good tool to think with—offers a way out of this dilemma. Reflecting on the sometimes laughable, sometimes infuriating dreams of changing America's bread in the past can help us grasp the possibilities and limits of efforts to change the way America eats in the present a little more clearly. In tracing the combinations of anxiety, longing, desire, habit, fear, benevolence, and greed that have propelled the history of industrial bread, I hope to show that dreams of good food are powerful social forces. They animate the actions of consumers, industry executives, advertisers, government officials, and food reformers. They have real material consequences. At the same time, they do not appear out of nowhere. Dreams of good food arise out of particular constellations of power and interests that can be analyzed and understood. To this end, the book is not arranged chronologically. Instead, it follows specific dreams of good bread through time. Each of the book's chapters centers on one particular dream of good bread and the arrangements of power that underpinned it. Each chapter then reflects on the consequences—intended and unintended, serendipitous and unfortunate, immediate and slow burning—brought on by that particular dream of good bread.

The past is not passed in this history. Even seemingly archaic ideas about saving the world through food have afterlives. They linger in the preoccupations of the present. To capture that play of the past in the present, each chapter of the book begins and ends with a contemporary story, a bridge of sorts between the concerns of the present and the ideas of the past.

Industrial bread, as defined in this book, began in embryonic form during the 1840s and exploded in the 1890s and 1900s amidst widespread anxiety about germs, gender roles, and "dirty" immigrants (chapter 1: dreams of purity and contagion). In this moment of upheaval, industrial bread was a perfectly shaped, perfectly clean, perfectly white spectacle of modern progress (chapter 2: dreams of control and abundance). During the Roaring Twenties it became the target of considerable anger and anxiety: modern bread appeared to be *too* pure, *too* perfect—and critics said that it was making the country fat, dumb, and lazy. "Responsible" citizens would have to demonstrate their social fitness through strict dietary discipline and white bread avoidance (chapter 3: dreams of health and discipline).

During World War II, however, synthetic enrichment campaigns, championed for reasons of national security, gave industrial bread armor plating and renewed appeal. Bread enrichment campaigns also trained Americans to crave added vitamin power in their food (chapter 4: dreams of strength and defense). After the war, industrial bread helped fuel the Manichean culture of the Red Scare and Cold War. Propelled by confident belief in the moral and physical superiority of industrial food, American bread went global in the early 1960s, a key ingredient in America's postwar dominance of the world food system (chapter 5: dreams of peace and security).

On the opposite end of the political spectrum, industrial bread emerged as a focal point for counterculture ire in the late 1960s. Antiwar activists, ecologists, and back-to-the-landers held up "plastic" white bread as a lethal symbol of militaristic hubris and cultural conformity. In the 1970s, industrial "health bread" went from counterculture to mainstream on a wave of consumer-oriented body consciousness. The 1980s and 1990s saw an explosion of elite niche market breads—"yuppie chow"—juxtaposed against industrial white, which had completed its trajectory from modern marvel to white trash icon. And, as I write these words in the spring of 2011, industrially produced whole wheat bread has, for the first time in U.S. history, outsold its refined white counterpart. Organic, artisanal-style, multigrain, and even gluten-free breads lead the industry today (chapter 6: dreams of resistance and status).

Exploring these stories, we'll see that dreams of good food play a unique role in the creation of social distinctions: they link individual consumption decisions to the health of the whole society in a way that seems natural and physiological, not socially produced. When someone else embraces our vision of good food, it isn't viewed as a culturally specific affinity; it is seen as acceptance of a universal natural truth—who wouldn't want to eat good food? On the other hand, when someone questions the universal goodness of our good food, it marks them as unfathomably different—what kind of person doesn't want good food?![19]

Seen in this light, the history of bread dreams is frequently a history of ambiguous achievements and evils committed for the most benevolent of reasons. Often the problem was not the food dream itself, but what the dream made invisible. In the 1830s, food guru Sylvester Graham—the man whose followers would give America both the humble graham cracker and the lofty belief that there is something morally virtuous about whole wheat—achieved celebrity status by blaming Irish and black New Yorkers for a cholera epidemic. The poor, he argued, brought disease upon themselves because they lacked the intelligence and self-discipline to embrace a "natural" diet. National health—both physical and moral—could be achieved only through a strict regime of healthy eating.

In retrospect, there was nothing wrong with Graham's prescription for healthy eating. It was a bit ascetic for my taste—whole wheat bread, fruit, nuts, fresh water, and no spices, meat, sugar, caffeine, or alcohol—but it was probably a reasonable reaction against the country's relentless diet of meat, boiled vegetables, white bread, and booze. The problem was that his vision of better society through better eating made such a neat panacea that he missed the real reason poor New Yorkers died from cholera: grueling labor conditions, low wages, corrupt government, and profiteering by vendors of clean water.[20]

Substitute "obesity" for "cholera," and I'm left wondering: Have we come that far since Sylvester Graham? This, in turn, raises the practical question at the heart of this book: Should we really try to change the world by changing what and how people eat?

My Tucson self says yes. My Berkeley self is more skeptical. And yet, I wrote this book in a third place: Walla Walla, Washington, where I now teach food politics to smart, eager students at Whitman College. The contemporary alternative food movement has been a force during most of my students' lives, so many of them arrive at college already deeply committed to changing the food system. And Walla Walla itself embodies all the contradictions they will have to grapple with if they are to succeed at that.

Tucked into the dry southeastern corner of Washington State, the town is surrounded by miles of wheat. Grown by heavily indebted family farmers in vast, capital-intensive farms and then exported to Asia by large multinational grain traders at low prices subsidized by the U.S. government, Walla Walla wheat is a river of gold in the global, geostrategic food system.

Ironically, from my perspective at least, Walla Walla mostly grows soft winter wheat—the wrong wheat for artisanal bread baking. But the "foodie" in me has other options here. Walla Walla is home to a fast-growing trade in high-end wines, produced in more than one hundred local wineries. The wine boom has brought vast amounts of money and tourism to this remote place, remaking the high desert landscape with an Old West-cum-Mediterranean aesthetic. It has also brought a new food culture and the alternative food movement: three community-supported agriculture businesses, grass-fed-beef ranchers, artisanal cheese makers, schoolyard gardens, and restaurants serving local produce. In Walla Walla, I don't just know "my" farmer and winemaker; they're my neighbors.

Still, while the wine boom has, to my mind, brought "good food" to Walla Walla, it hasn't brought good middle-class jobs—at least not as good as the stable, decent-paying jobs canning boiled vegetables and bottling mass-produced apple juice that have all disappeared in recent years. Ironically, good jobs making processed foods that many would disdainfully label "bad food" have been replaced by low-paid work serving eaters of "good food."

From my vantage in Walla Walla, I still believe that changing the food system is imperative. But the history of battles over bread suggests that real change will happen only when well-meaning folks learn to think beyond "good food" and "bad food," and the hierarchies of social difference that have long haunted these distinctions.

1

UNTOUCHED BY HUMAN HANDS

Dreams of Purity and Contagion

"I want to know where my bread comes from! I don't want bread from some nameless basement bakery. I want my bread from a bakery that's clean as my own kitchen. . . ." Know where your bread is baked and how. Don't take a chance with the bread you buy. You can't afford to.

—Holsum bread advertisement, late 1920s

A HAIR IN THE MILK

There are people who believe that drinking raw milk can cure illness and restore the body to natural harmony. There are people who think that drinking raw milk is like playing Russian roulette with microbes. There are a few farm families that drink raw milk just because it's what they have around, and a lot more folks who have never given raw milk a single thought because it's so unusual. Then there are those for whom raw milk is both scary and seductive, wholesome yet menacing. That's me.

A city kid, I grew up playing in vacant lots, not the back pasture. My idea of nature always involved a campground—I had no experience with the working nature of food production until I was in my twenties. The first time I saw milk come out of an actual cow, I was twenty-five and learning to do the milking myself while interning on a ranch in Arizona. "Red" was her name—the cow, that is. Red is not a particularly creative name for a cow, but my wife, Kate, and I came up with a lot more colorful monikers: the kind of names a cow gets called when it kicks over the milk pail, when it kicks over the feed

17

pail, when it intentionally stomps your foot or butts your shoulder with its ornery old lady horns.

Red's was the first clump of hair I ever saw floating in my milk. Before Red, I had never drunk milk with the scent of cow still lingering in it or wondered how much barnyard dust in the milk constituted "too much." I thought *Listeria* was something you used mouthwash to get rid of, not the bacteria responsible for a deadly milk-borne sickness.

Since then I have drunk a lot of raw milk, most of it illegal, thanks to strict government regulations slanted toward large high-tech dairies. I don't ascribe any particular natural virtue to milk's unpasteurized state, but I've come to like the grassy taste and the sense that I'm getting my milk direct from a local farmer. Despite all that, though, I have never gotten over the slight flutter of unease I first felt drinking raw milk—the modern intuition that maybe there was something dangerous about getting milk from a cow instead of a factory.

This unease has haunted Americans since they first began to grasp the existence of an invisible world of small, possibly threatening organisms. Not without cause. In the late nineteenth and early twentieth centuries, city residents got their milk from fetid, overcrowded "swill dairies" or off unrefrigerated train cars traveling overnight from the surrounding countryside. Until mandated pasteurization, milk was a key vector for typhoid and other serious diseases.[1]

Throughout U.S. history, anxieties about tainted milk have been matched only by concerns about meat. Most notably, *The Jungle*, Upton Sinclair's 1906 book about unsanitary conditions in Chicago's stockyards, galvanized a nascent consumer protection movement. Muckraking journalists, campaigning scientists, and an army of civically engaged middle- and upper-class women horrified by unsafe food took to the streets, courts, and legislatures, demanding change. Sinclair had hoped to spark outrage over the inhuman conditions experienced by immigrant meatpackers. Instead, the country fixated on germs and the frightening immigrants who appeared to spread them into the nation's food. "I aimed for the people's heart," Sinclair is said to have reflected, "and by accident, I hit them in the stomach."[2]

Still, when it came to protecting stomachs, the Pure Foods Movement, as it came to be called, achieved substantial reforms. Pure Foods activists forced manufacturers to change the way they handled and distributed food, boycotted unsanitary establishments out of business, forced state and local officials to take food safety more seriously, and passed what still serves as a the bedrock of all federal food safety regulation, the 1906 Pure Food and Drug Act. Unfortunately, their efforts were far from perfect and were steadily watered down over the next century.[3]

At the start of the new millennium, Pure Foods crusaders' concerns still seem shockingly contemporary. Serious food-borne illnesses affected millions and sent hundreds of thousands to hospitals during the 1990s and early 2000s. *E. coli* in beef emerged as an almost ordinary source of tragedy, while sensational outbreaks of food-borne illness in bean sprouts, strawberries, cilantro, eggs, peanut butter, and spinach gripped the media. Food safety regulations, some with roots in 1906, appeared impotent in the face of a far-flung global food system dominated by powerful corporations. In many cases, regulators themselves seemed to have been "captured" by the very companies they supposedly oversaw. It felt like the 1900s all over again.

On the other hand, few Americans alive today can imagine a time when the specter of unclean bread was as scary as germ-clotted milk or tainted beef. And yet, during the late nineteenth and early twentieth centuries, the menace of contaminated bread was no less a topic of public outcry than dirty meat or milk. Pure Foods crusaders targeted the nation's bakeries, government hearings convened around bread contamination, and Harvey W. Wiley, the country's most prominent Pure Foods advocate, warned consumers of serious threats to America's staple food.

Accurately or not, a simple loaf of bread from a small urban bakery seemed to many consumers a harbinger of death and disease. These fears ultimately changed the country's bread. An urgent need to know that one's bread was pure proved instrumental in convincing Americans to embrace industrially produced loaves. Early twentieth-century bread fears also confused food purity and social purity in a way that placed the blame for unsafe food on some of the food systems' greatest victims and distracted attention from more systemic pressures, creating danger and vulnerability. As we think about food safety in our own time, the story of America's bread panic suggests that visions of pure food can motivate desperately needed changes but also backfire in myriad ways.

THE MODEL PALACE OF AUTOMATIC BAKING

In 1910, the country's greatest bread bakery opened on the corner of Vanderbilt and Pacific in Brooklyn's Prospect Heights. Six stories tall with an alabaster white neoclassical facade, it was a shining temple to a new way of thinking about food "untouched by human hands." Gleaming surfaces, massive machinery, and light-filled halls proclaimed a new creed: industrial food is pure food, and pure food is the foundation of social progress. During the first decades of the twentieth century, tens of thousands of New Yorkers flocked to the Ward Bakery on school field trips and weekly tours to witness the spectacle.

The Ward Bakery in Brooklyn, along with its twin in the Bronx, was the flagship of a revolution in the way the country's single most important staple was produced and sold. In the early twentieth century, when average Americans got 30 percent of their daily calories from bread, more than any other single food, New Yorkers ate more bread than any other group in the country. New Yorkers also purchased more of their bread than the rest of the country, and they bought a lot of it from the Ward Baking Company. At the company's height, Ward's Brooklyn and Bronx factories supplied one in every five bakery loaves eaten in New York City. By the end of the 1920s, the company had extended that power across the entire country, coming astoundingly close to achieving monopoly control over every single sizable bread market in the nation.[4]

The Ward family achieved this dominance by pioneering key technological breakthroughs, running roughshod over union labor, laying waste to small competitors, and concocting financial machinations that would have dazzled Gordon Gecko. But the Ward Baking Company owed its uncanny ability to win over skeptical customers to a much larger sense of disquiet hanging over early twentieth-century America.

The Ward Bakery went up in Brooklyn at a moment when poor wheat harvests, commodity speculation, and the power of railroad monopolies had stressed bread supplies, causing occasional riots and widespread fear of famine. In the first decades of the twentieth century, "the bread question" was *the* question for many observers, and it wasn't just the bread supply that mattered. The country was divided on *how* bread should be produced in the first place. As one national household advice columnist wrote in 1900, "No subject in the history of foods has been of such vital importance or aroused so much diversion of opinion as bread making."[5] These specific concerns, in turn, reflected a larger set of perturbations agitating the country.

From the 1870s to the 1920s, a singular convergence of forces buffeted the United States, upending all sense of stability and order. Unprecedented influxes of southern and eastern European immigrants, rapid urbanization, explosive technological change, and a series of grave economic downturns strained old institutions built around the dream of an Anglo-Saxon nation of self-sufficient rural communities. Thrust into an emerging system of global grain trading and financial speculation, rural America reeled.[6]

Urban infrastructure collapsed under demographic pressures. Corrupt politicians and their private sector cronies stepped in to provide basic services at high cost. Great trusts—vast corporations with monopoly power—came to dominate nearly every important sector of the emerging industrial economy. Work, once carried out on an intimate scale, suddenly felt controlled by distant, impersonal forces. For white, native-born Americans, everything felt undone. Old elites struggled to maintain authority. The poor felt themselves tossed around by the whims of shadowy bosses and threatened by an invasion of foreigners. And elites and the poor alike searched for ways to make sense of a world turned upside down.

As many groups faced with great upheavals have done throughout history, late nineteenth- and early twentieth-century white Americans scapegoated—placing the blame for large-scale social change on immigrants and minorities. The period saw some of the ugliest nativism and most violent exclusion of minorities in U.S. history. Racial eugenics and white supremacist theories of human evolution flourished, providing scientific authority for the country's fear and harsh prescriptions for social improvement.

And yet, amidst all the exclusion and vitriol, other ways of responding to upheaval, championed by both working-class organized labor and an emerging population of middle-class professionals, produced some of the most important and inclusive social reforms in U.S. history: child labor laws, wage regulations, antitrust legislation, worker safety protections and, of course, food safety laws. This period saw the advent of social work and public health, expanded public education, nutrition programs, and investment in public green spaces—all explicitly aimed at relieving social tensions that might have incited more radical social change.[7]

Middle- and upper-class women, in particular, found a place for themselves in public life through campaigns and crusades aimed at bringing progress to the needy. Careful regulation, scientific expertise, and technological innovation, it seemed, could reknit the fractured nation and stave off class struggle. By the 1890s, this onrush of activism and landmark social reforms had coalesced under the banner of Progressivism.[8]

Two things are important about the Progressive Era for our purposes: first, the two impulses of the time—fear and optimism—did not cleave around opposed "good guys" and "bad guys"—they were two faces of the same coin. In reckoning with Progressive Era reforms, we must live with ambiguity. Like most great social movements, Progressivism challenged some elements of an unjust status quo, while reinforcing others. Second, we must appreciate the way concern over the purity of bodies—and, by extension, the purity of the food and drink consumed by those bodies—underpinned and unified nearly all of the diverse commitments that made up Progressivism. Temperance, the crusade against alcohol, was, in many ways, a key incubator for all Progressive reform efforts, but food mattered almost as much. A safe, pure, and efficient nation could not be built without safe, pure, and efficiently produced food. If people could only be enticed to consume pure foods (and stop poisoning their bodies and minds with alcohol), social problems would cease; the poor would find the physical and moral fortitude to lift themselves out of poverty; crime and violence would wane.

Legions of women heeded the advice of scientific nutrition and hygiene, changing the way their families ate. Legions more poured into the country's tenement zones and mountain hollers to spread what they called "the gospel of good food" to the turbulent masses.

Unfortunately, these efforts to improve the poor typically failed, often spectacularly. Middle- and upper-class reformers' eagerness to help was often matched only by their ignorance of what kinds of assistance the poor might actually want. Progressive advocacy for systemic change—consumer protections, public services, and accountable government—had a huge, and largely positive, impact on most Americans. On the other hand, eager attempts to "improve" the poor by teaching them about "good food" may have made reformers feel great about themselves but often missed the point. The emphasis on scientific diet and efficient household management as routes out of poverty was no match for the grinding structural forces keeping people poor: nativism, racism, political corruption, anti-worker laws, and monopoly power.[9]

Through their own militant embrace of scientific eating, however, middle- and upper-class reformers did sow the seeds of a new way of thinking about food that would have long-term repercussions. At the very least, by the 1930s, the bread question had been decisively answered: the country had abandoned its home-baked loaves and craft bakery bread, both scorned as dangerously impure, and embraced air-puffed, chemically conditioned, ultra-refined marvels of modern industry.

A BREAD REVOLUTION

In 1890, 90 percent of American bread was baked at home by women. From Perry County, Missouri, where German homesteaders made their own sourdough starters from beer mash and baked dark loaves in communal brick ovens, to the Deep South, where black and white field hands lunched on cornbread, to the country's Gold Coasts and Upper East Sides, where servants in starched aprons plated gleaming white rolls, homemade bread, in some form, was the country's staple. Despite periodic vogues for store-bought "French bread," the only people consistently purchasing the staff of life in the decades following the Civil War were affluent urbanites or recent immigrants living in tenement districts. The country's few commercial bakeries were nearly all tiny one-oven shops with five or fewer employees. Bread was—as it had been for millennia—the product of unstandardized ingredients, artisan labor, and unreliable technology.

Forty years later, this had changed completely. By 1930, 90 percent of the country's most important staple food was baked outside the home by men in increasingly distant factories. The few small bakeries left were rapidly disappearing, and bread had begun to take on the form in which we know it today: a standardized, homogeneous product of food science and assembly-line manufacture.

The industrialization of bread began haltingly after the Civil War, picking up speed as the century ended. By 1900, the country's largest bakeshops could produce fifteen thousand loaves a day. By 1910, large bakeries regularly churned out one hundred thousand loaves a day, and Ward's Brooklyn and Bronx factories together produced five hundred thousand. A model bakery set up by the American Bakers Association at its 1925 meetings in Buffalo was said to have topped 1 million loaves in twenty-four hours. Across the country, "model palaces of automatic baking" captured the public's imagination, each one a spectacle of scientific "system and order."[10]

Bread baking had been slow to industrialize compared to other sectors of the food system that saw major upheavals after the Civil War. There were cultural reasons for this, but it was also technically and economically difficult. Unlike most food industries, which deployed science to freeze food's living processes into an ideal state called "freshness," bakers had to work *with* bread's biological life.[11] Organic fermentation was essential to the magical alchemy that turned pasty globs of flour and water into light, sweet, aromatic loaves. This introduced a whole series of obstacles into the bakery assembly line: imagine how crazy it would have made Henry Ford if his Model T parts shrank or grew with slight variations in temperature, collapsed in air drafts, deflated after minor production delays, and depended on fickle microbes for energy. Before bakeries could become mass-production assembly lines, bread's living nature would have to be tamed.

With advances in microbiology, cereal chemistry, climate control, and industrial design during the first three decades of the twentieth century, bakers overcame these challenges. The Wards were early adopters of nearly every important technological development that drove this revolution. Perhaps more importantly, they pioneered the economic model of mergers and oligopoly that would define the industry for the rest of the century, as well as the cultural model of selling bread through the language of purity and hygiene that would convince Americans to eat the product of those powerful companies.

UP FROM BROOME STREET

During the Ward Baking Company's heyday in the 1910s and 1920s, Hugh Ward's well-heeled heirs loved to tell his story. Or at least their publicists did. Prominently displayed in newspaper ads and paraded out for interviews, the rags-to-riches tale of the company's founder gave an attractive aura of hard work and street cred to the Robber Barons of Bread.[12] As the story went, Hugh Ward and his father, James, landed in New York in 1849, fleeing Belfast and the Irish potato famine. Their first home was the Lower East Side, somewhere near Five Points, then a violent and squalid Irish and black quarter. At that time, opening a small bakery was still a relatively inexpensive affair—a seat-of-the-pants venture just within the reach of ambitious immigrant entrepreneurs with small stashes of cash and a penchant for long nights of hard work. Hugh Ward was one of them. A few months after landing in New York, he opened a small one-oven bakery in a brick building on Broome Street.

If it was like the city's other pre–Civil War immigrant bakeries, the conditions in Hugh Ward's shop would have been grim: he would have worked alongside his workers fourteen to sixteen hours a day in the building's stoop-ceilinged and vermin-infested basement. Twenty-three hours on Saturday. He would have slept what little he could with his family in a room above the shop, or alongside his workers on the bakery's dough-mixing tables. It would have been hot, living always in the glare of the oven. He would have worn a second skin of ash, flour, and sweat.

For six years Hugh Ward's bakery produced two hundred loaves a day for Lower East Side families. Then, in 1856, like so many others, Ward closed up shop and headed for the great American West. He made it as far as Pittsburgh. With its fiery coal furnaces and eternally black sky, Pittsburgh must have seemed to Ward like a city-sized version of his basement bakery. Certainly, with its population doubling every ten years, booming iron and glassworks, and glimmers of a prosperous future built on steel and armaments, it must have seemed like a good place to start a bakery.

Fueled by industry and immigrants, the Wards' new Pittsburgh establishment grew rapidly. Its secret, Ward's son Robert remembered later, was using low-grade flour to make the cheapest bread possible for Pittsburgh's poor. The bakery specialized in soot-colored "jumbo" loaves that sold for half the price of regular white bread. It was, in today's business parlance, a "bottom of the pyramid strategy." And it worked. The bakery required fifteen barrels of flour a week, more than triple the consumption of Ward's Broome Street establishment.

In 1897, the bakery, then run by Ward's sons Robert and George, combined with a profitable biscuit and cracker company, and capital from the merger allowed the company to open "Pittsburgh's first modern sanitary bakery" in 1903. Over the next eight years, Robert and George Ward oversaw one of the most remarkable periods of innovation and expansion in the history of baking. First in Pittsburgh, and then in a steady stream of new bakeries opened or acquired in St. Paul, Chicago, Cleveland, Boston, and Providence, the Ward brothers developed the country's most advanced mechanical mixers, kneaders, loaf shapers, and bread wrappers. While most of the country's bakeries still shuttled batches of bread in and out of hearths not that different from those that supplied the Roman Empire, Ward loaves flowed continually through long "tunnel ovens," assembly-line style. Less visibly, the Wards played a key role in bringing laboratory science to bear on baking, endowing the country's first research chair in bakery science at the Mellon Institute. As a 1925 paean to industrial baking in the *New York Times* beamed, "Each new invention eliminated labor, cut down the cost of production, and increased profits; and the Ward bakeries took advantage of every one."[13]

In 1909, when the first reports leaked to the press that the Wards had set their eyes on the New York market, the *New York Times* could easily call them Pittsburgh's "rulers of baking."[14] Hugh Ward had left Manhattan fifty-three years earlier a moderately successful immigrant baker. Now his sons and grandsons were returning, ready to invest $3 million outright and backed by a total capitalization of around $25 million, likely put up by Pittsburgh steel magnates (about $72 million and $600 million, respectively, in 2011 dollars).

This was appropriate. The man who would come to define the

Wards' New York operation—Hugh's grandson William—was born with flour in his blood, but it was the brute tactics of steel barons that defined his career. William began to rise in the company after his father died in 1915, and, by the early 1920s, he had muscled aside an uncle and assorted nephews to consolidate control. Wildly ambitious and often accused of stock swindles, boardroom thuggery, political corruption, and violent anti-union activities, all glossed with the sheen of high-profile charity work and benevolent paternalism, William put into motion the most audacious plan ever seen in American baking. Between 1921 and 1926, from his office in the company's New York flagship bakery, he executed a stealthily choreographed series of steadily larger mergers leading toward one final merger to end all mergers in which Ward would combine multiple giant bakery companies into a single firm with dominant positions in every bread market in the country.

It almost succeeded. By 1925, using millions of dollars staked by stock speculators, William had consolidated much of the industry into three massive companies: the Ward Baking Company, the General Baking Company, and Continental Baking. The General Baking Company, itself the product of several previous combinations, had dominant positions in some twenty-five hundred towns. Continental was even bigger. The Wards' first bakery in Pittsburgh had used 15 barrels of flour a week. Continental's forty massive plants spread out in thirty-five cities across the country consumed 57,500.

Most consumers hadn't yet noticed the changes, but Wisconsin's great Progressive politician Robert M. La Follette attacked the "Ward Bread Trust" in his presidential campaign rhetoric. Bakery workers' unions, bearing the brunt of Ward's growing power, railed against the "Ward Bread Octopus." And, for once, workers found common cause with many independent bakery owners, who decried the dirty tactics Ward's merger managers used to drive small firms out of business. Democrats in the House and Senate introduced resolutions against Ward, and federal regulators filed an antitrust complaint against Continental.

Unfazed, William Ward moved ahead without pause. In January 1926, he announced the formation of the Ward Food Products Corporation (WFPC), which would absorb General, Continental, and the family's New York flagship Ward Baking Company along with sundry interests in flour milling, yeast production, bakery equipment manufacturing, and transportation companies acquired over the years. In 2011 terms, the WFPC would be a $25-billion company, but more importantly, it would have a dominant presence in every important bread market in the country. Its gorilla weight and market presence would give it unprecedented power to determine the price of flour and bread. One company would, effectively, dictate the terms of access to the country's single most important food.

President Coolidge's pro-business administration was not known for its enthusiastic enforcement of antitrust laws, and Ward had actively supported the president's campaign—but the WFPC went too far. A month later the Federal Trade Commission (FTC) filed an injunction against the merger, ruling that the General, Continental, and Ward Baking Companies must remain independent.

The precise choreography of Ward's undertaking had come unglued. The pieces had begun to spin away from him. Faced with this, Ward retreated to home turf: the Ward Baking Company's flagship bakeries in Brooklyn and the Bronx. There, on February 6, 1929, almost three years to the date after the WFPC's incorporation, Ward's secretary found him slumped at his desk, dead of a heart attack three days short of his forty-fifth birthday.

• • •

Today, baseball buffs, interested in the Wards' short-lived Brooklyn Tip-Toppers major league franchise, are more likely to remember the Ward family than food historians. But the Wards' imprint lingers on our loaves and in our bakery aisles. The family revolutionized the technology of modern baking and created its business model. For, while the FTC balked at one company controlling the country's bread, it left untouched the larger structure of mini-monopolies. The giants General and Continental emerged from the fracas unscathed, living to combine and grow larger. Continental survived into the 1990s, when it was absorbed by Interstate Bakeries Corporation, an even bigger company—evidence that an impulse to combine and monopolize still dominates the industry. In his last year of life, however, William Ward gave us a more palpable icon to remember him by: probably hoping to distance the company from the scandalous taint of his last name, he adopted the brand name of an Indianapolis bakery he had acquired. In 1929, a new sign went up over many of his factories: although Ward's Tip-Top bread would continue to be made into the 1950s, the Ward Baking Company would henceforth and forever be better known as the Wonder Bakeries, makers of Wonder bread.

GREAT-GRANDMOTHER'S BREAD

An Irish American in Robert Ward's Pittsburgh, my great-grandmother Florence Farrell made twelve to sixteen loaves of bread a week, fifty-two weeks a year, for ten kids and assorted neighbors. Her husband, P. T., a small-time Democratic politician and self-taught draftsman, insisted on homemade bread. The store-bought stuff, he proclaimed, was just "sacks of hot air"—and he was not alone in this feeling. Yet, by the 1930s, like nearly everyone in America, the Farrell family no longer ate homemade bread every week. Even in the 1920s, the seeds of that shift were in place; as my great-aunt recalled, "It sounds like we [kids] appreciated [our mother's] homemade bread, but the truth is we loved any bakers' bread, in our contrary way."

At the start of the twenty-first century, a wave of neo-traditional food writers urged Americans to eschew anything "your great-grandmother wouldn't recognize as food." If your great-grandmother wouldn't have eaten it, they argued, it wasn't real food. This rule of thumb raised a few complications: I'm pretty sure my great-grandmother wouldn't have recognized Ethiopian *doro wat* or Oaxacan *huitlacochtle* as anything a human would eat, and yet they're two of my favorite foods. Neo-traditionalist's dreams of "real" food have racial and nationalist undertones, it seems. More importantly, they ignore the complexities and ambiguities of early twentieth-century Americans' relation to food: which version of my great-grandmother's bread am I supposed to treasure? The laborious homemade one her husband demanded, or the factory-baked one she eventually came to love? Food writers selling a particular dream of "great-grandmother's kitchen" rarely concern themselves with real people. What I want to know is how and why my great-grandmother's generation came to desire the store-bought staff of life.

"Convenience" is an easy answer, and certainly part of the historical explanation. While American preachers and social reformers (mostly male) had invoked "Mother's bread" as a symbol of all that was good and pure going back to the early 1800s, actual mothers had decried the relentless tedium of daily baking for just as long. Baking was arm-breaking work, complicated by fickle ovens and inconsistent ingredients. It kept women bound close to the home, tethered by the slow schedule of rising dough. As George Ward liked to brag, just one of his company's mixing machines "saved 1,600 women from tedium every fifteen minutes." Or, as a Polish immigrant put it more bluntly, bakery bread was a "godsend to the women. It saved their strength and time for work in the mill."[15]

Store-bought bread *was* a godsend, particularly in households without servants, and as economic pressures and new opportunities moved more women into the labor force. But convenience offers only a partial explanation for the popularity of store-bought bread. Florence Farrell never took a job outside the home, and her children recalled that she loved the sense of community created on baking days. Thanks to Florence's unpaid labor, homemade bread would also have been less expensive than even the most efficiently produced industrial bread until well into the 1930s. For the Farrells to have switched their allegiances, modern bread must have had some other appeal. None of my relatives remember exactly what that was, so we'll have to move from family lore to the terrain of history. To understand the attractions of modern bread more fully, we need to view it in a broader social context.

• • •

For bakers in the 1910s and 1920s, ever more efficient production of ever-greater quantities of bread was a decidedly ambiguous kind of progress. While consumers might buy newer, better automobiles as their prices fell thanks to industrial efficiency, they were unlikely to increase their consumption of bread, no matter how cheap and plentiful it got. Even worse, falling bread prices (or rising incomes) freed money in household budgets with which consumers could introduce more variety into their meals, displacing bread from its dominant place in the American diet. "Bread must compete with other foods for its place at the table," one industry observer wrote, capturing a widespread anxiety, but it had few advantages in that fight: lacking the movie star looks of newfangled fruits arriving by refrigerated train from California, the novelty of modern wonders like Jell-O, or the exotic appeal of tropical sweets steaming in from Central America, bread was just basic. "Declining consumption" was every baker's nightmare, and it was assumed to be inevitable.[16]

Instead, something remarkable happened during the first decades of the twentieth century: per capita bread consumption *increased*.[17] Modern factory bread wasn't just a more convenient version of the ancient staple—it was something new. Its ingredients may have remained more or less unchanged, its basic shape may have been preserved, its familiar taste maintained (in a watered-down form), but modern bread was somehow completely transformed. It had taken on shiny new meanings, found a new place on the American table and in the country's lunch pails.

Bakers worked hard for that increase, advertising relentlessly, doing everything possible to distinguish more or less identical loaves from one another through branding. They joined forces to promote bread consumption, collectively touting its healthful properties, sponsoring sandwich recipe contests, and even partnering with wheat growers and electric appliance makers to give toasters away at cost. But none of that would have saved bread if bakers hadn't capitalized on a new ethos of scientific eating spreading through the country. Scientific eating had several different facets, which we'll revisit in later chapters. For now, I'll argue that the appeal of modern bread lay in the way it resonated with a growing cultural embrace of science and industrial expertise as a buttress against rapidly escalating fears of impurity and contagion.

ANXIETY AND EXPERTISE

When Florence Farrell came of age at the turn of the century, the ability to make good bread was the mark of a good bride—her highest art. It was, in Victorian domestic ideology, "the very foundation of a good table" and "the sovereign" of the true housewife's kitchen, as Catherine and Harriet Beecher Stowe declared at the start of one of the century's best-selling books, *The American Woman's Home*.[18] In the early twentieth century, however, ideas about family and motherhood began to change, and this would make possible—even imperative—the shift from homemade to store-bought bread. Industrial bakers like the Wards had mastered baking technology and designed its cutthroat business model, but the ultimate source of their product's success lay in a new way of seeing the home.

In the last decades of the nineteenth century a "culture of professionalism" had begun to grip the country's emerging middle classes. Powerful visions of expertise and efficiency were colonizing every corner of daily life, from how babies were born (with doctors, not midwives, in attendance) to fashion (hemlines raised for sanitary reasons) and interior design (smooth, easily cleanable surfaces, not Victorian fringe and ruffle). This fervent new belief in science, social engineering, and industrial efficiency aimed to sweep away old forms of knowledge and authority perceived as grounded in craft, intuition, and tradition. Training in fields ranging from medicine to teaching was standardized and professionalized, and new disciplines—sanitation, hygienics, and public health—were created to extend scientific rationality into new realms.[19]

By the 1900s, a whole class of professional experts, armed with official certificates, fancy titles, and evangelical fervor, had secured a place for itself in the country's rigid social hierarchies. Emboldened by success and unwavering in its confident belief in the superiority of scientific expertise, this class set its sights on the country's hearth. In the eyes of nearly every branch of this new army of professional experts, mothers stood on the frontlines of the battle for national hygiene and efficiency. They conducted the care, feeding, and education of the population, and they governed the most intimate spaces of everyday life. Organized under the banner of "home economics," experts in household management and scientific motherhood believed that most of the nation's problems could be cured with careful attention to the workings of family life. "When the principles of hygiene are fully understood by women," Emma Sickels proclaimed to a large audience at Chicago's Art Institute in 1891, "there will be comparatively little disease."[20]

Scientific housekeeping, domestic hygiene, research-based meal planning, and efficient child rearing were supposed to liberate women from drudgery, but home economics aspired to even greater goals: by eliminating contagion, moral weakness, and inefficient energy use that sapped the stamina of the population, scientific household management would improve the very fabric of society from the hearth up.

For the mostly middle-class women who pioneered the field of home economics, the professionalization of domestic labor meant liberation and recognition. According to one of the movement's founders, Ellen Richards, women's work should properly be conceived as a professional occupation no different from doctor or engineer.[21] This professionalization of housework was, in theory, a way to place *all* women's work on par with that of men. In practice, however, it was primarily a way for women social reformers to gain respect for *their* work. If household management was a science, every housewife was a scientist of sorts, but home economists were the real experts.

Home economists' authority required the existence of a population deemed in need of education and reformation. Luckily, thanks to tremendous influxes of "unclean" southern and eastern European immigrants as well as the growing visibility of other minority groups, the nation appeared replete with mothers mired in tradition and ignorance. Thus, for the bulk of the nation's mothers, the ascendance of home economics meant less that their work would receive recognition as a vital contribution to the nation and more that their perceived backwardness and resistance to expert advice would be seen as threats to the nation.

The new disciplines of domestic expertise buttressed their authority by propagating an emergency mentality—painting vivid pictures of looming dangers and imminent disasters that would befall the nation if their advice weren't heeded. Household cleanliness, or rather the lack thereof, topped social reformers' lists of impending threats. By the turn of the twentieth century, the hypothesis that invisible microscopic organisms caused many illnesses had gained widespread scientific acceptance and was, thanks to the efforts of Progressive reformers, beginning to take hold in popular culture. In the 1900s, diverse groups, ranging from the Boy Scouts to the International Ladies Garment Workers Union, worked to preach this "gospel of germs" to the masses.[22] School curricula impressed the "laws of scientific hygiene" on young minds, and public signage warned of the dangers of kissing and spitting. Public health had been entirely reconceived. It was no longer the solitary concern of government officials, but rather the duty of all. In this era obsessed with the dangers of contagion, "the slightest deviation from perfect cleanliness was a cause for social anxiety since the invisible passage of germs could put the health of the family, companions, and even the entire nation at risk."[23]

The country's diet proved just as frightening as its cleaning habits, if not more so. Poor diet was a quiet killer and a silent drain on the country's stamina. By sapping the nation's vitality, inefficient diet appeared to be the root cause of nearly all of the nation's moral, physical, social, and mental problems. As health columnist W.R.C. Latson wrote in 1902, "The question of what to eat is one of the most important practical considerations of life. To know what to eat, how much and how often would go far toward solving some of life's gravest problems—poverty, weakness, disease, crime, and ultimately death."[24]

It's not hard to understand the fervor with which early twentieth-century social reformers approached the question "What to eat?" Cholera, botulism, typhoid, and other food-borne diseases killed in large numbers across class and race lines. And while historians disagree whether America's food supply actually grew more dangerous as it industrialized after the Civil War, one thing is clear: starting in the 1870s, Americans strongly *believed* that their food system was getting less safe. This sentiment opened the doors to what food historian Harvey Levenstein called "the Golden Age of Food Fads," as individual consumers sought safety in charismatic visions of better eating. It also underpinned collective mobilization, bringing together women's groups, consumer advocates, temperance unions, and other reformers for one of the most organized and sustained attempts to change the food system that history has known—the campaign for pure food, waged from the 1880s to the 1910s.[25]

Then, as now, the question of what to eat was always more than a culinary matter. As historian James Harvey Young noted, "The crusade for food and drug control shared with overall Progressivism a deep worry about 'purity': business, government at all levels, social conduct, even the bloodlines of the nation's populace seemed threat-

ened with pollution and required cleaning up."[26] In the face of looming danger, social reformers' visions of food purity cross-pollinated
easily with nativist politics and ideologies of racial purity. Indeed, as
Howard Markel and Alexandra Minna Stern argue in their history of
germ scares, it often became difficult to distinguish between descriptions of food-borne contagion and the terrifying prospects of racial
contamination.[27]

Food-borne diseases were widely associated with eastern and
southern Europeans, Mexicans, and other "dirty" groups. Those
groups' hunger was just as commonly, and perhaps more rightly, associated with political instability. Jacob Riis's widely read 1890 ex-
posé, *How the Other Half Lives,* gave most comfortable Americans
their first glimpse of this looming danger. The book took readers on
a tour of New York's tenement slums filled with the babble of foreign
tongues, ragged children, tubercular parents, and "queer [dietary]
staples found nowhere [else] on American ground." It offered a vision of a world where the masses clawed and fought for sustenance,
where "the cry for bread" filled the air. America need not care about
its poor for altruistic reasons, Riis argued. It was a question of self-
preservation: "In my mind there is a closer connection between the
wages of the tenement and the vices and improvidence of those who
dwell in them," he warned. "Weak tea with a dry crust [of bread] is
not a diet to nurse moral strength." In the book's much-discussed
final pages, Riis graphically drove this point home with an account of
a ragged father driven to violence against wealthy Fifth Avenue shoppers by his children's desperate need for a crust of bread.[28]

This was no idle threat. Most major cities had, at some point, experienced riots sparked by interruptions in bread supply or rising prices.
The connection between good, plentiful bread and social peace was
intuitively understood. Indeed, New York's first large bakery, the
New York Baking Company, was formed by a group of wealthy citizens hoping to prevent future eruptions of unrest like the one experienced during the citywide bakery strike of 1801.[29]

During the first decades of the twentieth century, industrialists like
William Ward would not raise wages or bow to union pressures, but
they were smart enough to know that thugs and guns could maintain
social stability only for so long. When the Wards built their New York

bakeries, the memory of Jewish bread riots in 1903 and 1905 had not yet faded, and the experience of a widespread 1910 bakery strike was fresh in the minds of many. So, while Ward increased his workers' hours and lowered their pay despite record profits, he also endowed a home for the city's elderly poor and a workers' retreat in the Hudson Valley—a bucolic wonderland where Ward bakery workers could rent subsidized summer cabins and their children could escape the corrupting influence of tenement life for a time. In the factory itself, on-site doctors cared for workers' health and taught them "healthy habits."[30]

This was precisely the approach that most food reformers took as well. Outside of labor and socialist-leaning movements, the social tensions evoked by Riis and others were understood as a problem not of exploitation but rather of a lack of education and the corrupting influences of poverty itself. The issue wasn't that workers couldn't afford food, but that they didn't know how to use their food budget efficiently, didn't understand scientific principles of good eating, or didn't have the means to cook properly.

Racial eugenicists, reaching the apex of their popularity during the 1910s and 1920s, believed that solving these social problems could be achieved only by purging society of inferior stock. Poor diet, in their minds, constituted clear evidence of unfitness. As Michael Williams argued in *Good Housekeeping,* alluding ominously to forced sterilization and other coercive measures favored by American eugenicists at the time, immediate action must be taken to eliminate "the dregs and waifs of our population" who simply could not "maintain true economy in nutrition."[31]

Most home economists, however, inclined toward the more optimistic euthenics movement. For them, racial fitness didn't begin and end with genes. It could be achieved by changing physical environments and teaching new habits. Social work and education would teach modern eating habits to the poor, while better urban planning and provision of what we today call "appropriate technology" would overcome the physical obstacles to proper eating. In a fashion reminiscent of many community-garden and anti-obesity campaigns designed to teach the poor about "healthy eating" today, reformers poured into the country's urban tenements and rural hill countries. What they achieved was not an attack on the economic root causes of poverty, but the spread of a gospel of progress through healthy habits and hygienic eating.

These were well-meaning efforts. Even George Ward's championing of cheap whole wheat bread for the masses can't be glossed merely as a cynical attempt to increase market share—indeed, by all accounts it hurt the company. Yet, ideas about scientific eating were also metrics by which populations could be measured for worthiness. Following expert dietary advice became not just a matter of good practice but a requirement of competent citizenship. Even when reformers' efforts to spread the gospel of good food failed, these failures had the effect of reinforcing social hierarchies. Rather than use these failures as an opportunity for self-reflection (maybe the poor actually need higher wages, not our gospel of good eating), reformers felt confirmed in their belief that poverty stemmed from the poor's ignorance (only a fool wouldn't want to eat hygienically).

Even when reformers failed to convince others to eat correctly, they themselves had deeply internalized their doctrine. Indeed, the greatest impact of this movement to shape how the masses ate was not on the masses, but on the habits and desires of the country's professional classes. Thus, while many of the food reformers' most ambitious projects—communal kitchens in tenement districts, for example—failed miserably, the power of hygienic eating flourished.

With this in mind, the choice of bakery over homemade can be understood as something more than just a question of taste or ease. Preference and convenience must be understood in relation to a whole series of deeply inculcated desires, responsibilities, and aspirations. Centuries of European tradition had linked bread choices with class and status, but the movement for hygienic eating added a whole new level of consequence: individual decisions about bread didn't just mark class differences, they placed eaters' behavior in relation to the larger health of the nation and proclaimed, for all to see, whether one was fit and responsible—or in need of help. The problem was that it was far from clear what kind of bread was most hygienic.

HOW OFTEN DO YOU INSPECT *YOUR* BAKERY?

To any late nineteenth-century observer, the answer to the question of what bread was most hygienic would have been obvious: *home*-baked bread was better. Bakery bread was one of the few processed foodstuffs widely associated with poverty rather than affluence, and bakeries themselves suffered under a cloud of suspicion. Except for a few "sanitary bakeries," the vast majority of the country's bakeries were more dark satanic mills than shining palaces.[32] Poorly capitalized and facing cutthroat competition, the country's small bakeries slashed any cost possible. They stretched and whitened cheap flour with plaster of Paris, borax, ground bones, pipe clay, chalk, alum, and other nefarious compounds. They invariably sold underweight loaves, and they worked laborers as hard as they could. As the lyrics of an 1884 union anthem from St. Helens, Oregon, asked, "Full eighteen hours under the ground, / Toiling and making bread! / Shut off from air and light and sound, / Are we alive or dead?"[33]

Beginning in the 1870s, labor organizations were able to bring these abuses to light and raise public outcry about "Slavery in the Baker Shops"—but not the outcry they hoped for.[34] Rather than rousing sympathy for exploited workers, unions and their allies succeeded in focusing the country's outrage on dirty bread and the dirty hands that made it. Reports of "disease-breeding bread" had circulated since the 1880s, but with the attention called to Chicago's meatpacking industry by Upton Sinclair's muckraking journalism, concern about bread exploded in the mid-1900s. Months after *The Jungle* hit bookstores in February 1906, the city's chief sanitary inspector declared that bakery "conditions rival those discovered in the worst of the packing houses."[35] Sensationalist descriptions of unventilated and pestilent cellar bakeries filled local newspapers and echoed through the city's lecture halls. Sanitary inspectors painted pictures of dark, vermin-infested caves with raw sewage dripping from pipes into dough-mixing troughs, street dust and horse manure blown onto dough, bread cooling on dirt floors, and whole families sleeping on rag piles in bakeries, alongside their chickens. In the worst cases, bakers worked ankle deep in water and sewage when storms backed up city drains.

As pressure for a federal pure food law mounted, Chicago civic organizations, women's groups, and self-styled sanitary activists conducted surprise bakery inspections and drew up "white lists" of acceptable establishments. Under pressure from these groups and driven from within by crusading health officials, the city government stepped up regulation. A 1907 ordinance established guidelines for bakery construction, outlawed sleeping in bakeries, and mandated regular inspections. Later, a second ordinance banned cellar bakeries outright.

These were the first such ordinances in a major city, and Pure Food activists around the country took Chicago as a model. There was still much work to be done, though: in 1908 only thirty of one thousand bakeries inspected under Chicago's new ordinance passed without citation.[36] At least they had been inspected. In New York, thousands of cellar bakeries went virtually unregulated. By 1910, however, with sensational accounts of filthy bakeries filling newspapers and stories of progressive action flooding in from Chicago and elsewhere, pressure mounted. Blue-ribbon commissions were appointed and "professional sanitarians" deployed.

In November 1911, the New York State Factory Investigating Committee convened days of hearings on the city's bakeries. Consumer protection advocate Frances Perkins, who would later become FDR's secretary of labor and the country's first female cabinet member, lent the proceedings celebrity status. During 1910, she had personally inspected one hundred New York bakeries, and found conditions revolting.[37] In her testimony before the committee, Perkins repeatedly emphasized bakeries' criminal lack of ventilation. The toll poor air quality took on the lungs of journeymen bakers was horrific. As a public health doctor confirmed later in the hearings, nearly 100 percent of bakery workers in New York showed signs of tuberculosis, bronchitis, and other lung infections. When dealing with other industries, the committee showed concern for workplace safety, but when it came to bread making, it was more interested in hearing about workers' hygiene.

With a few exceptions, committee members darted around witnesses' appeals for workplace safety regulations, restating the bakery problem as a question of how best to control immigrant workers. Commissioners' questions focused on immigrant bakers' beer drinking, tobacco chewing, sleeping habits, and spitting, their scabs, their lice, their sweat, their filthy hands, and their unwashed clothes. As the city health commissioner, Ernst Lederle, argued, cellar bakeries themselves were not the problem, the problem was that "the people were dirty and careless."[38]

Indeed, in both Chicago and New York, public uproar about cellar bakery conditions was hard to separate from larger anxieties about the habits of the nation's new Jewish and Italian immigrants. Thus, even when Perkins and other witnesses defended workers' hygiene habits, the commission voiced skepticism. In one revealing exchange, state assemblyman Cyrus Phillips argued with a public health doctor. "These men you have described are naturally and inherently unclean; aren't they? And they don't know how to do anything else?" the assemblyman queried. "Why, I guess that's true," the doctor ventured cautiously, but the assemblyman pressed on with his point about the nature of immigrant bakers: "No amount of inspection will improve them very much?" Then the doctor surprised those present in the hearing by responding that yes, he did believe that bakers' habits *could* be changed. Assemblyman Phillips replied incredulously, "[You think] that they could counteract their natural and inherent tendencies?" "I certainly do," the doctor repeated. The two officials weren't talking about bread anymore, they were debating the nature of new immigrants. Sensationalist accounts of dangerous bread likely reflected unease about newcomers more than any real hazards posed by eating the product of their ovens. And this is, in the end, the grain of salt with which we must take fears of cellar bakeries—and a clue to why bakeries like the Wards' flourished.

Whether or not bread from small bakeries was actually unsanitary, the moral panic around dirt, germs, and immigrant habits was a gift for industrial bakers. "I want to know where my bread comes from!" an affluent woman demanded in a national advertising campaign for Holsum bread. "I don't want bread from some nameless basement bakery. I want my bread from a bakery that's clean as my own kitchen. . . . I've stopped baking but I still want clean bread." Or, as an ad from Los Angeles more bluntly put it, "Many bakeries in New York, Chicago, and other cities are being condemned by health officers as unclean and unsanitary. How often do you inspect *your* bakery?"[39] Strange as it might seem to contemporary foodies, in the early twentieth century the language of "knowing where your food comes from" was a public relations coup for industrial food.

Bakeries across the country overwhelmingly adopted the new language of clean bread in their advertising, but it was the Wards, once again, who set the bar. Alongside reprinted news reports on the "shocking state of cellar bakeries," the Wards invited New York to visit its bakeries. "You can see every detail in the making of Ward's Tip-Top Bread. The human hand never touches bread at these, the greatest bakeries in the world—daylight bakeries, snow-white temples of cleanliness." Transparency, cleanliness, and modernity displaced taste, cost, convenience, and even freshness in bread advertising. The "bare hand" became the greatest enemy of bread. As a Ward Bakeries ad in the *New York Times* stressed in italics, *"Bread kneaded by hand or mixed by hand can never be made a truly clean sanitary product."*[40] Of course, even bread "untouched by human hands" still required the presence of a few workers, and this bothered consumers bombarded by images of disease-ridden bakers. So the Wards' advertising also trumpeted the company's meticulous inspection of workers' health and habits—even their moral character.

Consumers around the country flocked to witness the spectacle of sanitary baking. They crowded around the glass of smaller "window bakeries," where all operations could be viewed from the street, and lined up for tours of larger factories. One Ohio bakery even encouraged teachers to plan hygiene lessons for their students around tours of its factory. A trip to Stolzenbach's scientific bakery, the company claimed, would instill pupils with "the great, lifelong value of a thorough understanding of the inestimable advantage of perfect cleanliness."[41]

By the end of the 1900s, progressive concern with bakery conditions had spread throughout the entire nation. In Montgomery, Alabama, for example, progressive women's groups drew up a white list of acceptable establishments and launched a boycott of offending bakeries that caused an immediate 25 percent drop in sales.[42] By 1913, every major city was home to several sanitary bakeries, and small towns were close behind. In 1915, the *Ogden Standard* in Utah proudly declared that the town's thirty thousand people enjoyed access to no fewer than six sanitary bakeries producing "loaves of bread that our ancestors of only a generation ago would think beyond the power of a baker."[43]

YOU AND YOUR LITTLE OVEN CAN'T COMPETE

At first, changes in bakery facilities themselves—the introduction of shining surfaces, crisp white uniforms, medical inspectors, and mechanical mixers—seemed like enough to assuage most anxieties about bread. But doubts lingered, and old fears resurfaced. Consumers and their expert health advisors knew that germs and bacteria were invisible, but not much else. They believed that bread could be dangerous, but didn't know *how*. Thus, fear remained fairly amorphous and questions abounded. Did baking really kill all germs? Editors at the influential *Chautauquan* didn't think so: "Dough kneaded with the hands always runs the risk of contagion," they wrote in a special section on preventing disease. "The germs of cholera, typhoid, and scarlet fever, for example, might be carried in this way easier than in most others."[44] And what about bread mold? One Chicago civic group railed against "disease germs arising from moldy bread," while Ellen Richards warned housewives to stand ever vigilant against molds and bacterial growth that infected bread with "sticky masses" and blood-colored clots.[45]

Yeasts were microscopic. Were they also germs? Fascinated by the new world of microbiology, the authors of late nineteenth- and early twentieth-century writing on baking science frequently adopted the language of disease. *The Complete Bread, Cake, and Cracker Baker,* for example, casually noted that leavening contained "numerous organisms of disease," which produced "numerous sources of disease action."[46] And raw food guru Eugene Christian, known for his incendiary tract "Why Some Foods Explode in Your Stomach," offered this memorable image of bread's living biology: "Bread rises when infected with the yeast germ, because millions of these little worms have been born and have died, and from their dead and decaying bodies there rises a gas just as it does from the dead body of a hog or any other animal."[47]

Seen in that light, fermentation did seem a little scary, and this made easy fodder for food faddists. C. H. Routh, an influential British doctor, argued that yeast-leavened loaves created "a fit nidus [nest]" for the growth of bacteria. And he was but one voice making this connection. During the late nineteenth century, fear of fermentation led to a small craze for chemically leavened "aerated bread" on both sides of the Atlantic. New York City health commissioner Cyrus Edson went as far as to declare, "Bread which is wholesome should not be raised with yeast, but with a pure baking powder."[48]

Faced with associations between bread and the scary world of microbes, ordinary people tried to make sense of a paradox: how could bread baking, something people had done for millennia without apparent ill effects, be so horribly, horribly dangerous? *Undercooked* bread offered an easy way to reconcile this contradiction. Failure to cook bread properly must be what unleashed nature's living bestiary into innocent stomachs. As *Mother's Magazine* warned, children's "bread must be thoroughly cooked, for if the yeast spores escape the heat, as soon as they come into contact with the sugar in the stomach they grow and produce fermentation."[49]

With little actual evidence that poorly baked bread made people sick, the generalized cloud of anxiety around bread production gradually converged into one (slightly) more reasonable fear: by 1913, the country's food experts and health campaigners fixed their attention on the handling of bread *after* it left the bakery. Consumers could view bakery cleanliness with their own eyes and, at least in theory, pure food laws guaranteed the integrity of ingredients—but nothing protected the loaf itself. "While most bakeshops are now sanitary," a speaker observed at a national convention of state health officials, "the conditions under which [bread] is handled after it leaves the place is subject to serious criticism . . . [even the purest bread] may be swarming with the germs of filth."[50] Readers of *Good Housekeeping*, the country's leading Pure Foods advocate, voted unprotected bread one of their top five food safety concerns, and the *Journal of the American Medical Association* concurred. In a 1913 statement reprinted by newspapers around the country, America's leading medical journal warned that even bread baked in sanitary bakeries risked contamination by deadly microbes during delivery.[51]

The solution to this problem was obvious: bread must be wrapped. As the public cry for wrapped bread spread across the country between 1912 and 1914, however, bakers balked. Wrapping bread was complicated and labor intensive. Materials and machines were not yet adequate for the job, and it would probably damage flavor, they argued. It would certainly raise costs. Even some bakers who had eagerly adopted the mantle of "sanitation" blamed demands for wrapping on "zealous inspectors," "pure foods magazines," and fickle consumers lured by the novelty of "sealed package food preparations." Nevertheless, backed again by women's and consumers' organizations, state and local governments across the country pushed aside objections from the national baking industry lobby to pass laws requiring bread wrapping, and by 1920, store-bought bread was almost universally wrapped.[52]

Not surprisingly, these new regulations favored larger, more automated bakeries that could afford wrapping machines. Those companies, in turn, fanned the flames of consumer fear. Perfection Bakeries, for example, ran a national ad campaign warning in bold type, "State health authorities condemn unwrapped bread. . . . They know that dust, heavily laden with the germs of tuberculosis and other diseases is easily blown onto unwrapped bread. . . . When you eat bread that leaves the bakery unwrapped you are eating disease and dirt."[53] Once again, the language of cleanliness had become a club with which big bakers bludgeoned smaller competitors.

In the end, the language of "clean" bread made big bakers appear the heroes, when they could so easily have played the villains. Thus, even while plotting to control the nation's bread, William Ward could also, in good conscience, bask in the glow of commendations from mayors and public officials all over the country calling the Ward Bakeries champions of "civic hygiene" and the "public weal."[54]

Small bakers simply could not compete against the massed economic and cultural power of the trusts. Thus, even as the country's consumption of bakery bread soared in the first decades of the twentieth century, the number of bakeries fell dramatically.[55] Ironically, the language of "knowing where your food comes from" had facilitated the *distancing* of consumers from their bread production, as underground but local bakeries and home baking gave way to centralized palaces of industrial efficiency. Married to brute economic power, the language of health and purity swept away small bakeshops and skilled jobs like so much flour dust. Lung-stricken journeymen in New York's cellar bakeries had long held out against misery in the hopes of one day opening their own shops. Now they—and their former bosses—could only hope for a place on the unskilled assembly line of a bread factory. There they would enjoy better working conditions, perhaps, but no hope of starting their own bakery.

Even that stalwart icon of all that was good—"Mother"—came in for harsh criticism under the banner of hygienic diet. *Scientific Amer-*

ican, women's magazines, and home economics textbooks portrayed careless home baking as a threat to family health, while other observers wondered whether even the most careful housewife could produce safe bread. "The modern bakers' oven has a germ-killing power that is far beyond that of a household oven," the *Atlanta Constitution* warned, and a New Castle, Pennsylvania, reporter confirmed that baking factories' "great white ovens . . . properly kill the yeast germs." "You and your little oven cannot compete. . . . It is scientifically proven that home baking is a mistake from every standpoint."[56]

Ellen Richards compared home-baked loaves with "laboratory bread" and found the former lacking. For Richards, tradition and lack of control meant that home-baked bread was not just inferior but also potentially dangerous. "The custom of some housewives of wrapping the hot loaf in thick cloth that the steam may soften the crust is entirely wrong from a bacteriological standpoint," she argued, and extra care was needed for coarse breads, which contained particularly resistant bacteria. She urged housewives to follow strict sanitary procedures and educate themselves by conducting yeast gas experiments in test tubes and Petri dishes. To drive home the weight of her warning she stressed, *"Every case of typhoid fever is due to somebody's criminal carelessness."*[57] Faced with these risks, why experiment or chance the criminal carelessness of homemade bread when the scientific bakery was near?

Backed by the urgent language of food purity and public health, dramatic changes in the way the country got its bread seemed reasonable, even necessary. The destruction of craft baking, the replacement of skilled labor with machines, and the concentration of baking into ever larger and more distant factories were not solely the product of insatiable greed or capitalist competition. They arose out of often well-meaning and earnest concern for food safety.

THE TRIUMPH OF INDUSTRIAL BAKING

In 2010, the only trace of the Ward Baking Company's sparkling palace of automatic baking was a faint white gleam shining off the concrete rubble in a chain-linked vacant lot. In an age of resurgent artisan baking, Ward's Brooklyn bread factory was demolished to make way for high-end real estate development. Looking around

Prospect Heights, though, with its retro-chic bars, vintage stores, and yoga studios, it was clear that it wasn't just the bakery building that was gone. In an age marked by nostalgia for old ways and artisanal authenticity—when consumers living in expensive condos associate purity with small scale and the touch of human hands, not the reverse—the very utopian dreams of scientific eating embodied in the Ward Bakery seemed preposterous.

It's easy, from our vantage, to discount the wondrous appeal of industrial purity and hygiene, but this attitude does disservice to a time when food-borne illnesses were the leading causes of death, when disruptions in the provision of a single staple could unleash fears of famine and rebellion. We should think twice before dismissing consumers who flocked to sanitary factory bread as mere dupes of corporate propaganda. Nostalgia for Great-grandma's bread and neighborhood bakeries omits a few details.

Yet, for all that it made food safer or brought more air and light to bakery workers, the great wave of efficiency and hygiene sweeping through the United States during the early twentieth century did not address the root causes of food insecurity. Thanks to the combined efforts of social reformers and food scientists, the country's loaves would no longer carry typhus (if they ever really had), but they would still be the stuff of poverty. Food reformers' confidence in the gospel of hygienic eating fueled great victories, but also helped buttress social discrimination.

Thanks to widely circulating discourses of scientific expertise and efficiency, bread consumption choices became a way in which people positioned themselves and were positioned within social hierarchies. Of course, bread choices have *always* been about positioning oneself and being positioned within social hierarchies. Combined with the language of purity and contagion, however, it acquired powerful new stakes: early twentieth-century bread choices were not just about class and distinction in general, but rather about a specific form of social difference constructed around the very lines of life and death, health and disease.[58]

In the 2000s, as in the 1900s, Americans had many opportunities to contemplate food safety. And yet, compared to the 1900s, Americans had very little to fear. Thanks to modern medicines and, yes, government regulation, food-borne illness was no longer one of the nation's top killers. Even some food safety advocates conceded that widely cited estimates of the prevalence of food-borne illness might be exaggerated. Still, fears continued, sometimes escalating into panic.[59] These fears were not without basis. In a world of cutthroat competition and broken oversight, food processors take short cuts. They accelerate production lines to breakneck speeds, and accidents happen. They cut costs by recycling unsafe waste products as animal feed, sourcing fresh produce from distant corners of the planet, and cramming livestock into unsanitary feedlots. Avoidable illnesses sicken and kill real people. But resurgent anxiety about food safety also reflects other, more social dynamics. History suggests that anxiety about food contamination generally intensifies during periods of perceived upheaval: in moments of expanding globalization, rapid demographic changes, immigrant influxes, and swiftly evolving technology. The early twentieth century was one of those moments of upheaval, as was the early twenty-first.

That levels of anxiety about food can be correlated with concerns about immigration or urbanization does not make them less real. It does, however, challenge us to think about the social life of food fears in more nuanced ways. What unintended legacies will early twenty-first-century food safety anxiety produce? Will it yield consumer action and government legislation that address root causes of food-borne illness? Will it give rise to new, alternative networks of trust and accountability? What social disparities will it alleviate or amplify?

• • •

Red's milk never made my wife and me sick. We were young and not at any special risk, and everything seemed to work out, despite my apprehension. Soon we were driving glass jars of milk to friends in Tucson every week. A few people we knew balked outright at the idea of unpasteurized milk. Some signed on, enthusiastic about local milk in theory, but never mustered up the guts to drink their weekly jar in practice. Most people thought it was the best milk they'd ever had, and asked for more. They trusted our milk, and I've never fully understood why. In part, our friends trusted Kate and me, and that sufficed. More importantly, they trusted the experienced older couple teaching us. But, in a lot of ways, our friends were also placing their faith in a dream of good food. It's an old dream, and one that has left a deep imprint on America. It's the idea that food from small, local producers is pure and virtuous, that the best way to ensure food safety is to know exactly where it comes from.

Proponents of industrial food like to mock this dream, reveling in every instance of sickness traced to a small producer. Hard-to-pin-down relations of trust enmeshed in face-to-face connections, they argue, are no match for industrial-scale Hazard Analysis and Critical Control Points. During the early twenty-first century, however, a growing and diverse segment of the U.S. population, from liberal to libertarian, suburban soccer moms to rural survivalists, aging hippies to young urban elites, didn't share the food industry's confidence.

Prompted by the very real failings of a scientific regulatory system effectively controlled by powerful corporations, they sought alternative ways of knowing that their food was safe. Rather than rely on formal procedures and government audits, they wanted to know more intimately where their food came from. "People around here like farmers' markets," the past director of my local farmers' market told a public gathering, "because you never know what those Third World people are putting in imported food." Less xenophobically, my food politics students trust the meat from Walla Walla's organic grass-fed beef producer, not because they've checked the ranch's paperwork, but because they've gotten to know the owner and toured the operation.

I find this logic convincing and appealing, but what does it leave out? Among other gaps, reducing food safety to consumer-owner relations ignores a whole world of food chain workers—the people who, in most cases, actually grow, pick, process, and pack our food. This, despite the fact that the intense systematic pressures to cut corners that lead to contaminated food are often inseparable from the forces that make food chain work the most exploited and dangerous sector of the U.S. economy. As Eric Schlosser argues in *Fast Food Nation,* worker safety concerns are food safety concerns and vice versa.[60] The alternative food movement has had a hard time grappling with this idea. When we seek out "where our food comes from," we want to see a smiling farm-owning family, not a poor immigrant labor force. As Slow Food USA president Josh Viertel acknowledged in 2009, "Historically this movement has focused on the environment, health and preserving small farms. But we've completely missed the boat when it comes to work."[61]

Some segments of the diverse alternative food movement have, in fact, found ways to incorporate labor into their agrarian vision of good food. Others at least pay lip service to workers, but hope that a new system of local farms would make them redundant. In the worst cases, however, food safety concerns react with racism and xenophobia to enflame hatred. As in the case of my local farmers' market director, it is sometimes hard to separate food safety concerns from fear of strangers. Noted raw milk advocate Dr. William Campbell Douglass, for example, issued a widely cited statement in 2008 arguing that dirty illegal immigrant food chain workers were making Americans sick, infecting the country's sustenance with diseases ranging from tuberculosis to leprosy to STDs. That these diseases are not typically spread through food didn't matter. Douglass had touched a deep chord in American history. As sociologists Lourdes Gouveia and Arunas Juska discovered, well-meaning activism against contaminated meat in the 1990s often had the unintended side effect of fueling fear of "dirty" immigrant meatpackers.[62]

Food purity discourses may achieve wide-ranging improvements in the health and security of a defined population (typically wealthy white consumers), but they are not innocent. They structure the world of life into comparable ranks and actionable hierarchies, safeguarding privileged spheres while targeting outliers as enemies. There is nothing particularly wrong with this on a certain level—who mourns the elimination of typhus from milk? What becomes clear from the story of bread, however, is that fears of threat to the social body don't remain neatly moored in purely alimentary realms. They overflow, combine with larger social anxieties, and reinforce other kinds of exclusion and distract from root causes.

Perhaps what is needed in the face of this is a new model of food safety—one that doesn't just flip the old model around, privileging the dream of small-scale producers over large-scale, raw over pasteur-ized, while retaining the same underlying architecture of purity and contagion. We need a vision of food safety aware of its own social collusions and attentive, first and foremost, to the complex power relations flowing through our food system.

THE INVENTION OF SLICED BREAD

Dreams of Control and Abundance

The housewife can well experience a thrill of pleasure when she first sees a loaf of this bread with each slice the exact counterpart of its fellows. So neat and precise are the slices, and so definitely better than anyone could possibly slice by hand with a bread knife that one realizes instantly that here is a refinement that will receive a hearty and permanent welcome.

—Reporter's account of the first automatically sliced bread
sold in the United States, Chillicothe, Missouri, July 6, 1928

THE BEST THING SINCE SLICED BREAD?

Brasserie Four in Walla Walla, Washington, serves up regional cheeses, *pâte de foie de poulet* handmade from local organic chickens, and roasted bone marrow from a nearby ranch. Tourists, drawn to this out-of-the-way town by its hundred-plus wineries, stop in for French country cooking, but the vibe is hipster-salon. "Townies"—affluent early retirees and young urbanites who fled to the country with kids in tow—fill the place most nights. The art on the wall is by their kids and grandchildren. This is a place for sopping up herbed broth enveloping Northwest mussels and scraping every last bit of seasonal root vegetable puree out of a bowl. It is a place where you need lots of good bread. And for several years, until Walla Walla hatched a good European-style bakery of its own, Brasserie Four—this shrine to the local and artisanal—served baguettes made by Japanese robots twelve hundred miles away.

For such well-traveled bread, it had many of the marks of artisanal quality: a creamy yellow crumb, alveolate with large irregular holes, each bubble's thin, shiny membrane testifying to skillful work with a finicky wet dough and the absence of commercial yeast. The taste was nutty, with tang but no artificially sour sourdough notes. Brasserie Four's baguettes, produced by La Brea Bakeries in Los Angeles and shipped frozen to groceries and restaurants around the world, were clearly the product of care, slow fermentation, and simple ingredients, not a chemically pumped speed dough like most ersatz "French bread" in town.

As someone interested in good bread and food politics, I had long wondered whether it was possible to produce high-quality European-style breads in the United States at affordable prices. The dream of good bread for the masses is the most ancient of bread dreams. And living in Walla Walla, far from the artisan bakeries of Portland, San Francisco, or New York, this relatively inexpensive and widely available bread almost seemed to fit the bill. Not all my foodie friends shared my optimism: when I told one die-hard champion of handmade bread that I planned to visit La Brea's factory, he exploded, "Why would you want to go to La Brea Bakery? It's the evil empire!"

Some of the country's most prominent artisan bakers shared that sentiment. Dan Leader, owner of upstate New York's famed Bread Alone bakery, complained about La Brea to the *New York Times,* "With all due respect, bread that's mixed, shaped, and baked in a factory, untouched by human hands, is not artisan bread."[1] I was inclined to trust Leader because it was his cookbook that first introduced me to the art of baking European loaves. But I was still resolved to head to L.A. with my question: Could bread that's mixed in a sixty-thousand-square-foot factory owned by a Swiss multinational, shaped by high-tech machinery mimicking the sensitive fingers of a village baker, partially baked in a seventy-foot-long tunnel oven, and then flash frozen for shipment to stores and restaurants from Singapore to Walla Walla be "good"?

Jon Davis, La Brea Bakeries' vice president for concept development—the company's idea man, I was told—agreed to help answer that question by showing me around La Brea's operations. We made two preliminary stops before heading out to the Van Nuys industrial park where Brasserie Four's baguettes were born. First, we paused for coffee at the tiny La Brea Avenue storefront Nancy Silverton opened in 1989. That space still has a neighborhood bakery feel, with a steady stream of regulars ducking in for bread, coffee, and pastries, but no actual bread is baked there now. When it first opened in 1989, Angelinos, accustomed to sterile supermarket bread, called Silverton's European hearth loaves "dirty," "too holey," and "burnt," but something clicked quickly. In less than two years La Brea had outgrown its original space, and Silverton decided to open a larger bakery to fill skyrocketing orders from L.A. grocery stores and restaurants.[2]

That second bakery—the Direct Store Delivery plant producing fresh bread for the Greater Los Angeles market—was the next stop on our tour. "The DSD" is the heart of La Brea Bakeries, and Jon Davis's affection for this place was palpable. It is here where he "plays," getting out of the office and putting his hands in the dough to develop and refine new product lines. Although some of the work here is automated, this is not an industrial bakery by any stretch; it's a small artisanal bakery that has been "scaled up," the way a cook might double or triple a recipe. Instead of the original bakery's one worker scurrying around with one bucket of sourdough starter, the DSD has more workers and buckets than I can count. Instead of a couple of plastic tubs of fermenting dough, the DSD has scores of plastic tubs stacked in precarious towers. The overall effect is organized chaos, a precisely orchestrated ballet of weaving carts, moving loaves, and flying hands. The place still looks and smells like a craft bakery—even though it produces thousands of loaves a day.

Finally, after battling northbound traffic on the 405 expressway, we reached our third stop—the part of the tour I had traveled twelve hundred miles to see: quite possibly the world's most innovative industrial bakery. On the outside, La Brea's global production facility was a beige shell in a bland industrial park. Nothing immediately screamed "bakery." Inside, with its massive stainless steel tanks, circulatory system of tubes and pipes, cool, clean air, and humming conveyor belts, the place might as well have been a large milk bottler or apple-processing plant. But then I saw the baguettes.

La Brea's Van Nuys, plant is an M. C. Escher optical illusion come to life: impossibly long lines of dough trailing into the visual vanishing point, becoming impossibly perfect squares, rolling themselves into perfectly uniform baguettes, marching off in impossibly long lines again, rotating into towering Ferris wheel contraptions, filing around corners, parading through tunnels, and spiraling up almost forty feet in the air. When the 80 percent–baked baguettes finally descend to earth, it is through the machine that makes La Brea's far-flung distribution possible: a massive blast freezer that inserts fresh, preservative-free bread into the global food system. Human hands touch the loaves at exactly two points: each loaf is hand straightened and hand slashed before baking. Is this an artisan bakery? "Yes," Davis replied without hesitation.

"Artisanal," Davis argued, is a commitment to integrity, not the use of any particular technique. He pointed to La Brea's insistence on slow, cool fermentation to build rich flavor and texture out of just flour, water, starter, and salt. La Brea could easily speed up the line by turning up the temperature to accelerate fermentation, eliminating the loaves' long sojourn in a cool retarding room, or adding chemicals that condition dough to higher speed mixing and rougher handling. It won't. And, Davis admitted with a note of pride, the company has lost several major contracts because of this commitment. Unlike most large bakeries, he explained, La Brea has changed its machinery to conform to and nurture the delicate, living nature of bread, rather than adjusting its bread to suit the requirements of efficient automation. Moving steadily along its assembly line, the dough looked, felt, and smelled just like what I make at home.

Awed, I asked Davis how La Brea's industrial-artisanal power might affect small bakeries. Would it, Goliath-like, annihilate the country's fragile new culture of local baking? What were the environmental costs of transporting frozen bread thousands of miles? Davis had answers to those questions, but by then I was lost in my own reverie. The idea that a company like La Brea could make high-quality bread accessible to a much broader group of people intrigued me. "If you have a good small artisan bakery in your neighborhood or town, by all means, buy your bread there," Davis insisted, "but unless they live in San Francisco or someplace like that, most people just don't have that kind of access." La Brea loaves still cost more than standard store-bought fare and appeal to a relatively narrow band of consumers, but what could it become? Was this a model for a future of artisanal-industrial abundance, a technological fix for the failings of our food system?

It seemed improbable, but then that reminded me of another watershed moment in industrial baking that appeared equally inconceivable in its time. Perhaps by delving into the political life of another moment in which industrial abundance, once deemed impossible, felt just within reach, I can gain some purchase on my dream of affordable artisan bread in the United States. And, in the process, we can understand a bit better the hidden costs of seeking technological fixes to food system dilemmas.

THE INVENTION OF SLICED BREAD

On July 6, 1928, what would become the world's first loaves of automatically sliced bread steamed out of the ovens of the Chillicothe Baking Company in northwestern Missouri. The slicing machine's inventor, Otto Rohwedder, unappreciated and down on his luck, had achieved something nearly every member of the industrial baking establishment thought impossible. Retail bakers had used machines to slice loaves at the point of sale for years, but few people in the industry believed that bread could be automatically sliced as it came off the assembly line. Bread was too unruly. What would hold the sliced loaves together? How would slicing affect the chemistry of taste? What would prevent sliced bread from rapidly molding or staling? Many bakers actively opposed factory slicing. Otto Rohwedder's initial design for a five-foot-long "power driven multi-bladed bread slicer" dated back to 1917, but he found no takers for the idea and had almost given up hope. For Rohwedder's friend Frank Bench, owner of the Chillicothe Baking Company, installing the machine was a favor and a last shot in the dark. Bench's bakery was teetering on the verge of bankruptcy—what did he have to lose?[3]

The results astounded all observers. Sales of sliced Kleen-Maid Bread soared 2,000 percent within weeks, and a beaming *Chillicothe Constitution-Tribune* reporter described housewives' "thrill of pleasure" upon "first see[ing] a loaf of this bread with each slice the exact counterpart of its fellows . . . definitely better than anyone could possibly slice by hand."[4] The news spread rapidly. Sliced bread took off first in Missouri, Iowa, and Illinois, then spread throughout the

Midwest by late summer 1928. By fall 1928 mechanical slicing hit the West Coast, and appeared in New York and New Jersey by October. Slicing got easier too, as bakers realized that the wooden pins Rohwedder and Bench had used to hold sliced loaves together were not necessary; the wrapper sufficed. By 1929, an industry report suggested that there was practically no town of more than twenty-five thousand people without a supply of sliced bread. Some bakers dismissed sliced bread as a fad, comparing it to other Roaring Twenties crazes like pole sitting, barnstorming, and jazz dancing. Nevertheless, as bakers wrote in frantic trade magazine articles, anyone who resisted the new technology would be crushed by the competition.[5]

The Arnot Baking Company in Jacksonville, Florida, learned this the hard way. For two long years it tried to hold out against the new technology, even as it hemorrhaged customers to bakers offering sliced bread. Arnot reduced prices and increased the richness of its doughs, but still the company's unsliced loaves lost market share. Finally, in 1931, Arnot installed a slicer and reported an immediate 600 percent increase in sales.[6]

By 1930, half a dozen companies manufactured commercial bread slicers, and by 1936, 90 percent of the country's commercial bread was sliced.[7] The industry's conservative estimates showed that bakeries offering sliced bread increased sales 100–300 percent. Anecdotal reports spoke of increases of up to 3,000 percent.[8]

While awaiting deliveries of mechanical slicers from hopelessly backordered manufacturers, bakers asked themselves a logical question: What's so great about sliced bread? "Why does anyone want sliced bread anyway?" one baker wondered in an essay for a trade magazine. "The housewife is saved one operation in the preparation of a meal. Yet, try as one will, the reasons do not seem valid enough to make demand for the new product."[9] He had a point. How much extra work is it really to slice your own bread?

Quite a bit, as it turned out. And the reason for this difficulty lay in the very processes of industrialization bread had undergone in the preceding decades. Recall that in the 1920s, instead of baking their own bread or buying it face-to-face from a neighborhood baker, consumers were increasingly purchasing loaves from far-off factories. Instead of seeing, smelling, and touching bread directly, they were picking up loaves sealed in hygienic wrapping. Despite all the emphasis on "knowing *where* your bread came from," consumers had no good way of judging *when* it had come. They needed a new way of judging freshness, and they found it in squeezable softness. More squeezable loaves appeared fresher, even if they weren't. Marketing surveys revealed that while consumers didn't always like eating soft bread, they always bought the softest-feeling loaf. Softness had become customers' proxy for freshness, and savvy bakery scientists turned their minds to engineering even more squeezable loaves.[10]

As a result of the drive toward softer bread, industry observers noted that modern loaves had become almost impossible to slice neatly at home. Without exaggeration and with only a little bit of whimsy, we can speak of a messy collision between the preternaturally soft loaves of machine-age baking and the dull cutlery of turn-of-the-century kitchens. Consumers, marketing experts, and baking industry research all agreed: neat, perfect—toaster and sandwich ready—slices could only be achieved mechanically.[11]

Practical considerations, then, played a key role in sliced bread's rapid acceptance. But what about housewives' "thrill of pleasure when . . . first see[ing] a loaf of this bread with each slice the exact counterpart of its fellows"? A little saved labor couldn't explain a thrill like that. How did this simple invention become America's "best thing"? To understand that, we must return to the ethos of scientific eating, to a different manifestation of the early twentieth-century veneration of industrial food. Sliced bread may have endured because of the convenience it offered, but its immediate exaltation speaks to something more visceral: a powerful emotional resonance between the spectacle of industrial bread and a larger set of aesthetics and aspirations gripping 1920s America.

THE STREAMLINED LOAF

Consider the precise symmetry of the sliced loaf, each of its pieces "the exact counterpart of its fellows." Calibrated within a sixteenth of an inch, the loaf's tranches articulate a perfect accordion, a white fanned deck. Note the plane of the slice. Each face reveals an intricate lacework unmarred by aberrant holes. There are no unneeded flourishes, no swags added by the baker. If we could, for a moment, let go of our postmodern attachment to the roughed-up and irregular landscape of artisanal bread, the sight would take our breath away. Industrial bread exudes a modernist aesthetic, and it didn't get that way by accident.

During the 1920s and 1930s, an obsession with machines and progress changed the look of America's material life. Streamlined design channeled a love of industrial efficiency into the nooks and crannies of Victorian frill and Craftsman style. It began with vehicles—smoothing, tapering, and lengthening their lines to help them slip efficiently through air. It was a seductive look, all speed and glamour, and it spread quickly to objects with no need to foil drag. Irons, pencil sharpeners, and kitchen mixers got lean and smooth. The country's first pop-up toaster, the 1928 Toastmaster, looked like an Airstream camper. Even vegetables got remade in the image of rocket ships. As historian Christina Cogdell notes, "Carrots were being transformed [by plant breeders] from 'short chubby roots' into 'far' more 'attractive' 'long slim beauties.' "[12]

Bakers responded to this trend by smoothing out bread's bulges, squaring off pan bread's flared "balloon tops," and lengthening loaves into Zephyr trains. Industry experts believed that "stubby, plump loaves of bread, the old fashioned design" would increase bread consumption because their slices were broader and thicker, but they were forced to accept consumers' desire for streamlined loaves. "Skinny bread is here to stay," a gathering of professional bakers confessed in 1937, and, from Charleston, West Virginia, to Kingsport, Tennessee, bakeries touted the sleek design of their loaves. In advertising images of bread from the 1920s and 1930s, loaves look for all the world like Bauhaus office blocks or Le Corbusier chairs.[13] This was more than just a visual style. It was a political statement about the future. Tellingly, at the peak of the streamline aesthetic in 1938, a food industry expo in Zanesville, Ohio, presented a loaf of sliced bread under the theme of "Utopia."[14]

This combination of food, technology, and the future would not have seemed unusual. At the turn of the century, Americans' appetite for utopian thinking seemed limitless. Hundreds of utopian manifestos and novels filled bookstores, utopian clubs debated the means of achieving progress, and utopian communities sprang up, attempting to turn the dream into practical reality. Of all the writing on utopia, Edward Bellamy's *Looking Backward* captured the country's imagination most. In the 1888 novel, which remained popular for decades, Julian West, a young Brahmin of Gilded Age Boston, falls into a deep sleep and awakens in the year 2000 to find the United States transformed into a socialist utopia. Centralized factory production meets all human needs and resources are publicly owned. People are educated, long-lived, and free to pursue whatever leisure activities they desire. War and crime have disappeared. As West explores this new world, he comes to understand how cruel and inefficient his own era was. *Looking Backward* was a not-so-subtle indictment of robber barons, speculation, and greed, a paean to cooperation and redistribution. It sparked Bellamy Clubs, inspired experiments in collective living, fueled growing interest in cooperatively owned enterprise, and sold more copies than almost any other book of its time.[15]

Bellamy's utopian socialism was not without critics, in large part because a competing utopian vision had begun to grip the country's most influential circles: the dream of universal prosperity achieved through cutthroat competition and unregulated markets that would take early twentieth-century elites by storm. The themes of *Looking Backward* did not sit well with proponents of economic "survival of the fittest," a harsh interpretation of Darwinism popularized by Herbert Spencer and fervently embraced by American industrialists. Still, the novel remained popular because it captured a feeling that everyone from Andrew Carnegie to the most militant Red could agree upon: that rapidly emerging technological progress held out the possibility of a world of social harmony built on abundance and efficiency.

In the late 1920s that utopia seemed just within grasp. Wireless radio, liquid-fueled rockets, long-distance air flights, and talking pictures offered dramatic evidence of a world to come. High-tech foods like streamlined sliced bread promised a future of ease, one in which the very material constraints of biological existence that had limited humans for millennia were overcome by science. This Promethean dream looked different from competing political perspectives: Socialists hated industrial trusts but envisioned a world of shared abundance made possible by industrial food production. Capitalists, on the other hand, relished cheap industrial food as a means of placating increasingly organized and militant workers. Either way, it was the same vision: technology would usher in good society by conquering and taming the fickle nature of food provisioning.

This was another incarnation of the ethos of scientific eating. And, as in the previous chapter, delving into it will help us understand one more piece of Florence Farrell's switch to store-bought bread.

NOTHING LEFT TO CHANCE

"To begin then with the very foundation of a good table—*Bread: What ought it to be?*" Catherine and Harriet Beecher Stowe posed this question in their path-breaking compendium of domestic advice, *The American Woman's Home.*[16] The book, which quickly found a place as the essential primer of Victorian domesticity in the United States, promised modern answers to modern problems. Yet, the Beecher sisters' thoughts on bread had a timeless air: "Bread-making can be cultivated . . . as a fine art," guided by "the divine principle of beauty," they argued.[17]

Less than fifty years later, however, the Beechers' invocation of art and aesthetics as the basis for "what bread ought to be" had all but vanished from cookbooks and other food writing. Mary D. Warren, one of countless purveyors of domestic advice who followed in the Beechers' footsteps, captured the new spirit of bread. In a 1923 *Ladies' Home Journal* article, "Science of Oven Management," she insisted, "Modern inventions have made an exact science of baking, and there is no reason whatever for failure. . . . One simply cannot bake by guesswork and expect to secure results, any more than one can ascertain with certainty a sick person's temperature by merely feeling his brow."[18]

Thus, by the 1920s, bread making was widely imagined as a techno-science. References to art, craft, and instinct in the making of bread would remain subordinate to rules and exactitude until the late 1960s. Like family health care, baking was to be a terrain of control and expert measurement rather than art and aesthetics. "Modern baking is scientifically done. Nothing is left to chance," an elementary school textbook read. "The baker has studied the principles of baking and understands the working of the laws that govern his product. In his bakery there is a laboratory with microscopes, tubes, balances, and other instruments, the materials to be used are tested by experts. . . . [The modern baker] is guided by scientific laws."[19]

Baking's traditional apprenticeship model gave way to formal study. The Wahl-Heinus Institute of Fermentology, the Wahl Efficiency Institute, the Chidlow Institute, and the Siebel Institute of Technology championed the scientific study of bread chemistry, biology, and engineering. Founded in 1919 and chaired by George Ward, the American Institute of Baking emerged as a center for research and education.[20] Meanwhile, plenary sessions at meetings of the National Association of Master Bakers informed bakers of the latest scientific thinking on wheat chemistry, rational cost accounting, the effects of salts on fermentation biology, accurate measurement, efficient movement, the physiology of taste, bacteriology, and "bakeshop entomology," among other topics.[21]

Industrial bakers did not conjure up the public's infatuation with scientific progress out of nothing to serve their own interests. Nevertheless, the ethos of scientific eating definitely helped bakers. And they certainly nurtured it. During the first decades of the twentieth century, displays of scientific expertise would provide a key weapon in professional bakers' all-out war against home bread making.

MOTHER WAS A RANK FRAUD AS A BREAD MAKER

With small-scale bakeries effectively dispatched by machinery and oligopoly power, the fate of industrial baking turned on large-scale bakers' ability to outcompete women making bread at home. "For every master baker there are a thousand housewives, and every housewife is either a competitor or a customer," George Haffner, president of the National Association of Master Bakers, warned at the group's 1915 annual meeting. Winning over housewives, he argued presciently, would require a full-scale mobilization, and science would be bakers' primary ally in this battle for bread.[22]

Convincing the country to fear small bakeries and their immigrant workers was one thing. Casting doubt on the safety of Mother's bread was a bit harder. Home bakers had tremendous sanitary advantage over distant factories. You didn't have to take a tour to see how your bread was baked, or guess at the health and habits of your baker.

People had baked bread at home for millennia without disaster. As a result, industrial bakers and their allies in home economics could get only so far depicting homemade bread as a biohazard. Bakers would have to outcompete housewives on other fronts. They would have to make scientific bread appealing in its own right.

In this sense, bakers' mastery of science was a cultural performance, a theater of charisma, authority, and power. Carefully scripted displays of precision, control, and efficiency served two functions: they validated bakers' confidence in their own greatness, their special role in the march toward social progress. And they projected this self-image into a world of women deemed in need of education. "The average housewife today who bakes bread is living in the dark," a speaker at the 1916 convention of the National Association of Master Bakers proclaimed. "She is ignorant of what the up-to-date method of baking consists; she has to be educated, the same as a child is educated to eat from a plate—the only difference being that our task is far harder than teaching a child, whose mind is receptive to instruction and learning."[23]

A 1904 *New York Times* story echoed this sentiment, quoting "the manager of a big bread factory" triumphantly and at length: "I am tired of hearing about that wonderful bread that mother used to make. Mother was a rank fraud as a bread maker. . . . Don't you remember how often her bread went wrong? . . . Mother sometimes blamed that on the weather, or maybe on fairies . . . but it was neither the weather nor the fairies. It was because mother didn't know how to mix dough properly, or because there was something wrong with her ingredients, and she didn't know enough to remedy it."[24]

Bakers' smug paternalism might have infuriated the ranks of middle-class women championing food reforms and social improvement—except that they were just as ensorcelled as bakers. They had staked *their* authority on scientific expertise and its world-changing potential. This sparked considerable debate among home economists. Many believed strongly that housewives could efficiently make bread at home, and dedicated themselves to teaching women the science of baking. In general, however, the country's largely female purveyors of domestic advice and household education mostly embraced bakers' efforts to win over women.

According to leading home economists, Mother could still compete with even the largest bread factories on price, as long as one considered her labor "free." She couldn't hope to compete on quality or consistency, however—not against the massed forces of assembly-line production, temperature-controlled fermentation, chemical dough conditioners, standardized ingredients, and professional ovens. By 1920, William Panschar contends in his history of American baking, the superiority of industrial production was widely accepted. "As engineers rather than craftsmen, bakers were able to produce consistently a high quality, uniform loaf of bread. The degree of control exacted over formulas, ingredients, and production processes were now far beyond the skills of a housewife to match."[25]

Home economists' support for professional baking, in turn, reflected an important change in the beliefs about women's role in the family. As a Pennsylvania journalist explained in 1914, "The modern woman has out-grown the idea that a mother can best serve her children by slaving for them over the hot stove. Self-improvement is the mother's first duty." Indeed, the reporter continued, time and effort squandered on pointless home baking was "responsible for most domestic misery." Women should concern themselves with things they could do relatively well—looking beautiful, raising healthy children, and efficiently administering a modern household.[26]

In this new vision of domesticity, a good housewife was a professional manager making smart choices to maximize her family's health and prospects. As the chair of the University of Chicago's home economics department predicted: in the past, women were judged by their ability to *make* good bread, in the future they would be judged by their skill at *buying* it. "For after all, real efficiency in housekeeping is coming to be measured rather by good administration than by simply the power to do."[27] Responsible mothers delegated their family's staple food to more appropriate experts—professional bakers— and focused their time on policing the quality of competing bread brands. Housewives should be expert consumers, not bread makers. Nevertheless, at a moment when commercial baking was taking place farther and farther from homes as a result of industrial consolidation, a serious question remained: by what signs should expert housewives judge store-bought bread?

WHITE IS A MORAL COLOR

By the 1930s, America's loaves were slender beauties: long, white-wrapped packages. On the inside, however, slicing put bread's structure on display as never before. Crumb irregularities and unevenness that were once acceptable, or easily blamed on customers' deficient skills with bread knives, were now immediately apparent to anyone opening a package of bread. This alarmed bakers. Large uneven holes, so esteemed by artisan bread lovers today, had no place in the modernist aesthetic. Each one was an unacceptable reminder of bread's natural life, a tiny realm of imperfection unconquered by science. The perfect tapered loaf, the ideal slice thickness—all that came to nothing if bread's face looked worm-eaten. Thus, scientific bakers threw themselves into developing new dough-mixing equipment, loaf-shaping technology and, most importantly, chemical dough conditioners to ensure that every slice revealed the exact same architecture of tiny even cells. Consumers, for their part, admired the new look of bread, and accepted uniformity as a mark of quality.[28] Indeed, only one aspect of the high modernist reengineering of bread's appearance stirred major controversy during the first decades of the twentieth century: flour whitening.

White bread had long stood as a symbol of wealth and status—and in America, racial purity—but during the first decades of the twentieth century this association expressed itself in a unique way. Thanks to the way industrial bakers positioned their product as an icon of scientific progress, the superiority of white bread didn't appear to be a matter merely of taste or culinary preference. It was an expression of responsible citizenship. To eat white bread was to participate in the process of building a better nation.

The very whiteness of modern bread helped confirm this dream. At least since the early medieval period, whiteness has had a Janus-faced social and religious symbolism in the West; the color could equally stand for life or death, purity or pallor. In the early twentieth century, however, the meaning of white was increasingly stabilized around notions of purity and control. At a time when white America's collective sense of the ambiguous shades of racial whiteness was more unstable and fractious than at any other time in its history, the simple color white provided a safe and reassuring haven—an uncontaminated field. Whiteness, as never before, had become synonymous with control over threatening disorder, and this association manifested itself in multiple arenas, including food production. Whether in clothing, kitchens, appliances, or water closets, the color of scientific control was white.[29]

Dr. Woods Hutchinson, a leading national pundit on matters related to health, for example, wrote in praise of the color white in an *American Magazine* article: the color white—particularly from whitewash and white paint—represented an important means of forcing immigrants to adopt higher standards of cleanliness. "Anything in the way of dirt or garbage which showed up against this shiny [white] background was so conspicuous," Hutchinson argued, "that shame alone compelled the Polacks and Hungarians in the district to get rid of it in some way." If, as early twentieth-century experts loved to repeat, "dirt was matter out of place," white had been normalized as the defining measure of whether something was in or out of place. "Whitewash," Le Corbusier, one of the most influential modern designers of the early twentieth century, proclaimed, "is extremely moral."[30]

Even Alfred W. McCann—one of the country's fiercest anti–white bread crusaders—understood the visual discipline of the white loaf. McCann ardently promoted whole grain bread, but attacked corrupt bakers who took advantage of the "dusky color" of their darker loaves to conceal impurities. If this didn't happen, he argued, "The white bread maker would not then point to his immaculate loaf, free from the faintest tint of color. He would not contrast the 'chastity' of that white loaf with the 'defilement' of the dark one."[31] In a time when bread production was increasingly taking place outside the home and out of consumers' sight, the whiteness of loaves increasingly substituted for the direct ability to monitor the baking process and reassured consumers of bread's compatibility with modern conceptions of purity, control, and progress.

Luckily, white bread was widely available. The invention of efficient porcelain and then steel roller mills in the mid-1800s had made highly refined flour inexpensive and available to the masses for the first time in human history. From the 1840s on, white wheat bread was no longer only for elites. Refined flour became standard fare for most consumers, and even the poorest Americans would have enjoyed an occasional white loaf. Still, these loaves were not particularly white by twentieth-century standards. Contemporary accounts described them in shades of creamy yellow—hardly the stuff of a modernist palette. This is where the trouble began.

SHINING WHITE OR WAXY AS A CORPSE

Making the creamy white of white flour match the bright titanium shade favored in other objects of scientific housekeeping, from appliances to cooks' aprons to kitchen tiles, required more than efficient milling and sifting. Until the early 1900s, it required something more precious: time. All wheat flour whitens naturally through oxidation as it ages, and millers had traditionally matured their best product for one to two months. But natural aging took up valuable space, slowed inventory turnover, and inevitably led to losses from spoilage. Chemical bleaching, achieved by exposing flour to chlorine or nitrogen peroxide gas, on the other hand, produced oxidation instantly. As *Scientific American* proclaimed, with the 1904 invention of the Alsop bleaching process, "The uncontrollable and time-consuming aging and maturing of flour by nature . . . has been superseded by a safe, rapid, and far more effective process based on scientific principles."[32]

Bleaching may have been practical and efficient, but even the science-obsessed American public didn't like hearing words like "chlorine gas" in conjunction with their bread. Accustomed to outcry against pre-industrial bakers' use of chalk, borax, and alum to whiten dark flour, many consumers and consumer advocates quickly decided that chemical bleaching constituted yet another form of bread adulteration. Influential progressive leaders and publications took up the anti-bleaching cause, and Harvey Wiley entreated his broad following to stand against those who "fool with flour." "Save the bread of the nation!" he urged.[33]

The controversy came to a head in 1910 with a case that would last into the 1920s and influence food safety legislation into the twenty-first century. On April 9, 1910, looking for an opportunity to challenge flour bleaching in court, Harvey Wiley, then chief of the U.S. Bureau of Chemistry, precursor to the FDA, ordered the seizure of 625 sacks of bleached flour sold by the Lexington Mill & Elevator

Company of Lexington, Nebraska. The flour had been shipped across state lines into Missouri, placing the case in federal jurisdiction. This allowed the Bureau of Chemistry to charge Lexington Mill & Elevator with selling "adulterated, misbranded flour containing poisonous and deleterious ingredients."[34] The bureau hoped to establish two things with the case: that bleaching allowed millers to sell, or "misbrand," inferior flour as white, and that nitrate residues from the bleaching process constituted a dangerous ingredient.[35]

A Missouri jury quickly agreed with the government on both counts, but from there, the case wound its way through a drawn-out process of appeal. A federal court of appeals eventually reversed the jury's decision, and in 1914, the U.S. Supreme Court unanimously upheld the reversal.[36]

The Supreme Court's decision hinged on the meaning of the word "may" in a line of the 1906 Pure Food and Drug Act. The act had clearly empowered the government to condemn food that contains "any added poisonous or other added deleterious ingredient which *may* render such article injurious to health," and the Bureau of Chemistry argued that nitrates of the type found in flour subjected to the Alsop process were clearly injurious to health. The Supreme Court, however, sided with Lexington Mill & Elevator's argument that, although nitrates may harm health in large quantities, the government must prove that they do so in the specific amounts present. In a ruling that still guides government actions in arenas from genetically modified organism (GMO) labeling to herbal supplement regulation, the Supreme Court declared that it was incumbent on the Bureau of Chemistry to show that an ingredient may be harmful *in the quantity typically present* in a normal serving or dose.[37]

Forced to retry the case, the government brought a new set of charges against the mill, cleansed of references to health dangers. This time the government accused Lexington Mill & Elevator only of misbranding inferior flour, and, when the case finally came to trial, the bureau won. In a 1920 ruling that stood unchallenged, a lower court agreed that the mill had used bleaching to make a brownish flour look finer. The bureau won that battle, but had already lost the war.[38]

Wiley, long since forced out of government by a general shift away from aggressive consumer protection, was heartbroken. After the 1914 Supreme Court ruling, he had written in *Good Housekeeping* that the country's flour would forever be "as white and waxy as the face of a corpse."[39] By the early 1920s, it was clear to him that nothing could hold back bleaching. The Supreme Court ruling and lower court victory took away the government's ability to ban bleaching outright, forcing it to bring adulteration charges on a case-by-case basis. Even Wiley conceded that this was impossible given the vast quantity of flour shipped in the country.[40]

A few Americans retained enough of a Progressive Era skepticism about the practices of food processors to ensure a sizable niche market for unbleached flour. Gold Medal and other flour millers with roots in the Pure Foods Movement could still tout the health benefits of unbleached flour and seek out Wiley's support for their product. But it was clear that the larger public had lost any doubts it had about bleaching. By 1930, when *Scientific American* introduced readers to the latest whitening agent—"Do-White . . . a finely-ground powder with a pleasing leguminous taste"—nearly all commercial flour was treated with chlorine gas, nitrogen trichloride, or nitrogen.[41] As one Iowa miller committed to unbleached flour complained in a letter to Wiley, the public just wouldn't buy anything that wasn't "chalky white."[42]

This would change in a few years, as the country latched onto a new set of health fears related to refined flour, which we'll address in the next chapter, but for the time being, dazzling white bread was something to celebrate.

THE FINAL FRONTIER

One more great threshold of techno-scientific baking remained to be crossed, and sold to the public as the best thing since sliced bread— one aspect of baking remained largely untransformed by science, even as advanced machinery, precise measurements, temperature controls, and chemistry molded loaves to assembly-line production. Until the early 1950s, even the most cutting-edge bakers still fermented dough in much the same way as ancient Egyptians: they mixed a batch and waited for it to rise, mixed another batch and waited for it to rise. Temperature controls and chemical yeast nutrients could speed up batch fermentation, but dough's biological rhythm still punctuated the otherwise smooth assembly-line flow of industrial baking. No matter how fast a baker could mix dough or speed it through ovens, production capacity was limited by the space available for giant troughs of dough just sitting around.

Beginning in the 1920s, scientists and engineers scrambled for a way to circumvent natural fermentation, but all failed. It was, in a sense, the seemingly unachievable Holy Grail of bakery science. Technology could speed up fermentation, but it was too much a part of bread's flavor and structure to avoid altogether. Then, in 1952, John C. Baker, a chemist who first grew interested in bread while studying the effects of chlorine gas bleaching on flour, approached the problem from a new angle. Previously, scientists had worked to eliminate fermentation altogether, which was impossible, or to speed it up, which still left bakers waiting for batches. What if, Baker speculated, instead of eliminating or speeding fermentation, the microbial action of yeasts could simply be separated into its own industrial process removed from actual baking?[43]

In 1953, Dr. Baker released the first prototype assembly line based on this theory. In the Do-Maker Process, as he called it, an independent assembly line continually produced vats of liquid ferment—a broth of yeast, water, and yeast nutrients not unlike a French artisan bakers' preferment, or *poolish*. The broth required four hours of fermentation time, but some was always on hand, ready to be injected into an ultra–high speed mixer, where it combined with a steady stream of flour and other dry ingredients. The result was a nonstop stream of "fermented" dough ready for panning and proofing. The Do-Maker Process cut three hours of waiting time off every loaf. More importantly, because transferring batches of dough required more hand labor than any other aspect of industrial baking, it reduced personnel costs by as much as 75 percent.[44]

Continuous-mix baking—or "no-time" baking, as it was dubbed—spread quickly and, like all significant advances in bakery technology, had an immediate and dramatic effect on competition. In 1967, a USDA study showed that astonishing growth in the productivity of large bakeries thanks to continuous-mix technology was putting small bakeries out of business in record numbers.[45] Industrial bakeries without capital to install expensive continuous-mix equipment simply couldn't compete.

The 1950s and early 1960s saw periods of sustained bread price spikes, so it's not clear that consumers felt the benefits of cost saving and consolidation. They did like no-time bread, though. As a probably unintended side effect, the Do-Maker Process produced loaves with incredibly fine and uniform cell structure.[46] Bakers immediately latched onto the marketing potential of this innovation, calling the product of continuous-mix baking "batter-whipped bread," and hailing the fact that science had finally banished all holes from the country's bread. Wonder bread advertising called batter-whipped bread "revolutionary," and most consumers seemed to agree. The white shirts of the nation were finally safe from drips of jam leaked through unruly holes. No longer would haphazard gas bubbles remind eaters of bread's natural origins.

INDUSTRIAL ABUNDANCE CONSIDERED

At the head of the La Brea Bakery production line in Van Nuys, towering steel vats hold liquid sourdough culture, the microbial progeny of Nancy Silverton's original starter. Piquant and frothy, it is a liquid ferment like the Do-Maker's broth, but once it's mixed into batches of dough, all resemblance to continuous-mix baking ends. La Brea dough undergoes long, slow fermentation at cool temperatures in stainless steel troughs. Sumptuous amounts of time allow the dough's flavors to fully develop. High-tech machinery handles the risen dough, but in exactly the opposite way as on most industrial production lines: tiny wire filigrees, steel fingers, and ingenious paddles divide and shape each piece without pressing out gas bubbles formed during fermentation. Jon Davis tells me that it took years of collaboration with a Japanese high-tech manufacturer to develop equipment that would encourage the natural holes that automatic dough handling typically sets out to destroy.

With its different approach to time and nature, the La Brea Bakery appears to channel a new industrial food aesthetic in which slowness and tradition are as important as speed and progress. Hominess and high modernism mix quite well at La Brea. This, in turn, seems to answer a question that a number of skeptical bakers and food writers posed during the 1920s and 1930s: Must we sacrifice quality ingredients and flavor in the name of industrial efficiency? Can't we have both?[47] La Brea, with its carefully made loaves and simple ingredients, suggests that maybe we can.

At the same time, much of the old aesthetic persists at La Brea. An industrial, scientific spectacle of perfectly controlled irregularity simply stands in for the old love of perfectly controlled regularity. Both aesthetics of control evince an equally strong confidence in modern technology's ability to usher in a utopia of abundant good food. At the start of the twenty-first century, the idea that high-tech food holds the key to a better world has been tarnished by decades of experience with the health, social, and environmental consequences of industrial agriculture and food processing. But it still casts its spell. While La Brea's dream of abundant good bread is harmless enough, the larger confidence in industrial food production has real consequences. At the very least, it narrows Americans' sense of what kinds of changes in the food system are practical or possible.

Steeped in the dream of industrial plenty, for example, many skeptical observers of the alternative food movement voice doubts about the ability of small farmers and artisan producers to feed a rapidly growing world. Food historian James McWilliams captured this attitude in his book *Just Food: Where Locavores Get It Wrong and How We Can Truly Eat Responsibly.* Although he admitted to sharing the culinary pleasures of slow, organic eating, McWilliams berated members of the alternative food movement for believing that it could amount to anything more than an elitist trend. Heirloom farmers' market tomatoes and handmade *pain au levain* were wonderful, but tackling world hunger required industry, efficiency, and scale.[48]

McWilliams was correct in one sense. Many expressions of the alternative food movement appear precious and far removed from the daily grind of poverty. But while defenders of industrial food production can make easy sport of rich locavores, they conveniently ignore the far greater elitism of oligopoly agribusiness, the myriad ways in which the dream of industrial plenty often made life worse, not better. Scientific household management, as Ruth Schwartz Cowan showed in her aptly named book *More Work for Mother,* placed more pressures on women, not fewer.[49] Ever-larger and more efficient bakeries churned out ever-cheaper bread, but often at the cost of good jobs and community businesses. Cost savings from efficiency were not always passed on to consumers. And, as we will see in a later chapter, massive expansion of food production facilitated by technological advances sometimes created more hunger, not less.

Most early twentieth-century food writers, domestic advisors, and consumers couldn't have imagined these counterintuitive outcomes of their dream of industrial plenty. Nevertheless, the ambiguous nature of industrial plenty was not completely lost on American bread eaters of the period. As industrial baking triumphed over small shops and home ovens, the country began to disagree about the nature of this new bread—first quietly and then, by the end of 1920s, vehemently. As the Great Depression took hold, community groups urged consumers to buy local bread from small bakeries or make it themselves.[50] They also began to doubt the high modern aesthetic altogether. Had bread become *too* modern: too soft, too white, too defiled and denatured? Would soft bread make for a soft country?

Tapping into a much older line of American religious tradition, noted food gurus of the late 1920s and 1930s worried that industrial bread might erode moral behavior. In 1929, in bold type arrayed around a large picture of white bread, the *New York Evening Graphic* declared, "Criminals are made by the food that they eat as children—Science finds that white bread develops criminals."[51] For many household advisors and dietary experts, as the next chapter shows, industrialization had gone too far.

THE STAFF OF DEATH

Dreams of Health and Discipline

The whiter your bread, the quicker you're dead.
—Dr. P. L. Clark's *Home Health Radio*, c. 1929

GRAIN DAMAGE

Professional cyclists spend a lot of time thinking about what to eat. Burning seven thousand calories in a race will do that. And, for many decades, cyclists' obsessive solution to the food question focused on building muscle and storing up energy. This meant carbohydrates and protein piled on top of carbohydrates and protein. Giant carb-loaded dinners of pasta and bread were an essential pre-race ritual. In the mid-2000s, however, elite cyclists began to think about food differently—not just as the building block of muscle and energy, but as a kind of medicine.

Pro racers and their amateur emulators began to seek out "anti-inflammatory foods," like raspberries, ginger, and salmon, believed to speed recovery from injuries. And they began to avoid foods deemed "pro-inflammatory"—foods that purportedly irritated bodily tissues, caused aching joints, and sapped stamina. Shockingly, for a group of people accustomed to large amounts of carbohydrates, wheat, along with other foods containing the protein gluten, topped cyclists' list of inflammatory agents.

Christian Vande Velde, a popular rider from the Chicago suburbs, led the break away from gluten. A pro cyclist since the late 1990s, Vande Velde had helped Lance Armstrong to two of his Tour de France victories and racked up an impressive record of race wins of his own. But he was also plagued by injuries, and, by 2007, he was no longer a young rider. It would have been easy to write him off—until the wins started rolling in again and 2008 turned into Vande Velde's best season ever. That year he claimed stage wins in the Tour de France, the Giro d'Italia, and the Paris-Nice spring classic. He took the overall winner's jersey at the important Tour of Missouri, third place in the Tour of California, and third place in the U.S. Pro National Time Trial Championship.

Many observers attributed Vande Velde's success that year to his switch to a strong new team. Vande Velde, however, pointed to his diet. That year, following the advice of sports physiologist Allen Lim, Vande Velde had gone "gluten free."[1] Though the shift was painful—Vande Velde found giving up bread particularly difficult—it was worth the suffering. As he told reporters, on a gluten-free diet he slept better, felt mentally fresh, and performed at a higher level than ever before. "Physically I am a lot leaner. . . . I am less lethargic and my energy levels have been quite good. . . . I recover quicker and maybe have less inflammation in my back and hips." Soon Vande Velde's teammates copied his diet, and then other pro teams followed. In 2010, Lance Armstrong's RadioShack crew rode gluten free all the way to its overall team victory in the Tour de France.[2]

This story repeated itself in other elite endurance sports, but by the late 2000s, it wasn't just professional athletes who were going gluten free. Celebrities, ranging from Hollywood darlings Gwyneth Paltrow and Zooey Deschanel to cable news tough guy Keith Olbermann, praised the benefits of avoiding gluten: the diet aided weight loss, unleashed untapped reservoirs of energy, stabilized insulin levels, and even promoted mental acuity. Already familiar with the low-carb Atkins diet, soccer moms everywhere and affluent residents of the East and West coasts followed close behind. According to one widely cited market report, 15–25 percent of American consumers wanted to purchase more gluten-free foods in 2009.[3]

In just a few years, the market for gluten-free products had emerged as one of the grocery industry's fastest-growing sectors. Books with titles like *Going against the Grain, Grain Damage, The Grain-Free Diet,* and *Dangerous Grains* filled bookstore shelves. Cable news programs warned that wheat might inflame joints, worsen autism, lead to cancer, or send insulin levels soaring. If you visited an alternative health care specialist with sore knees or digestive trouble, you'd have been almost certain to hear that giving up wheat might help.

To me at forty, dogged by my own seemingly endless sports injuries, all this sounded really appealing. So, in the middle of researching and writing a book about bread and despite my obsessive love of baking, I went gluten free. This meant a lot more than just giving up bread, as I soon learned. Other grains—rye, barley, spelt, and sometimes oats—contained gluten. Worse still, in our industrial food system, gluten had found its way as an additive into thousands of foods, from powdered spices to ketchup. Really going gluten free required constant vigilance, endless research, difficult sacrifices, and ceaseless self-control. I only lasted two months—but in that time, I felt real results. I felt energetic and sharp, and during the first weeks of the diet, I experienced what can only be described as euphoria. Reading gluten-free websites and online testimonials, I discovered that my experience was not uncommon: many people reported feeling euphoric in the first weeks after going gluten free.

My experience didn't synch with the findings of mainstream science, however, or my gastroenterologist's recommendations. According to most mainstream medical experts, gluten should rightfully concern only about 1 percent of the population—the percentage of people thought to be afflicted with celiac disease, a serious autoimmune disorder. For people with this disorder, consumption of even tiny amounts of gluten causes the villi of the small intestine to literally smother themselves in mucus. The result is damaging inflammation and impaired ability to absorb nutrients, leading to seriously elevated risk for a wide range of cancers, neurological diseases, and other autoimmune disorders.[4] Except for that 1 percent, gluten was harmless, my doctor assured me (and mainstream medical research confirmed). So I got tested for celiac, and the results were negative. I was free and clear—but why did giving up gluten make me feel so good?

The historian in me came up with what I thought was a good explanation: over the past hundred years, relentless fine-tuning of individual health through dietary discipline has become something of a national obsession. Whether through rigorous dieting, intense exercise, or almost religious attention to the latest missives of nutrition science, rituals of control over one's body are a key marker of elite status and responsible personhood.[5] And nothing made me feel in control of my body more than following the challenging strictures of gluten-free eating. I knew that my various aches and complaints probably stemmed from the daily grind of self-imposed pressures, work and family stress, and the accumulated trauma of decades of competitive sports more than they did from my diet, but I didn't feel that I could control those parts of my life. I *could* control the way I ate, and it felt good. History plus psychology explained my results.

But, as anyone who has ever typed a health-related search into Google knows, there are always experts ready to offer some other explanation. In this case, a whole army of alternative health care providers, physical therapists, diet gurus, and holistic healers, armed with everything from critiques of capitalist agribusiness to the latest insights of genomic medicine, rejected my quick self-psychoanalysis. Gluten didn't just hurt celiacs, they warned. According to these alternative health experts, many if not most people had their health and stamina sapped by the stuff. Thus, gluten-free diet proponents cautioned their audiences to "think outside the celiac box"—to imagine a whole spectrum of gluten sensitivities and systemic effects that can't be objectively identified by science yet, but *can* be perceived (and remedied) by individuals carefully attuned to their bodies.[6] We have slowly discovered genetic markers and mechanisms for *other* low-grade autoimmune disorders, the argument went; what's to say that low-grade gluten intolerance wouldn't eventually be made verifiably "real" in the same way someday?[7]

That kind of talk could easily be dismissed as pseudo-science, relegating the gluten-free craze to a long line of fashionable pseudo-ailments sported briefly by "the worried well."[8] Without tests accepted by mainstream science and relying only on a patient's bodily intuition, self-diagnosis of nonceliac gluten intolerance was easy to gloss as psychosomatic. On the other side of the gluten divide, however, a collection of ever-more-mainstream voices had begun to pose gluten avoiders as canaries in the coal mine—people who were, for some reason, more attuned to something fundamentally askew with our health care and food systems. Gluten problems, from this perspective, spoke to a larger problem of health hazards lurking in modern food, concealed from us by Big Agribusiness and the failings of mainstream medicine. The staff of life may have sustained Western diets for thousands of years, but no longer. Modernity corrupted the staff of life.[9]

Exactly what had changed varied in different accounts, but all argued that, in some important way, our wheat, or the way we eat it, had become "unnatural." Some writers blamed modern plant breeding. Others pointed to pesticides, endocrine disrupters, high-speed dough handling, industrial fermentation, genetic modification, or the unbridled use of wheat-based additives in foods that never before contained gluten. Some of the claims were clearly specious, but others contained a tantalizing basis in truth: driven by food processors' need for grains adapted to the rigors of industrial processing, modern plant breeding *has* dramatically increased gluten levels in wheat. Powered by the relentless acceleration of corporate baking, high-speed dough handling and rapid-fire fermentation *have* changed the molecular makeup of bread.[10] What wasn't clear was whether those changes actually impacted eaters.[11]

As a student of food history, I knew that diet gurus often operate like this: introducing small grains of doubt into the comfortable confidence of mainstream science. These small grains of doubt are always just within the realm of the plausible, and they always gain traction by playing on already existing anxieties. They thrive by taking big, looming, seemingly impossible to control social forces and giving them a quick and easy individual dietary fix. Gluten-free proponents might be right about structural problems in the U.S. food system, I concluded, but their individualistic "Not in my body" solution was all wrong.[12] And yet, as someone upset about the U.S. industrial food system, arguments regarding agribusiness and the harmful effects of gluten resonated with me. Was gluten free a fad or a warning bell? Or both?

In the end, I gave up on that question, just as I gave up on gluten-free eating. I realized that, as a consumer, I could weigh evidence on either side of the scientific debate all day without getting anywhere, but as a student of history, I could offer another way of looking at the problem: regardless of whether I believed that widespread gluten intolerance was "real" or not, I knew that we could learn a lot by thinking about the decidedly social dreams rolled up in debates about gluten and health. In going gluten free, I was participating in a very old and very American dream: a deep and abiding belief in the ability to fine-tune and maximize the moral and physical health of my body and my nation by eating the right food—an irrepressible confidence in the power of proper diet to cure almost all physical and social ills. This dream, in turn, has long reflected deeper concerns about the nature of industrial progress, society's relation to nature and, of course, anxiety about status. Not surprisingly, wheat and bread have played a major role in this history.

Indeed, for almost as long as Western culture has existed, it has been accompanied by anxieties about wheat or its refining. Recall, for example, Plato's discussion in *The Republic* about the impact of refined wheat on society's moral health, and consider the seventeenth-century celebrity diet guru Thomas Tryon, who warned Britons that eating overly refined or poorly baked loaves upset Nature and Reason.[13] During the past two hundred years, however, as bread production has grown increasingly industrial and increasingly distant from homes, suspicions about the staff of life's effect on life itself have grown even more frequent.

Usually these concerns focused on the components of bread like vitamins or fiber. Typically they cleaved between critics and backers of refined white flour, but sometimes, as in the 2000s, they broadened to encompass *any* wheat. Disagreements about refined flour's relation to constipation date back centuries, but battles over bread have spotlighted a wide range of other effects, from blood impurity, antibody formation, and chemical poisoning to discussions of nervous inflammation, corporeal enervation, tissue sweetening, and acidosis. The specifics change over time: Atkins turns into gluten free, gluten free turns into . . . ? But much remains the same, and this is where history can offer some perspective.

In 1924, the industry magazine *Baking Technology* warned readers of rampant "amylophobia" sweeping the country.[14] Literally the fear of starch, amylophobia, in the writer's usage, encompassed an amorphous, spreading sense that modern bread—either all wheat bread or just its white, refined form—did something bad to bodies.

In 1924, the baking industry was emerging shining white out of forty years of moral panic over bread cleanliness and contagion. Here, however, was a different kind of concern: not fixated on external contaminants but on the nature of bread itself and its effects on human metabolism. Something about modern bread—and critics differed about what that something was—appeared to be making the country fat, sick, lazy, and weak.

This chapter suggests that, as strange and exaggerated as 1920s and 1930s "amylophobia" might seem, it has a lot to teach us about the political and psychic costs of our national fixation on achieving perfect health through dietary discipline. But before we can understand the wheat fears of the early twentieth century, we'll need to appreciate the even deeper and older roots from which they arose. There's nowhere better to begin that than with Sylvester Graham, America's first great white bread critic.

THE CRUSADE AGAINST MORAL INFLAMMATION

Today, if we remember him at all, we remember Sylvester Graham as the inventor of the graham cracker (which he wasn't) or "the father of American vegetarianism" (which he may have been).[15] Almost two hundred years ago, however, the man whose devoted followers later gave his name to the dull brown cracker used for s'mores inspired scandal, controversy, and riots. Thousands of people read his essays or squeezed into packed auditoriums to hear him speak during the 1830s and 1840s. Tens of thousands followed his teachings religiously, and far more decried them just as dogmatically. Medical journals ran tempestuous debates about his principles, while mob violence stalked his speaking engagements up and down the East Coast. Even after his death in 1850, controversy raged about what an autopsy revealed about the condition of his intestines.

Before all that, though, Sylvester Graham was the seventeenth son of an elderly father and an insane mother, born sickly and not expected to thrive. As a child he showed signs of consumption. As a youth he suffered general physical debility, nervous exhaustion, and "sensitivity." But, after an apparent breakdown in his late twenties, Graham retreated to Rhode Island where he embraced a strict dietary regimen and miraculously recovered. In his triumph over infirmity,

Graham found religion—not just the Protestant creed he had studied at Amherst College, but also a deep and abiding physiological faith, a fervently optimistic belief that disease was a choice and that anyone could achieve health as he had.

Armed with this conviction, Graham entered public life in the late 1820s, against a background of social upheaval and flourishing fervor for reform. Like many health crusaders of the time, Graham embarked on his activist journey through the temperance movement, which served as a stepping-stone into a web of reform-minded networks including abolition, suffrage, transcendentalism, vegetarianism, and animal rights. Exposed to this wide range of commitments, Graham came to believe that diet held the key to them all.

Under the influence of increasingly popular critics of early nineteenth-century "heroic medicine," with its affection for blood-letting and mercury purgatives, Graham believed, not without cause, that health was best achieved by avoiding doctors. As part of a larger religious current sweeping Jacksonian America, Graham combined evangelical revival with scientific study of the body. Called "Christian physiology" by historians of religion, this was not faith healing, but rather a conviction that all disease arose from a failure to conform one's bodily habits to the Laws of Nature, a scientific order designed by the Creator.[16] Under the influence of the celebrated French physiologist François Broussais's "gastroenterological theory," Graham's particular version of Christian physiology located humans' primary connection to Nature and Creator in the alimentary tract.

More specifically, Graham imagined the body as a network of fibers radiating out from the intestines, connecting and feeding every organ. Ingesting "stimulating" food and drink—particularly animal flesh, white bread, alcohol, caffeine, and spices—irritated and inflamed those fibers from the gut outward, producing overall ill health. On the other hand, because all health was connected to the gut, cooling the body's fibers through bland, disciplined eating could cure any ill. Avoiding stimulating foods was, Graham proclaimed, "nothing less than the application of Christianity to the physical condition and wants of man . . . the means which God has ordained for the redemption of the body."[17] Even the worst cases of bodily derangement could be eased by an ascetic diet of whole wheat bread and water.

For Graham, health and bodily inflammation were more than physiological. Central to Christian physiology was the conviction that careful study of scientific law would inevitably confirm biblical law and vice versa. God created Nature, therefore Nature—the workings of human physiology—must logically work according to the laws of God. And because particularly vital fibrous connections linked the intestines, genitals, and brain together in "morbid sympathy," intestinal inflammation also held the key to the nation's moral health. In this holistic view, the maintenance of individual health and moral virtue went together. Thus, Graham's best-selling *Lecture to Young Men on Chastity* famously blamed masturbation for a long list of civic woes. But the compulsion to masturbate itself arose out of poor physical hygiene and diet. Even chaste youths resisting "the solitary vice" with all their might could not triumph against "involuntary nighttime emissions" unless they harmonized their bodies with Nature through austere eating.[18]

In a social milieu crowded with competing health gurus, Graham's big break came in the form of a global cholera pandemic that reached the United States via Canada in 1832.[19] As the disease radiated out from the East Coast's crowded cities and claimed lives with awe-inspiring speed, the nation panicked. Roads out of affected areas were choked with refugees fleeing quarantine. Business in New York City came to a standstill that summer, and public health officials around the country flailed to find ways to slow the disease's spread. Health officials shoveled chloride of lime on every surface they could and in some towns burned tar pitch to "purify the air"—efforts that may have reassured the public, but did little against cholera. In New York, city officials banned the sale of nearly all fresh fruits and vegetables. This draconian measure may, in fact, have helped slow food-borne cholera, but it also took a terrible toll on the poor's already meager diet and livelihoods.

Medical authorities, for their part, offered even less help. Some of their prophylactic recommendations—heavy doses of port wine and the opiate laudanum, for example—may have dulled the senses, but probably helped cholera kill. Others, like calomel, a toxic mercury compound prescribed to children in doses "fit for a horse," needed no help from King Cholera.

The impotency of medical treatment only confirmed the wide-spread popular sense that cholera had been sent by God to strike down the wicked and test the virtuous. In this desperate context, Graham, speaking to breathless audiences up and down the East Coast, offered a hopeful message of personal empowerment. For Graham, cholera was not a punishment sent from on high. Nor did he give much credence to the nascent ideas of sanitation science, which blamed the epidemic's spread on miserable tenement conditions, the poverty of the country's new industrial working class, and corrupt city political machines' inability to remove urban waste or protect the food supply. Further still from his mind was the minority view that economic inequalities might play a role in the spread of disease. Despite the fact that poor New Yorkers drank dangerous city water while wealthy residents, who could have pressured for better infra-structure, simply bought expensive clean water from private contrac-tors, Graham proclaimed that cholera—and all other diseases, for that matter—stemmed from a lack of what we today might call "per-sonal responsibility."

As historian of religion Catherine Albanese writes, "No longer was disease the result of God's punishment. . . . Rather, it was one's own decision."[20] People brought disease upon themselves by yielding to the temptation of physiological stimulation and they could banish it just as easily. Instead of framing cholera as a righteous force inevi-tably clearing out "the scum of the city," Graham offered a relatively simple and practical defense against the disease. In theory anyone could follow Graham's prescription and, he argued, it worked not just for cholera, but for all ailments, from headaches and cancer to *ennui* and anxiety. In an era when mainstream medicine harmed more than it helped, his prescription may have seemed prudish, but at least it didn't kill: no meat or white bread, less worry about what doctors say, sexual abstinence, more exercise, temperance, and lots of pure water (assuming you could afford it).

While Graham's conclusions went against conventional medical wisdom, they left dominant assumptions about society unquestioned. Indeed, the fact that cholera struck first in cities' poorest quarters seemed positive proof to him that moral failings fueled the outbreak. This view resonated with East Coast elites eager to wash their hands of responsibility for the poor's suffering, but Graham didn't limit his criticism to the poor Irish and blacks at the heart of the outbreak. Instead, he assailed all Americans' addiction to debilitating foods. Meat eating was human violence and bestiality incarnate, he argued—the embodiment of blood-dripping depravity. But the country's seemingly unstanchable craving for refined flour was almost equally abhorrent. Although Graham grasped the importance of dietary fiber long before it was scientific common sense, his critique of white flour aimed much higher. Separating white flour and bran, he preached, epitomized civilization's degenerate impulse to undo God's natural goodness. All food processing "put asunder what God has joined together," in Graham's eyes, but refining wheat ruptured God's perfect food. Refined wheat was a shattered covenant—the estrangement of humanity from its biblical staff of life. Because white flour was so de-natured—so out of harmony with Creation—it took a particularly devastating toll on the bodies and souls of those who ate it, inflaming every joint and fiber and unhinging every rectitude.[21]

In contrast to debased diets of meat and white bread, Graham preached the perfect meal, "highly conducive to the welfare of bodies and souls": locally grown whole wheat, recently ground and baked into bread by a loving wife, accompanied by fresh fruit and vegetables grown in virgin, unfertilized soil, and washed down with pure water. "They who have never eaten bread made of wheat, recently produced by a pure virgin soil," he proclaimed, "have but a very imperfect notion of the deliciousness of good bread; such as is often to be met with in the comfortable log houses in our western country."[22]

In this evocation of local wheat, loving wives and mothers, log cabins, and virgin soil we begin to get a glimpse of the politics of Graham's vision of good bread. During the early nineteenth century, the country had begun to urbanize and industrialize. Although these changes would not really reach breakneck pace until the end of the century, Graham, like many Americans, perceived an erosion of hearth and home. Corrosive pressures of the rapidly expanding national market seemed bent on destroying independent agrarian households as the country's primary units of social life and economic production. The explosive industrialization and commodification of food provisioning would happen later, but Graham had glimpsed the future and didn't like it. Changes in family sustenance were harbingers of moral decline.

Raised by an affectionless mother, he pined for "mother's bread" as edible proof of love and kindness. Like so many food reformers today, he longed for a mythical time when mothers, kneading bread, firmly anchored in the home, held the nation's moral fabric in place. Graham railed virulently against urbanites' emerging taste for bakery bread because professional bakers lacked mothers' moral sensibility. Though he moved in the social circles of suffrage activism, Graham's elegies to "good bread" rested on a resoundingly conservative bedrock of traditional family values. As *Little Women* author Louisa May Alcott trenchantly observed in an account of the Graham-inspired commune Fruitlands founded by her father, Bronson Alcott, men sat around discussing the ethics of eating and farming, while women did all the work.[23]

In time, the cholera epidemic extinguished itself, vanishing as quickly as it had come. Graham's message, on the other hand, proved more long lasting. By 1839, noted cookbook author Sarah Josepha Hale could confidently declare that whole wheat bread was "now best known as 'Graham bread,'" thanks to his "unwearied and successful [work] in recommending it to the public." Graham-inspired banquets serving "simple farmer-like repast[s]" attracted East Coast luminaries such as the influential newspaper editor Horace Greeley, an early and ardent convert, and key abolition and suffrage activists like Lucy Stone, Frances D. Gage, and the Reverend John Pierpont.[24]

As Graham's fame grew, he teamed up with the charismatic and influential reformer William Andrus Alcott to spread the word. Indeed, William Alcott deserves much of the credit for popularizing Grahamism. Together they lectured across the country, edited health magazines, and founded the United States' first health food store, providing Bostonians with whole wheat bread, fresh fruits, and "vegetables grown in virgin, unfertilized soil." They created the American Physiological Society to promote Grahamism and supported the establishment of "physiological boardinghouses," where unmarried or traveling male Grahamites might find appropriate food and a pure moral climate. By 1854, four years after his death, the *New York Daily Times* could depict Grahamism as a ubiquitous form of youth rebellion found on college campuses.[25]

For many followers, Graham's prescriptions simply offered a route to individual health. In an age when meals were gargantuan and greasy, vegetables brutalized by endless boiling, and constipation a national plague, Graham's dietary recommendations must have offered some relief to stuffed diners. But this was not the end point Graham intended. Bountiful energy, set into motion by physical discipline, was to be used for something greater—full-scale social transformation.

It wasn't just that the ranks of the abolition, suffrage, temperance, and antivivisection movements overlapped extensively with Grahamism; for true Grahamites, good society and good diet were inseparable. Progressive educator and Grahamite Bronson Alcott would have argued, for example, that his unpopular decision to subsist on bran bread and raw fruits arose from the same place as his scandalous decision to allow a black girl to attend classes at his school. Grahamites hated sugar for its enervating effects *and* its origins on slave plantations. As Horace Greeley challenged a New York audience of abolitionists, temperance activists, and suffragists: imagine how righteous our efforts would be if we could each mobilize more vital energy by shedding our violent attachment to animal flesh.[26]

This was heady stuff. After following a strict regimen of coarse bread and rigorous exercise, one convert, Thomas Ghaskins, wrote, "My mind underwent a most surprising change, and a flood of light was poured upon it. It appeared to me that I could see into almost every thing, and I was constantly led to their true causes. I was able to see into the real nature and moral bearing of the various institutions of Society, and the domestic and religious habits and practices of the busy world around me. . . . I was a new creature, physically, morally, and spiritually."[27]

Not surprisingly, many members of "Society" were less than excited about this kind of scrutiny into their institutions, domestic habits, and religious practices. High-strung testimonials like Ghaskins's made easy targets for satirists. As critics were quick to note, for a movement premised on the avoidance of stimulation, Grahamites sure seemed to get worked up about diet.

While critics reserved their strongest vitriol for Graham's vegetarianism, bran bread came in for considerable derision. Medical authorities lined up to testify that bran itself was indigestible—an inflammatory agent, scouring intestines and stimulating gastric nerves, the opposite of what Graham desired. His diet was naught but "sawdust and sand" the *Wisconsin Herald and Grant County Advertiser* declared. And the *Chicago Daily Tribune* humor column quipped: "Graham bread is said to be excellent food for the children on account of its superior bone-giving qualities. You can feed a child on that bread until he is all bones."[28] Capturing the tenor of anti-Grahamite sentiment perfectly, the writer J. J. Flournoy predicted that Graham's diet would produce "a nation of pigmies to be warred upon by cranes," whereas meat and white bread generated "strong, large, hale men . . . better sailors, workmen, and soldiers, and majestical Christians."[29]

Faced with such widespread opposition and torn apart by its own fundamentalism, Grahamism waned after the 1850s, although it never quite disappeared. By 1874, a columnist in the *Chicago Daily Tribune* could state confidently that Graham would have been hard pressed "to muster a baker's dozen of followers."[30] But this wasn't quite true. Enclaves of Grahamism appeared here and there until the end of the century. Bronson Alcott's short-lived Fruitlands experiment was just one example. Equally ill-fated but far more ambitious, the Vegetarian Settlement Company tried to build an entire city in Kansas supported by sales of Graham flour and Graham crackers. During the 1860s, the founders of the Seventh-Day Adventist Church adopted Graham's dietary prescriptions almost exactly. Eight million Adventists around the world today live out Graham's legacy. The church also gave rise to Grahamism's most famous twentieth-century preacher: John Harvey Kellogg, the breakfast cereal king. Harder to trace directly, but still palpable, Grahamism, channeled through 1960s counterculture, lingers in tens of millions of Americans' instinctive belief in the virtues of "natural food."[31]

So what are we to make of this legacy? It would be easy to make a joke of it, as many have: to laugh at Graham's sexual prudery and loathing of sensual pleasure. I prefer to stress the more complicated politics smuggled in with calls for "simple repast." The disparity between suffragist ideals and a diet dependent on unremitting female labor was just the tip of the iceberg.

Under the guise of good bread, Graham peddled a sentimental

utopia of rural simplicity that conveniently ignored the many forms of exploitation, debt bondage, and global connections that had always plagued supposedly "independent" frontier households—not to mention the human and environmental costs of the conquest of Indian Territory. Calls for local wheat sound pleasant today, but, in the 1840s, Graham's exaltation of "virgin soils" and "comfortable log houses" would have clearly read as a warrant for westward expansion. For Graham and his followers, building the Kingdom of God on Earth from the stomach out was inseparable from the emerging imperial ambitions of their young Republic. As Kyla Tompkins, a scholar of nineteenth-century food movements, has explained, whole wheat bread, locally grown and produced by whites, "signified domestic order, civic health, and moral well-being; ingesting more [good] bread, [Graham] promised would . . . ensure America's place in the pantheon of civilized nations."[32] Strange as it may seem, for Graham, the destruction of Native American peoples and their indigenous foodways represented a necessary step in the country's quest for harmony with nature.

This raises awkward questions about the power to declare things "natural" or "unnatural." If we honestly and passionately love the taste of store-bought white bread, why isn't that a natural craving? More disturbingly, Graham's assumption that property-owning, small-scale farmers living in white, male-headed, heterosexual households and grinding their own "local" wheat were the most "natural" Americans—the ultimate expression of moral virtue, democratic spirit, and natural harmony—still resonates strongly today. But what—and *who*—gets left out of this picture?

We might, like some contemporary vegetarian activists, forgive these elements of Grahamism as unfortunate but understandable products of their time. But we would do better to appreciate the tensions inherent in the movement. Grahamism demanded justice for animals and slaves, while longing for land cleared of Native Americans. It challenged the abuses of an industrializing food system in ways that reinforced women's subordination. And it questioned the entrenched authority of medical experts, while reinforcing divides between "virtuous" elite eaters and the "intemperate" poor.

By the end of the nineteenth century, however, America's utopian impulse to perfect society from the intestines out would lose some of the radical social critique that makes Grahamism attractive. Early twentieth-century bread critics drew heavily on Graham's coupling of bodily health and civic virtue, but theirs was a more worldly approach. As debates about the effect of modern bread came once again to prominence between 1910 and 1930, all sides would rely on the unsavory premises of social Darwinism and racial eugenics. Concerns about white bread's effects on bodies would increasingly channel earthly anxieties about the survival of the fittest. Christian physiologists' spiritual dreams of social and inner harmony, for all their flaws, would give way to obsessions with external appearance and material success. Two early twentieth-century food gurus, Alfred W. McCann and Bernarr MacFadden, epitomized the evolution from Christian physiology to more ruthless dreams of social fitness demonstrated through bodily discipline.

MCCANN'S PARABLES OF WHITE BREAD POISONING

In the late 1920s, just two miles away from the Ward Baking Company's Brooklyn factory, another family was making its fortune selling a very different kind of loaf. The Dugan brothers began baking bread in 1875, as a complement to their pushcart grocery business. By the 1920s, their business had outgrown a series of ever-larger bakeries, and was likely the country's largest producer of 100 percent whole wheat bread.[33]

Large-scale production of whole wheat bread faced technical challenges that had long dissuaded most manufacturers from attempting it: whole wheat flour spoils quickly compared to white and its tiny bran particles slice gluten strands to pieces, making it hard to raise a light, airy loaf. As a result, even bakers producing "whole wheat" breads frequently used blends of white and whole wheat. David H. Dugan, on the other hand, insisted on 100 percent whole wheat— even when his own workers protested that it couldn't be made by machine.

Even more challenging, however, whole wheat bakers had to convince a skeptical public to eat the stuff. And in this, the Dugan Brothers Bakery received invaluable assistance. It came in the form of one of the country's most popular dietary advisors, Dr. Alfred W. McCann, who pitched Dugan Brothers bread daily on his WOR radio show. The Dugan brothers were known for the religious roots of their health bread empire, and McCann's daily fulminations against processed foods likewise drew heavily on Graham and the Christian physiologists. McCann's arguments and examples, however, would eventually provide the foundation for a wide range of decidedly secular attacks against white bread.[34]

As the longtime food editor of the *New York Globe* and head of his own pure food laboratory, McCann was a bottomless source of studies, experiments, and anecdotes. He packed his broadcasts and books with accounts of tests in which dogs, chickens, pigs, and even orphans or refugees were fed nothing but white bread for weeks, their declining health meticulously observed. More importantly, he had a genius for parables of "white bread poisoning."

Two such stories in particular captured the early twentieth-century imagination: in "the Madeira-Mamore case," purportedly conveyed to McCann by the survivor of a South American railroad project gone awry, four thousand tracklayers were said to have perished on the Brazil-Bolivia border after subsisting on nothing but white bread rations for months. Actual evidence for the Madeira-Mamore deaths was secondhand and scant, but McCann himself played an eyewitness role in the second story, which he dubbed "the *Kronprinz Wilhelm* incident."

In 1915, hundreds of sailors on the German battleship *Kronprinz Wilhelm* nearly died of fatigue and heart failure after 255 days at sea eating plentiful rations of white flour, white potatoes, white sugar, and red meat. When the ship sought refuge at Newport News, Virginia, McCann offered his services as a health expert, insisting that the source of the sailors' affliction lay in their highly refined diet. As McCann told the story, the ship's surgeon and U.S. medical authorities quickly rejected his theory. The *Kronprinz Wilhelm* sailed under the steam of a classic American diet—nutrition couldn't be the cause of its affliction. Eventually, though, McCann's theories were confirmed, and he crowed that the *Kronprinz Wilhelm* incident proved conclusively "the inadequacies of the very foods on which America relies for the protection of her troops, as well as the protection of her so-called middle and lower class civilians."[35]

These were compelling just-so stories, and during the 1920s, white bread critics invoked them so frequently that they didn't have to rehash the details. Just referring to their legendary names—"the Madeira-Mamore case," "the *Kronprinz Wilhelm* incident"—sufficed to strike terror in the stomachs of health-minded bread eaters.

Today these tragedies would likely be diagnosed as the result of severe thiamin deficiency (which causes loss of muscle control, confusion, and eventually heart failure), but for McCann, malnutrition had more complex pathways. It resulted not from absolute deficiencies, but rather from imbalances between "base-forming" and "acid-forming" foods, leading to dangerous "acidosis." Refined sugar and "bread bled white" were acid-forming foods eaten in such large quantities by Americans that they skewed the country's metabolic balance toward acidosis, sapping national vitality while triggering cancer, kidney disease, early childhood mortality, tuberculosis, and heart disease. As McCann argued in a best-selling book reprinted by newspapers across the country, "Millers will never know how many babies they have handicapped . . . from their commercial disregard of the laws of Nature [and] interfer[ence] with the inexorable laws which the Creator has ordained."[36]

By the time Alfred McCann himself died young of a heart attack in 1931, shortly after delivering a two-hour radio tirade, fear of acidosis had become a national obsession—much like early twenty-first-century concerns about gluten. A 1932 survey of new health and dietary advice books, for example, reported skeptically on the overwhelming consensus: "Nearly every disease in the world [seems] not to be the result of eating improper food, but also of eating proper foods in improper combinations. . . . If a person is so ignorant as to permit [white bread and sugar] to pass his lips, he is doomed."[37]

WEAKNESS IS A CRIME

Alfred W. McCann instilled Graham's Christian physiology with a Progressive distaste for bread trusts and food oligopolies. Refined white flour was the product of greedy industrialists whose violations of "the provisions of the Creator" accelerated the country's moral decline. America must defy these "Moneybags," he argued, and return its eating practices to the basic laws of God.[38] Nevertheless, by the

1920s, a decidedly more pecuniary philosophy of health would out-shine McCann's ideas. The real prophet of 1920s amylophobia was Bernarr MacFadden, a sinewy entrepreneur with a genius for self-promotion and a love of big business. MacFadden adapted Christian physiology to preach a more optimistic and secular creed—the gospel of personal improvement.

Like all good diet gurus of his time, MacFadden was born a sickly child. And, of course, like all good diet gurus, MacFadden overcame his weakness through strict physical discipline—his version marked by relentless exercise, heroic fasts, and a Graham-influenced diet. By 1899, at age thirty-one, his muscles rippling and constitution brimming with vitality, he founded a secular church called "Physical Culture" and began to preach. "Weakness is a crime; don't be a criminal" was his worldly commandment.[39]

Half social movement, half business empire, Physical Culture would eventually come to include a health and diet publishing conglomerate, the country's most popular lineup of pulp fiction magazines and books, newspapers throughout the country, a Physical Culture restaurant chain, several Physical Culture spa resorts, a model for Physical Culture schools, and a planned residential community in New Jersey based on MacFadden's principles. When he died in 1955 (a respectable eighty-seven, but still a bit shy of the 150 birthdays he had vowed to celebrate), the unabashed egomaniac had been a popular-culture icon for four decades, unsuccessful Republican politician, advisor to presidents, the subject of countless scandals, and a guru to Hollywood celebrities. He had taken on patent medicine makers, a nation's sexual prudery, and the American Medical Association. He had denounced constrictive clothing, shoes, alcohol, cigarettes, Communists, Jews—and, of course, white bread, "the greatest humbug ever foisted upon a civilized people."[40]

MacFadden inspired many imitators, some of whom, like Charles Atlas (groomed by MacFadden) and Jack LaLanne (taught by Mac-Fadden's star pupil), would eventually eclipse his memory. But Bernarr MacFadden was the original. With his high brow, aquiline nose, and muscular physique posed nearly naked on thousands of posters and magazine covers, he was the early twentieth-century's image of what health should look like—and how to achieve it.

Although MacFadden presented himself as a real-life Superman, he insisted that anyone could achieve the same results. Powerful physique, sexual virility, worldly success, and long life were all within the reach of the average American. His prescription was rigorous but relatively simple: all disease arose from blood impurities caused by poor diet and metabolic imbalance. Strenuous exercise and regular fasting cleansed the blood and sculpted a successful-looking body, while good diet prevented the buildup of blood impurities and unattractive fat. Maintaining outward appearance was just as important as inward harmony, he argued, because it gave visual testimony of one's virtue and vigor.

MacFadden's specific dietary advice changed over the years, with certain steadfast exceptions: "As nearly as possible foods should be used in their natural condition," uncooked, whole, and with as little variety as possible.[41] Nuts, fruits, and water made the best meals. One should eat little meat and avoid alcohol, caffeine, and white bread. When he was a youth, MacFadden claimed, white bread had sickened him horribly, so the cause of its elimination was close to his heart. For forty years, he would fight a personal, passionate battle against the nation's bakers and millers. A few bites of what he called "the staff of death" might not actually kill the strong, but it weakened them. People with sickly constitutions were to avoid all bread. For the rest, whole wheat was best.

This was, if you will, a testosterone-charged Grahamism. But it was also a decidedly profane Grahamism. The "crime of weakness and the sin of sickness" MacFadden railed against were not offenses against God's commandments. They reflected a new kind of moral imperative emerging in the early twentieth century. The physical labor of maintaining perpetual vigor had become intertwined with the social labor of demonstrating one's privileged place in the hierarchies of cutthroat capitalism.

In Physical Culture we see contemporary obsessions with externally displayed and internally honed perfect health at a formative moment. To the extent that the quest for the perfect, enduring body has emerged as one of the governing ideals of our age, early twentieth-century gurus like MacFadden, enthralling audiences in his leopard-skin tunic, laid the foundation for our obsessions. Physical Culture was, as R. Marie Griffith argues in her history of Christian health movements, the perfect marriage of Protestant moral obligation and consumer capitalist vanity.[42] Its lasting power speaks to something fundamental and enduring about the United States, but in order to really understand the social implications of this seductive dream of food and health, we must understand the unpleasant context of racial thinking out of which it emerged.

SAVING THE RACE THROUGH DIET

During the first decades of the twentieth century, visceral fear of racial decline gripped northern European Americans. America's genetic heritage—assumed, of course, to be pure northern European, and the pinnacle of human evolution—appeared threatened from all sides. With declining birth rates among the country's upper classes and large influxes of darker-skinned immigrants, the country seemed headed toward what pundits of the day ominously labeled "race suicide." Failure to confront this peril would, as Albert Edward Wiggam, a regular contributor to the magazine *Physical Culture* and champion of white supremacist pseudo-science, warned, "silently and slowly wreck the race that built [civilization]."[43] In a time marked by rapid urbanization and demographic change, the doctrines of racial eugenics took on enormous appeal, even to many of the country's most progressive reformers.

While we often associate eugenics with Nazi Germany, the prewar United States served as a crucial proving ground for campaigns to "improve the race." The American eugenics movement's most infamous achievements came in the form of large-scale government policy—widespread state laws mandating forced sterilization of "dysgenic" groups and new federal immigration policies seeking to limit the taint of inferior blood. But eugenics was also a bottom-up movement lived out in everyday popular culture—in the world of pulp fiction and dietary fads.[44] Bernarr MacFadden's career followed eugenics' arc through popular culture perfectly.

During the 1920s and 1930s, eugenic ideals circulated through Hollywood movies, self-help manuals, novels, museum exhibits, and newspaper advice columns. Chic pageants, many sponsored directly by Physical Culture, pitted individuals and even families against each other in eugenic fitness competitions. And across the country, state fair displays informed visitors what they could do to improve the race, offering helpful advice on how to observe and assess the genetic vigor of family and neighbors.[45]

In eugenics-obsessed America, straying from what was deemed the "standard" path had serious, earthly consequences. As B. G. Jeffries, a popular health book author, admonished, it was wrong to regard bodily weakness caused by "disobedience to nature's dictates" as mere "grievances." Taking MacFadden's dictum that "weakness is a crime" quite literally, Jeffries argued that physical infirmity should be seen as a willful act of criminal conduct. "Though the evil consequences inflicted on their descendants and on future generation are often as great as those caused by crime, [people with poor bodily discipline] do not think themselves in any degree criminal."[46] Given the urgency of the problem, Jeffries argued not just for forced sterilization of people who dragged down the nation's stock, but also criminal punishments for officials who allowed marriages between people of inferior stock.

But what about people of "normal" genetic makeup who failed to do their best to maintain perfect health? Did Aryans need to strive for improvement, too? Conversely, could people with inferior genes improve themselves through discipline and hard work?

These were tricky questions for eugenicists, and a key place where Physical Culture supplemented pessimistic ideas about racial predestination. Although MacFadden was deeply committed to the principles of eugenics and regularly directed his readers toward race-betterment manuals, he inclined toward a different interpretation of evolution. In this view, more Lamarckian than Darwinian, vigorous effort could offset the curse of bad genes. Indeed, as the son of a drunken Ozarks farmer of Irish descent, MacFadden should not have been allowed to be born, according to eugenic principles—yet he had achieved superhuman vitality. So MacFadden offered a compromise between eugenics and Physical Culture, nature and nurture: "No matter how strong the hereditary influence may be toward vigorous bodies, if people do nothing on their own initiative, through the idea that they are so well born that they do not need to make any effort toward obtaining or maintaining health, much that has been gained by inheritance will be lost."[47]

In one sense, MacFadden's emphasis on the power of effort was libratory, granting "inferior" peoples a chance to overcome genetic predestination. At the same time, it extended the coercive power of eugenics to everyone: even affluent white Aryans needed to demonstrate their worthiness. In this context, what food people chose and how it affected their bodies mattered. In an era when politicians openly advocated letting weaker people die out in the name of the greater good, conforming oneself to dominant ideals of beauty and vigor mattered.

The so-called normal white American might not fear the worst manifestations of eugenics, but there were smaller, quiet consequences to every bodily choice. Paul Popenoe, in his popular 1925 handbook of advice for young men, even warned that no eugenically minded girl would choose a constipated man because one's innards didn't lie. They inevitably revealed the soundness of one's character and the intelligence of one's choices.[48] In this context, a person's bread selection mattered. And, as readers' letters to *Physical Culture* revealed, switching from white bread to brown bread, or no bread at all, demonstrated fitness. One previously feeble man wrote that by substituting whole wheat for white bread, he was able to hike eighty miles in two days through California hills "without the slightest stiffness of joints or soreness of muscle."[49]

Seen through the lens of eugenics, we can now appreciate Mac-Fadden's macho antics a little better. As R. Marie Griffith suggests, whereas earlier reformers saw dietary discipline and fasting as gateways to spiritual virtue, "MacFadden took for granted that [its] . . . real appeal . . . was the experience of absolute power evoked by a fast. Through fasting, MacFadden promised, a person could exercise unqualified control over virtually all forms of disease, while revealing a degree of strength and stamina such as would put others to shame. In short, fasting was a stunning weapon of mastery, an instrument with which to prove one's superiority over menacing perils ranging from microbes to men."[50]

RED MEAT, WHITE BREAD, AND BLUE BLOOD

Of course, defenders of white bread could wield the exact same language of racial vigor. Dr. Woods Hutchinson, for example, a widely read New York health writer, directed eugenics-infused vitriol at nearly every aspect of claims that white bread destroyed the white race. Touting the "triumphant vindication of white bread" by science, he argued that "all this torrent of denunciation and prophecy of evil, to the effect that we are undermining the constitution of the race and devitalizing our tissues by the use of this attractive and toothsome but nutritious pale ghost of real bread, is pretty nearly moonshine."[51]

To the contrary, Hutchinson reasoned, one need only compare strapping, tall Americans with specimens from any rice- or brown bread–eating nation. In strength, valor, and intelligence, the American surpassed them all. So eat what you want, Hutchinson intoned; "white flour, red meat, and blue blood" are the emblems of global conquest. To *not* eat them would threaten America's place in the pantheon of nations. Indeed, as one of Hutchinson's fans quoted him in the *Los Angeles Times,* brown bread and vegetables were "the diet of the enslaved, stagnant and conquered races." A cartoon advertisement for Whitmer bakeries appearing around the same time drove this point home visually. In it an American doughboy towers over a rice-eating Asian. "Bread eaters lead the world," it affirmed, and among them, "the most progressive" eat white wheat bread.[52]

Thus, as memoirs and novels of Jewish life in 1920s America confirm, consuming dark rye bread marked one as racially inferior, and eating white bread represented a key step toward "Americanization."[53] It wasn't just that white bread was culturally associated with white civilization—a symbol of progress or Americanness. White bread was believed to have *made* white American civilization possible. Superior men required superior fuel.

This raised an important question: how could consumers be sure that white bread offered the best foundation for racial fitness? Hutchinson willingly conceded whole wheat bread's superior endowment of vitamins and minerals. So how could he, and so many like him, argue for the nutritional superiority of white bread? On one level, Hutchinson simply rejected what he viewed as "food faddists' " misreading of nature. Flipping Graham on his head, Hutchinson argued that "the unconquerable preference of the human stomach for white bread" was entirely natural. "Never was [there] a better or more convincing illustration of the sound common sense of unregenerate humanity than the irresistible way in which wheat bread has swept the board as the staple bread-stuff of civilized man."[54] To shill for rough brown bread was to rebel against human instinct.

On another level, Hutchinson helped popularize a key scientific argument against whole wheat bread. While whole wheat bread contained more nutrients than white, many early twentieth-century scientists believed that they could not be absorbed as well by the body. As Hutchinson explained, whole wheat bread's nutrients came "in an utterly indigestible and unutilizable form, namely bran and husks. So weight for weight, white bread is more nutritious than brown as well as free from the irritating effects of the husks upon the food tube."[55] From the vantage of early twentieth-century medicine, whole wheat backers' logic seemed flawed. "What the faddists apparently do not see at all," popular health author Dr. Logan Glendening charged, "is that the two parts of their argument are self-contradictory. The roughage is valuable because it contains vitamins, but the only reason it is valuable as roughage is because it goes through the intestinal tract undissolved or undigested. If the bran does any good as roughage it does no good as vitamin container."[56] This concept did not stand the test of time—or new understandings of nutrient absorption— but it made intuitive sense to many people and became something of an early twentieth-century health axiom. Nevertheless, by the mid-1920s, a growing field of food gurus and dietary advisors had begun to sow serious doubts among ordinary consumers about the damaging effects of industrial white bread.

THE QUICKER YOU'RE DEAD

By the mid-1920s, despite Dr. Hutchinson's efforts, anti–white bread forces were gaining ground rapidly. As one columnist observed incredulously, the "man in the leopard suit" (MacFadden) was "hoodwinking" audiences across the country. And to MacFadden's voice a chorus joined: Delle Ross, a well-known dietician, wrote in the *New York Telegram* that "white bread kills more than any other food," and Eva Osgood of the League of Women Voters warned mothers that "giving [too much] white bread to children will cause blindness before they are six." Charles Froude's *Right Food* proclaimed white bread the wrong food, responsible for "morbidity of mind and body." And an editorial in the *Chicago Journal of Commerce* observed that "wide open expressionless eyes, a pinched nose and contracted jaws [are typical characteristics of the] woman who has been disfigured by the use of white flour."[57]

These were not a few fringe comments. In 1927, Louis Rumsey at the American Institute of Baking assembled a nearly book-length compendium of accusations against white bread.[58] Critics pinpointed white bread as the source of, among other ailments, anemia, cancer, diabetes, criminal delinquency, tuberculosis, polyneuritis, neurasthenia, gout, rheumatism, liver disease, kidney failure, overstimulated nervous systems and, of course, acidosis. Constipation, an obvious example, rarely made the list, although one "Mr. Sibley," writing for a Chicago newspaper, denounced white bread as a feminine plot "to choke the intestines of men with starch paste." In the golden age of the radio jingle, great slogans caught the ear: white bread was "corpse-white," "the broken staff," "grain minus life," and "the food that doesn't feed." Most famously, Dr. P. L. Clark, a Chicago radio personality, gave us a ditty still repeated today: "The whiter your bread, the quicker you're dead."[59]

As always, it's hard to gauge the impact of this onslaught on everyday consumer decisions, but by 1929, Philip Lovell could observe, "Fifteen years ago it was only the 'freak' or the health 'nut' who would go into the bakeshop . . . and ask for whole wheat or rye bread. . . . The darker flours were known only to the foreigners who had been accustomed to them from their mother country. True Americans used only white flour. Today—what a change! Every up-to-date restaurant or cafeteria carries two or three different kinds of whole wheat breads. . . . A visit to any downtown cafeteria will also show that at least four out of five of its patrons choose the dark flours for their breadstuffs."[60] Lovell's enthusiasm doesn't quite synch with data on bakery production—whole wheat and rye bread accounted for less than 20 percent of the nation's output during this period.[61] But even accounting for exaggeration, something *was* changing. At least enough to send bakers into a defensive frenzy.

THE GOSPEL OF MODERATION

During the 1920s and 1930s, a few industrial bakers embraced the new demand for darker breads, trying, usually unsuccessfully, to mass-produce and mass-market whole wheat loaves. Most simply refused to change, resisting attacks on their product with all their might. Trade organizations churned out pamphlets and posters countering "food quackery," distributed guides to the nutritional benefits of white bread, and funded research into the same. The American Institute of Baking even offered biting cartoons lampooning "food fakirs and faddists" free to any publication that would run them.[62]

In 1930, capitalizing on the government's desire to help farmers by promoting wheat consumption, industry representatives and the National Food Board pressured the USDA to make a definitive statement in support of white bread. Other breads were fine foods, they argued, but white bread better suited the economic crisis: white flour kept better than whole wheat, was cheaper to mill, and more efficient to bake. Because fine flour used less of each kernel than whole wheat, it helped farmers by increasing demand. Leftover bran could even be sold as animal feed, aiding another branch of agriculture. Couldn't the USDA clear up, once and for all, the fuss about nutrition?

A. F. Woods, chief science officer at the USDA, agreed to a statement supporting bread in general, which he wrote and distributed to nine of the nation's top nutrition experts for endorsement. H. C. Sherman, a leading expert at Columbia University, wrote back immediately. Something must be done to moderate the influence of "cranks and food fakers," he agreed, but "millers and bakers are now engaged in a more active propaganda in favor of the white than is anyone in favor of the whole wheat." Without radical changes, he warned, the USDA statement would clearly "take the side of the white bread."[63]

The other eight experts signed without qualms. On this issue, the baking industry, the USDA, and mainstream nutrition science were largely in accord. White bread critics' most convincing evidence, they argued, had a fatal flaw: no one could deny that dogs, chickens, rats, railway workers, or sailors fed only white bread for extended periods would sicken. But, as E. V. McCollum, discoverer of vitamins A, B, and D, demanded on the pages of *Everybody's Health* that same year: who eats only white bread?[64] White bread is not a perfect food, he argued, but *no* food is perfect alone. The now-axiomatic mantra that, in moderation, any food can be a healthy part of a balanced diet won the day for industrial white bread.

H.C. Sherman eventually signed the USDA statement, convinced by his colleagues' gospel of moderation. But, looking back, he was correct about the statement. It reads like most government dietary advice today, presenting different sides so as to appear neutral, but in fact taking industry's side in subtle ways. "White and whole wheat breads are both wholesome foods," it declared. Whole wheat might be better, but "no person subsists on one food. . . . The form [of bread] eaten may be left to the choice of the individual when the remainder of the diet is constituted as to contribute the necessary minerals, vitamins, and any necessary roughage."[65] Both breads stood on equal footing as long as moderation and variety were observed, the statement declared. But this ignored the fact that many poor Americans, subsisting heavily on bread, didn't have the luxury of a diverse diet. Tellingly, one of the statement's industry-friendly endorsers successfully suppressed parts of the document suggesting that people relying heavily on white bread must take extra care to complement their staple with fruits and vegetables.[66]

When the government statement went out in May 1930, bakers beamed. "Another triumph for white bread," the headline in *Northwestern Miller* proclaimed. And Henry Stude, president of the American Bakers Association (ABA), wrote to the USDA's A.F. Woods thanking him for his work. The ABA, he gushed, "has received innumerable clippings where this item has appeared and innumerable editorials brought forth by this news item." Indeed, the statement, reprinted in newspapers around the country, was interpreted as a ringing endorsement of white bread. As a *Kansas City Star* headline declared, "Now we can enjoy our white bread."[67]

The USDA statement didn't silence white bread's most ardent critics, but it did crystallize an emerging commonsense view. As the 1930s progressed, the idea that white bread not only didn't cause disease, but could also be part of a good diet gained steady traction. Redeemed, white bread offered comfort in the dark years of the Depression. Amylophobia waned.

MODERATION'S DISCONTENTS

Mainstream policy makers, focused on the body's balance sheet of vitamins and minerals and leery of challenging any sector of the food industry, liked the idea that every edible contributed something to a healthy diet when eaten in moderation. But what if some forms of wheat caused harm when taken in *any* amount? By the 1930s, white bread's vitamin and fiber deficits were well understood, but Graham, McCann, and MacFadden—like gluten-free advocates today—discerned more insidious vectors of harm. From their vantage point, even infinitesimal amounts of white bread could unbalance metabolisms and inflame tissues; moderation was no shield against harm. For decades, gauzy claims like this have earned scorn and the label "quackery." Today, however, they're applied not just to refined flour but to all wheat products. They've returned, with some plausibility and much acclaim, in the present-day justifications for gluten-free eating.

This resurgence draws strength from new ways of imagining digestive health on genetic and molecular levels. But striking continuities between past and present speak to long-running clashes between competing approaches to health care. If there is one narrative that comes up again and again on gluten-free blogs, it is a story that pits a suffering woman, excruciatingly attuned to her body's response to wheat, against the seemingly deaf ears of medical authority. "My doctor doesn't believe me. He says my results are anecdotal because they haven't been proven with double blind studies."[68] This is the self-diagnosed gluten intolerant's lament: doctors and insurance companies don't want to take the time to treat me as an individual patient, with an individual genome and an intuitive understanding of my body.

As with Graham or MacFadden, we still see a clash between lay and expert authority. Although most wheat critics, by cultural necessity, sought to ground their claims in the language of science, at root we see an encounter between the privileging of supposedly objective laboratory science and a respect for natural intuition. And, in truth, while the more "natural" focus on health may not always have logic or legitimate double-blind studies on its side, it is very good at identifying blind spots in the vision of mainstream science. In their idiosyncratic way, fringe health movements help expose the unspoken cultural assumptions, political interests, and subjective decisions woven into science.

Graham's prescriptions, for example, were irrefutably kooky by the scientific standards of his day. Nevertheless, he grasped something important about heroic medicine's inability to address the afflictions of emerging modern life. In the same way, should it surprise us that today, when private insurance companies tyrannize health with all the subtlety of a bloodletter, many people want to take health care into their own hands through diet and self-diagnosis? All those elite athletes, Hollywood stars, and Wall Street brokers bragging that gluten-free gives them leaner, meaner performance? Perhaps they aren't kooks, just people who have perceived the power of individual self-control as a defense against the dangers of a modern food system and the failings of medical authorities.

If this were true, the pursuit of perfect health and vigorous bodies through dietary discipline would allow us to care for ourselves in a deeper and more thoughtful way. More often than not, however, it just embroils aspirants in taxing new fears and compulsions, new searches for expert insight, and new, more rigorous ways of fortifying one's body against decay. Dreams of perfect health through bodily discipline can easily become anxious nightmares.

The problem with this relentless quest for individual health through dietary discipline is not just the toll it takes on mental health. The problem, for society as a whole, is that America's dream of achieving health through dietary discipline frequently confuses self-control with moral virtue. Whether you're talking about Grahamites eating moral brown bread, a whole wheat bread eater entering one of Physical Culture's contests of eugenic fitness, or a celebrity raving about the way avoiding gluten sharpened her thinking and streamlined her body, celebrations of bodily discipline are always implicitly juxtaposed against the specter of unfit and irresponsible citizens. When weakness is a crime and sickness arises from individual choice, it's easy to cast people not conforming to prevailing ideas about health or body image as villains. In this way, even the most well-meaning efforts to spread the gospel of good bread (or no bread) run the risk of reinforcing social hierarchies and exclusions. By turning questions of public health into issues of individual discipline, the dream of perfect bodies achieved through diet also makes it easier to ignore the root causes of those problems. The dream of maximum health through self-control individualizes and medicalizes what, in many cases, are social and political problems.

To be sure, the current wave of gluten intolerance will fade away in time, leaving some significant mark on our dietary dreams but losing its urgency. The deeper underlying concerns won't go away. Amylo-phobias reflect half-articulated concerns about the pathologies of a modern food system, the rigors of competitive striving for status, and the failings of the health care system. They are an index of anxiety about modern life. These concerns won't go away until we begin to address them directly, rather than through individual food choices.

VITAMIN BREAD BOOT CAMP

Dreams of Strength and Defense

Nations that have bread are the nations that stand against the villainy of despots, tyrants, and fools. . . . Let's not forget that the real sinews of war are wrought by bread that builds muscle and brawn . . . bread shortens the war and lengthens the peace. If any man doubts the truth of this story, then he'd better get ready to be shot as a patriot or shackled as a slave.

—Spaulding Bakeries advertisement, Chicago, 1944

NATIONAL SECURITY FOOD

During Walla Walla's long, high desert summers, residents and wine tourists flock to a repurposed bus depot just off Main Street for the weekly farmers' market. To avoid the blazing afternoon sun, my family usually goes early in the morning, but we almost always end up getting caught in the heat. You can't shop quickly here. A dozen encounters with friends and acquaintances inevitably foil any attempt to just duck in briefly and pick up a few items. One conversation turns into another. I see former students selling produce. My kids run off with classmates. My wife, Kate, bumps into someone she's been meaning to call and begins to make plans to hang out later. A colleague introduces her parents visiting from out of town. Soon two hours have passed, and I still haven't gotten to the fruit stands. Visiting the Walla Walla farmers' market feels like an alternative food movement fantasy come to life. It's a wonderful picture: tight-knit social bonds and community ties forged over local produce.

One thing doesn't quite fit the alternative food movement stereotype, though: take a quick stroll around the parking area and it wouldn't be unusual to find NRA decals outnumbering Sierra Club stickers. Tea Party slogans may well grace more bumpers than Obama or Greenpeace. We tend to think of the alternative food movement as a liberal, Birkenstock-wearing lifestyle club, but that image doesn't quite pan out here. One of the local food vendors is our Republican state representative.

If you look hard enough, the liberal stereotype doesn't always hold up outside Walla Walla, either. As Rob Dreher writes in his book *Crunchy Cons,* legions of "Birkenstocked Burkeans, gun-loving organic gardeners, evangelical free-range farmers, hip homeschooling mamas, [and] right-wing nature lovers" have long been drawn to the alternative food movement. Right-wing talk radio personalities might rail against liberal locavores and out-of-touch Whole Foods shoppers but, as Dreher notes, conservatives who look carefully find that the alternative food movement expresses many of their values.[1] Participants on the left and right both sense something authentically "American" in the romance of Jeffersonian agrarianism—the idea that small communities of independent private-property-owning farmers form the backbone of democracy. The alternative food movement, like many conservatives, emphasizes the virtues of decentralization, self-sufficiency, and local independence. Images of community, family, and small-town life gracing alternative food movement literature would seem right at home on a brochure for Focus on the Family. Perhaps most palpably, a Libertarian anti-regulation streak runs deep through the whole alternative food movement, with conservative rancher Joel Salatin as its current celebrity spokesman. Considering that Salatin holds a degree from the ultra-conservative Bob Jones University and evinces fierce allegiance to the Christian Right, you wouldn't think his ideas would get far in the "liberal" alternative food movement. Yet Salatin's outspoken condemnations of bureaucratic red tape and what he sees as regulations hampering small-scale alternative food production earned him the title "America's most influential farmer" and made him a minor celebrity in liberal enclaves like Berkeley, California.[2] When it comes to lionizing the independent spirit of family farms, Left and Right can easily sit at the same table.

Since 9/11, liberal and conservative members of the alternative food movement have also begun to find common ground on the idea that "good food" and national security go hand in hand. Best-selling food writer Michael Pollan crystallized this new language of food and national security. On the eve of the 2008 presidential elections, Pollan's "Open Letter to the Next Farmer-in-Chief," published in the *New York Times,* roused thousands of urban gourmets and local foodies to unprecedented interest in the national politics of agriculture. Transforming the U.S. food system was not just necessary for health and the environment, Pollan declared, "it is a critical issue of national security." A centralized food system under the command of a few large companies was more vulnerable to attack and interruption than a small-scale decentralized provisioning network, Pollan argued. A system that specialized in producing gargantuan portions of junk food made the country weak and unfit to fight.[3]

Members of the alternative food movement quickly grasped the appeal of national security rhetoric. Organizers of farmers' markets, community gardens, and local food projects saw that they could use the language of security to give urgency to their causes. As a Seattle-based locavore blog advertised, lentils grown in the Palouse hills near my home weren't just tasty and light on carbon. Because they helped build healthy soils and food self-sufficiency, they "might just be the ideal national security food."[4]

In part, this turn toward national security was tactical—appropriating a powerful discourse from the right for the movement's own ends. But it also reflected a real desire. The alternative food movement seemed to pine for the passionate intensity and personal sacrifice generated by wartime mobilization. WWII-era posters entreating Americans to conserve food, eat less meat, and grow their own vegetables circulated through alternative food movement websites. How can we muster that kind of national purpose and urgency around *our* campaigns? food activists asked wistfully. As if in response to that question, new "Victory Gardens" sprang up on college campuses across the country and environmental organizations adopted WWII-era rhetoric, asking members to observe "Meatless Mondays" as part of the fight against climate change.

This urgent way of talking about food and security made for some strange bedfellows. For many, like Pollan, the diet-security connection gave teeth to appeals for liberal policy reform; for others, like the farmers' market director I quoted several chapters ago, it justified xenophobia. The racialized specter of contaminated foreign food and threatening foreigners hovered silently over many dreams of finding safety in local self-sufficiency. Meanwhile, public health officials and defense department strategists took the language of diet and defense in a totally different direction: they joined forces to frame the country's obesity epidemic as a national security threat—"the terror within," as Surgeon General Richard Carmona phrased it just months after 9/11.[5]

What do we gain and lose when we think of eating as an act of individual and national defense, or when we connect dreams of "good food" to military campaigns? Where did we even get this idea that eating could be seen as a kind of combat?

• • •

Connections between civilian diet and military mobilization are ancient, of course. Armies march on their stomachs, and civilian populations have always been asked to sacrifice to make that possible. Yet, during the world wars of the twentieth century, the United States found itself insulated from conflict's most fearsome camp followers: starvation, trammeled fields, and interrupted production. Americans conserved and went without, to be sure, but the geographical accident of unscathed food production also enabled the emergence of a different kind of relation between eating and defense.

Deliberately cultivated by military planners, food industry representatives, and public health officials, this new ethic didn't just ask civilians to reduce intake of certain foods so that troops might have more. It also demanded that civilians *increase* consumption of foods deemed essential to home front fitness—maximizing nutrition and energy intake on the home front in the name of defense.

The idea that patriotic civilian populations must conform to particular notions of scientifically determined healthy eating has its roots in the early twentieth century. After the Boer War, for example, Great

Britain instituted the Committee on the Deterioration of the Race to study the nation's diet as a way of improving physical readiness for future conflicts. During World War I, Americans were berated for carrying millions of pounds of excess fat that could be better used as rations or tallow. Well-known physiologist Francis Benedict questioned "whether a patriot should be permitted in times of stress to carry excess body-weight." And after the war, a Carnegie Institution study reflected that imperfect nutrition, particularly on the part of the civilian poor, "was a hindrance and danger to the state." By the eve of World War II, some officials had begun to speak of poor nutrition as a form of desertion.[6] If, for eugenicists and followers of Physical Culture, poor diet was seen as a crime against society in ordinary times, during wars the stakes were even higher—it was treason.

This idea is still with us today in modified forms. From the U.S. Army declaring "battle on the bulge" to vitamin supplements marketed as weapons in a war against ill health, diet and combat have blurred together in our minds in ways early proponents couldn't have imagined. Individual food choices, we are told, have far-ranging consequences for the national readiness, whether that readiness is needed for an actually existing hot war, a future war, or simply to gird us in all-out social struggles against myriad perceived threats. Given the importance of bread in the U.S. diet, it shouldn't surprise us that this consciousness—particularly the association between added vitamins and defense—was, in crucial ways, forged around bread. More specifically, it materialized out of educational campaigns surrounding the panicked introduction of synthetically enriched white bread on the eve of World War II.

By exploring the story of wartime bread enrichment, we'll see that forceful national security rhetoric can, in fact, inspire sweeping positive improvements for all eaters—not just for a privileged elite. At the same time, the sense of urgency generated by linking food to national security inclined consumers and policy makers to accept stopgap measures and hurried compromises. These urgent measures, perhaps necessary in the moment, ultimately ended up narrowing Americans' bread options and reinforcing the power of giant baking companies. What appeared only as short-term wartime expedience would set the stage for the 1950s and 1960s golden age of Wonder bread.

UNFIT TO FIGHT

In 1940, with U.S entry into Europe's war appearing ever more inevitable, Congress authorized the country's first peacetime draft. As men across the country lined up outside neighborhood draft boards, however, it was quickly evident that the country had a problem. After a decade of lean economic times, men aged twenty-one to thirty-five were dangerously unfit to fight.

In Chicago's tough Eleventh Ward—cradle of the city's Democratic machine, home to the stockyards and hard-working Lithuanian, Polish, Italian, German, and Irish men—draft boards found seven out of ten conscripts physically unfit to serve. In New York State, 30 percent failed their medical exams. In West Waterloo, Iowa, 124 out of 224 farm boys didn't pass muster. Nationwide, General Lewis B. Hershey reported gravely in 1941, draft board doctors and dentists had rejected five hundred thousand out of the first million men screened.[7]

The Depression had taken a brutal toll on the nation's health. Easily preventable problems with teeth and eyes topped the list of reasons for rejection, and a silent enemy lurked in the ranks of the un- and underemployed. Experts calculated that malnutrition, directly or indirectly, caused at least a third of all rejections.[8] While a spate of books written during the economic crisis of 2008 celebrated 1930s-era cooks for their thrifty use of authentic ingredients to make "real" American food, the reality of Depression-era diet was often more grim. Yes, the country was beginning to bake its own bread from scratch again, but it also suffered from a deep "hollow hunger." This wasn't outright starvation, but rather, as home economist Margaret Reid reported, a "hidden hunger . . . that threatens to lower the zest for living and to sap the productive capacity of workers and the stamina of the armed forces." A government commission convened after the Selective Service debacle of 1941 found that 75 percent of low-income high school students suffered from vitamin B2 deficiencies and 65 percent of Works Progress Administration workers suffered from scurvy or near-scurvy. Another study revealed that 54 percent of a sample of low-income whites and blacks suffered from night blindness characteristic of vitamin A deficiency—a statistic that terrified war planners looking ahead to combat conditions. "Nearly all" low-income students tested in another study experienced at least one vitamin deficiency, and time-series research at a community health center in New York City revealed that malnutrition rates there had risen steadily through the 1930s, hitting 37 percent in 1938. Pellagra—the vitamin deficiency disease most closely, if incorrectly, associated with bread-eating habits—killed twenty thousand Americans and debilitated well over one hundred thousand between 1933 and 1938.[9]

In the face of this crisis, the run-up to World War II saw intense focus on nutrition research. This was a time of great innovation in dietary surveillance, experimental nutrition, population surveys, and chemical analysis. New techniques for rapid blood sampling were developed and schoolchildren, prisoners, soldiers, and factory workers rolled up their sleeves to give planners the information needed to define a national standardized war diet. At the same time, government planners and nutritionists recognized that, no matter how efficient it was, this standard war diet could not be *imposed* by the state. It had to arise from the population's souls and desires.

This presented a serious problem: during the 1930s and 1940s, Americans got more calories from industrial white bread than from any other food, and in case after case, they refused to accept major changes in that staple. Even when industry leaders like the Ward Baking Company threw their marketing weight behind whole wheat bread, as they occasionally did, sales did not rise for long.[10] Efforts to promote alternatives to white bread as a form of patriotic wheat conservation had seen some success during WWI, but mostly they failed. And they certainly hadn't lasted. As one magazine writer observed in 1941, "Last time we had the slogan 'food will win the war' but precious few of the lessons which might have been learned from the wartime self-denial of 1918 carried over into peacetime dietetics. We went on cramming our tummies with bread so white it was almost blue." All this white bread, the author concluded, made the country fat, neurotic, and unprepared for battle.[11]

Thiamin topped everyone's list of concerns. Dubbed "the morale vitamin" because of its perceived effect on mental stamina and physical resilience, thiamin (vitamin B1) was deemed essential to readiness early in the war effort. Nutrition studies published in popular science magazines painted a dark picture of a thiamin-deficient nation. Subjects deprived of the vitamin displayed inability to concentrate, uncertain memory, awkwardness, self-consciousness, progressive feelings of inferiority, irritability, depression, and anxiety. Pointing out the obvious, but with great authority, the editor of the *Journal of the American Medical Association* observed that these traits were among the "least desirable in a population facing invasion." Unfortunately, industrial processing had mercilessly stripped the country's single most important food of thiamin. Eating refined white bread, a popular science writer suggested, did Hitler's work for him.[12]

Later, Cornell nutrition scientist Clive McCay would reflect back on the moment: bread's role in war had been clear to anyone who looked abroad, he argued. The secret of Germany's "husky soldiers" was its "excellent dark loaf"; the great resilience of Russia was its stubborn rye bread. France, on the other hand, a nation of puffy white bread eaters, had folded. What would become of the United States, where people simply would not eat whole wheat? Despite hopeful slogans like "America's Bread Front Has Never Failed," wartime food officials were worried.[13] Something had to be done, but what?

A NUTRITIONAL WEAPON DELIVERY SYSTEM

By 1943, this question had been decisively answered—at least as far as bakers and policy makers were concerned. The country would repair its broken staff with synthetic enrichment, the universally mandated addition of thiamin, niacin, iron, and later riboflavin to flour and bread. For war planners, public health officials, and baking industry executives, synthetic enrichment was the only "realistic" way to improve the nation's health in a hurry. Even prominent nutrition scientists long skeptical of white bread joined the consensus in the name of wartime expedience. Synthetic enrichment was, they conceded, the quickest way to rush vitamins to almost every American, almost every day—without needing to change the country's tastes or upset its milling and baking industries.[14]

This doesn't mean that synthetic enrichment offered the only or inevitable option for policy makers. As war loomed, the United States could have looked to a number of strategies for fixing its broken fighting staff. Other countries changed the extraction rate—the proportion of the whole wheat berry retained in flour after the milling process—of their bread. Britain, for example, had ordered millers to produce high-extraction flour for its "War Bread," creating a tough loaf despised by consumers, but probably responsible for saving the island from crippling malnutrition.[15] Canada went even further: not only did the government mandate high-extraction "Canadian Bread," starting in 1941, it declared that the addition of synthetic vitamins to bread constituted criminal food adulteration.[16] Homegrown options existed as well. Most famously, Clive McCay's "Cornell Bread," developed for the New York State Emergency Food Commission, counted on substantial backing from agribusiness lobbies and health food advocates. Drawing its nutritional boost from soy flour and milk solids rather than whole wheat, this bread could fuel home front fighters *and* satisfy their craving for soft, white loaves. Cornell Bread instantly won loyal adherents among both health food advocates and New York government officials. But while Cornell Bread has enjoyed repeated spates of popularity from the 1950s to the present, it consistently lost out to synthetic enrichment in high-level food policy debates—despite backing from powerful dairy and soybean lobbies.[17]

Self-styled nutritional realists countered that none of these foreign or domestic alternatives would work in the United States. Even government intervention couldn't change consumers' taste for pure industrial white bread, the realists argued. Look at Switzerland, they warned, deploying their favorite cautionary tale: in 1937, hoping to increase whole wheat bread consumption, Swiss officials imposed taxes making whole wheat bread 25 percent cheaper than white bread. It didn't work. Swiss consumers simply paid more to eat white bread.[18] Influential home economist Helen Mitchell summed up the realists' attitude for the *Journal of Home Economics:* "Enrichment seems a desirable compromise between a *theoretically* better nutritional practice and a *realistic* one based on the psychology of food habits."[19] Thus, the urgency of war settled a long-running debate about how to improve industrial bread, sweeping aside more radical alternatives in the name of expediency.

Unlike mandated high-extraction loaves or the use of natural additives like milk solids, enrichment was cheap and easy. It required no significant reworking of production lines, no new equipment, no need to learn new baking techniques and, once sufficient supplies of vitamin powders could be assured, little additional expense. Bakers couldn't believe their luck. One simple flick of a compressed nutrient wafer into every batch of dough could put to rest decades of condemnation and restore the busted staff to its former glory.

Millers balked at enriching flour at first but, like bakers, they eventually saw the advantages. As one millers' association told its members, in a time when better nutrition was "needed by all Americans to make them rugged and strong for the all-out war emergency," enrichment offered a chance to reverse decades of declining flour consumption. Because enriched bread and flour had "become corner stones in the national education program for better nutrition," they could sweep away "the scientific basis for former criticism of [our] fine foods."[20]

With bakers and millers on board, the industrial war food machine went into motion. And once it did, alternative health breads like McCay's Cornell loaf wouldn't merely be passed over—they could be denounced as national security threats by industry spokespeople along with USDA and FDA officials. Nevertheless, one important question still remained: How best to distribute enriched white bread? While many in the baking industry hoped to build demand for enriched white bread and boost corporate profits by selling premium-priced loaves to affluent tastemakers, nutritional realists rejected this route. True, they argued, poorer consumers might eventually spend more on bread to emulate wealthy eaters, but in a time of war, added nutrition was too important to leave to the whims of market forces and consumer choice. Synthetic vitamins didn't cost producers much and could easily be added to *all* bread.[21]

FOR THE AFFLUENT ONLY?

During the late 1930s and early 1940s, Robert R. Williams, a University of Chicago–trained chemist, found himself at the center of the debate over whether to mandate bread enrichment for all or to sell it as a premium-priced luxury. Born in 1893, the son of missionaries, Williams spent his childhood in southern India, surrounded by hunger. As a young teacher in the Philippines, scenes of deprivation haunted him. But it was during a stint as a low-level scientist with the colonial government in Manila that he first came to understand the moral and political weight of malnutrition.[22]

There, in 1910, spurred by the constant sight of listless, limb-twisted victims of endemic beriberi, Williams had set out to investigate suggestions that polished rice might cause the disease. He wasn't interested in colonial policy, or in the political reasons why millions of Asians might subsist on rice alone. Williams's goal was simpler and more technical: find a physiological cause and practical cure for the suffering he saw. After five years' work, he succeeded at the first part: beriberi was, as he had suspected, the result of malnutrition, caused by the lack of a factor he named "thiamin"—a plentiful substance in rice husks but completely absent in polished grains. The second half of Williams's dream—finding a cheap, politically viable cure to that problem—would take him more than twenty-five years.

In the meantime, Williams returned to the United States, where he joined the FDA to enforce Pure Foods laws and then helped lead national nutrition campaigns during World War I. During the Roaring Twenties, he entered the private sector as chemical director of the Bell Telephone Laboratories, then a hotbed of innovative applied science. In his spare time, however, Williams still pursued his driving passion. Finally, in 1936, after years of work, Williams announced that he had discovered an inexpensive method for creating thiamin in a lab.

True to his ideals, Williams registered the patent for thiamin synthesis to a nonprofit dedicated to funding humanitarian dietary research and set out to find industry partners who could deliver the product to people needing it most. At first, two companies answered his call: the pharmaceutical giant Merck, which agreed to mass-produce synthetic B1, and General Mills, which agreed to include it in select products. When the two companies approached Williams in 1938 with the idea of licensing synthetic B1 for use in flour, they tantalized him with the promise of massive economies of scale, a national advertising campaign, and direct access to the 15 percent of the U.S. flour market controlled by General Mills—but there was a cost. In return for pioneering the commercialization of B1 flour and enrichment products, General Mills and Merck demanded exclusive rights, a monopoly concession. Unless a government edict mandated enrichment of all flour products, General Mills' negotiators argued, no company would be willing to take the first step without guaranteed exclusive rights that would allow it to charge a premium price and recoup the costs of innovation.[23]

Williams's collaborators warned against the deal. "The advantages of licensing some large food company are obvious, but such a situation is charged with fulminate of mercury," Williams's boss at the Bell Laboratories counseled. Not only would General Mills and Merck use their exclusive position to profit outrageously from Williams's public-health research, they might not even deliver products to the country's neediest. "I have been plagued by a number of misgivings," Williams wrote to an ally in the USDA. "Perhaps the millers' genuine interest in the matter is limited to their specifically premium price flour; perhaps they even contemplate using the vitamin primarily for incorporation in even higher price package goods and are merely talking flour for its moral effect on us." If General Mills and Merck decided to limit enrichment to top-shelf flours, Williams concluded, "[enriched] flour would go to consumers who have a varied diet and less need for the vitamin restoration than to the consumers of the lower price flours."

A high-ranking FDA official friendly to Williams's cause concurred and raised the possibility of government action: "If the large flour producers could not afford to put B1 in their flour for the underprivileged, then possibly it should be a government function." But in the end, the official backed a more gradual model—not unlike the route taken by supporters of organic-labeled foods in the United States today. He argued for enriching premium-priced products first, and then counting on the market to provide for poor consumers later. Wealthy consumers would buy premium-priced flour and bread because they were more "susceptible to education." This would, eventually, lower prices, raise awareness, and "make itself felt among the lower income classes."

Despite Williams's misgivings, Merck cut a deal with Standard Brands to produce enrichment tablets for bakery use, and by 1940, General Mills was mass-marketing enriched flour. Profits boomed for both companies, but Williams's fears proved prescient. After touring the country to promote enrichment in 1941, he reflected sadly that millers and bakers who adopted enrichment did so almost exclusively with an eye toward niche markets and premium charges. The American staple food had not been enriched—only a small luxury subset. As he complained in his diary, enrichment held sway only in the country's "silk stocking districts," and even there interest was waning. Enriched bread, like organic arugula or patty pan squash, seemed destined to be an ephemerally trendy status item.

Only in the context of mobilization for total war could Williams and other nutrition scientists convince the country that enrichment mattered enough to make premium pricing unethical. By the time War Food Order Number 1 mandated across-the-board bread enrichment, many patriotic bakers and millers had already begun to internalize the minimal costs of adding vitamins to their products.

After the expiration of War Food Order Number 1 at the end of hostilities, more than half the country's states passed laws requiring bread enrichment, but they hardly needed to act. By 1947, a year after the repeal of mandatory wartime enrichment, industry marketing reports suggested that housewives had come to simply *expect* extra vitamins in their bread at no extra cost, and would continue to expect this in the postwar period.[24] As the war ended, Victory Gardens weeded over and Meatless Mondays morphed into barbeque parties, but with enriched bread something had stuck. Consumers had begun to crave extra vitamins in their food.

This remarkable cultural shift began with efforts to convince home front fighters that enriched white bread was a lynchpin of national defense, not the staff of death. In the context of wartime mobilization, the campaign for enrichment had served as a kind of vitamin boot camp, teaching Americans to think about nutrition.

VITAMIN BOOT CAMP

Early market research showed that bread buyers harbored deep-seated suspicions about bakers' enriched bread claims. Before the government made mandatory enrichment the norm, many housewives confused the word "enriched" with "richness," assuming vitaminized bread was more fattening than regular loaves. Some believed that enriched bread was a medicinal product best reserved for sick family members, while others simply dismissed "enriched" as a meaningless advertising word.[25]

Food manufacturers had enriched a few products since the 1930s, and home economists had lectured about the importance of vitamins since the 1910s, but most Americans had no idea what it all meant. A 1940 Gallup Poll found that only 9 percent of Americans knew what vitamins did. In 1941, another poll revealed that only 16 percent could distinguish between calories and vitamins. "Funny how we never knew nothin' about vitamins or calories or dietin' when we was young . . . we must a-been tough ones to live through it," admitted Mary Anne Meehan, a cook interviewed by a Works Progress Administration oral historian in 1939. "Now don't get me wrong. I believe in this vitamin and calory stuff alright," she continued—but it didn't sound that convincing.[26]

If Americans were to accept the idea that individuals had a patriotic duty to eat vitamin-rich foods, a national education campaign would have to convince them. Bread seemed like a good place to start. As U.S. surgeon general Thomas Parran argued, bread enrichment offered "a way in which necessary vitamins can be put into the diet of all our people, rich and poor; for all of us eat bread in some form three times a day."[27] Just as Selective Service applied to every fighting-aged man in the country, bread touched virtually every civilian family. Bread would make a good boot camp in which civilians could learn to think about how the vitamin content of foods they ate affected national defense.

In January 1941 the National Research Council for Defense announced that enriched bread would help the country "withstand the stresses and strains of war," and newspapers from Marysville, Ohio, to Brainard, Minnesota, from Amarillo, Texas, to Ogden, Utah, carried the story on their front pages. The surgeon general reinforced this message in a widely read *Better Homes and Gardens* article. Enrichment wouldn't just fix the busted staff of life, he insisted, it would turn bread into a weapon of national defense. "We are on the eve of a food revolution," the *Science News Letter* proclaimed. "Our staff of life, bread, will be restored to an ancient estate, making it more worthy of bearing this proud title. Vitamins are coming to the rescue. . . . The new vitaminized flour will give modern America strength for defense in war."[28]

The message echoed out from the advice columns of *Good House-keeping*:

The Army and Navy are using enriched flour and bread because of the extra health values they offer at no extra cost. You're in the Army, too! It's your patriotic duty to give your family these health values by using enriched bread and flour.[29]

to national advertising campaigns:

Enriched bread—a contribution to national defense. . . . The vitality, the vigor, and the health of our citizens is of prime importance in our national defense program.[30]

to local ad campaigns in cities and small towns across the country, like this one from Syracuse, New York:

Cabako Bakery—Defense Through Health[31]

to the bully pulpit of the U.S. Public Health Service:

The time has come when it is the patriotic duty of every American to eat enriched bread. Don't buy plain white bread.[32]

The message couldn't have been clearer. As a Fleischmann's ad run in thirteen cities and three national weeklies declared, vitamin deficiency was "a bomb so powerful that it could stun a whole city—leave all the people, young and old, dull, stupefied, fumbling." Bread fortified with Fleischmann's enrichment products was "the defense weapon the U.S. Government itself is urging the whole country to accept."[33]

Red Cross and Civil Defense nutrition classes instructed housewives across the country to choose enriched bread. *Listen America,* a national radio program broadcast weekly during 1941 and 1942, put the same message in living rooms. Anthropologists developed strategies to communicate the importance of enrichment to immigrant groups, and *The Modest Miracle,* a Hollywood short feature sponsored by the Federal Security Agency and Standard Brands, touted vitamin bread in theaters. Meanwhile, community "Nutrition Weeks" sponsored by bakeries and government agencies combined nutrition classes, educational film screenings, and bakery specials.[34]

These efforts didn't fall on deaf ears. Industry studies reported large increases in demand for enriched bread in the wake of propaganda campaigns. "Probably no other food and nutrition program has advanced so rapidly as the national movement to fortify cereal foods with vitamins and minerals," General Mills vice president R. C. Sherwood announced in an address to the American Public Health Association.[35] Through their combined efforts, government officials, the media, and private companies had built a foundation of awareness such that the significance of enrichment need no longer be explained.

Enriched bread had become "the biggest sales asset of recent times in the food field," according to a grocery trade magazine. When, after the war, a U.S. Department of Commerce pamphlet offered career advice to demobilized GIs, it could confidently recommend commercial baking because "the war-time bread enrichment program has done much to increase consumption." "Through vigorous advertising," it continued, "the American public has been led to a new conception of the healthful qualities of commercially baked bread."[36]

But this wasn't just about selling bread. Defense planners believed that the enrichment campaign would engender a broader consumer consciousness around nutrition and defense—and it did. As one study reported, "the flood of publicity on enrichment helped make the public 'vitamin conscious,'" and facilitated the efforts of other food industries working to connect their products with national defense. According to another source, white bread enrichment had "started a trend in food advertising and nutrition education that cannot fail to educate the American public to the value of truly 'protective' foods." As the influential nutritionist Hazel K. Stiebeling reflected after the war, bread enrichment campaigns trained Americans to take vitamins seriously. Indeed, this effort worked so well that government officials and bread advertising frequently had to remind consumers that enriched bread was not a medicine or miracle.[37]

The speed with which this message spread stunned even its most ardent supporters. Well before V-J Day, public health officials and war foods planners had a sense that they had achieved something remarkable and long lasting. Patting themselves on the back, they called bread enrichment "one of the most valuable and successful activities" of modern civil defense and the "beginning [of] a new era in nutrition for the American people." Bread enrichment, Thomas C. Desmond declared euphorically in the New York State Joint Legislative Committee on Nutrition's landmark 1944 report, *Food in War and in Peace,* had been "the key to the final solution of this Nation's nutrition problem." Should this achievement be carried into the postwar period, he predicted, bread "will compete with milk for the title of 'The perfect food.' "[38]

Desmond was right. The habit of associating enriched bread with strength carried over into the postwar period, even as former GIs moved to the suburbs en masse. And that association breathed new life into industrial bread. Celebrating enriched bread's tenth anniversary in 1951, the *Journal of Home Economics* marveled at how completely enrichment's success had silenced skeptics and "food faddists." A *Colliers* article written around the same time beamed, "On the tenth anniversary of enriched bread, many medical experts say that the accomplishment is one of the greatest nutritional advances in history." The American Medical Association, the National Research Council, and scores of local newspapers published glowing commendations, praising the bread enrichment campaign for making the United States stronger and healthier. Robert R. Williams, for his part, coined the widely circulated sound bite, "Enriched white bread is bargain health insurance for millions." A product of mobilization for world war, the association between industrial bread and security would continue into the Cold War.[39]

ROCKFORD FILES

After World War II, Rockford, Illinois, an industrial center built by European immigrants, daring inventors, and strong labor unions, was the stuff of middle-class dreams. Although Rockford's economy was far more industrial than the national average, it suited America's self-image to think of it as the country's most "typical" city, and sociologists obliged with the label. In 1949, *Life* shared sociologists' discovery with the country, declaring that Rockford was "about as typical as a city can be."[40] Market researchers flocked in droves to the shores of the Rock River to observe prototypical Americans in their natural habitat. So it was here, in mid-century Rockford, that the U.S. Department of Agriculture, the American Institute of Baking, and the Baking Industry Research Advisory Council collaborated on the most elaborate experimental study of bread consumption in history. The findings of the study, which ran from 1954 to 1955, spoke to a country's love affair with fluffy white bread: 95 percent of households bought white bread once a week; 75 percent bought it more than once a week. In total, Rockfordians ate about a pound and a half of bread per person per week, regardless of age or economic class.[41]

In repeated blind tests, consumer preference was clear and overwhelming: sweeter bread was better, but more importantly, fluffier bread was better. Comparing loaves of different densities, families almost always chose the lightest. But, strangely, this bread was not entirely well loved. About a third of housewives in the study described supermarket bread as "doughy; gummy; soggy; not well baked," about 15 percent thought the taste was terrible, and as much as 18 percent thought it too airy (despite the overwhelming preference for airy bread in blind tests). Depending on the year, between 60 and 75 percent of Rockford housewives registered major complaints about their staff of life.[42]

In the mid-1950s, it wouldn't have been hard to find these tepid responses affirmed by a whole range of white bread critics writing for popular magazines and newspapers. Whether you looked at *Better Homes and Gardens, Sunset,* or *Harper's,* homemaker advice columns in small-town newspapers or the more lofty *New York Times* food section, it would have been hard to find anything *good* said about the taste of industrial white bread. In a steady stream of newspaper articles, letters to the editors from housewives, and popular magazine features, industrial white bread was described as "cottony fluff," "cotton batting," "fake," "purposeless perfection," "inedible," "limp," "hot air," "a fugitive from a test tube," and "a doughy mass of chemicals."[43]

Yet nationwide, Americans ate a lot of industrial white bread in the late 1940s and early 1950s. As in Rockford, the vast majority of households in the United States ate store-bought white bread at all three meals—totaling some 8.6 billion loaves a year in 1954 (not including home-baked bread, and store-bought whole wheat, raisin bread, and "ethnic" breads). Most people consumed three to seven slices a day, but an astounding 33 percent of the population finished off more than eight slices a day. And this level of bread consumption cut across class: while the wealthiest 10 percent of the country consumed bread in slightly smaller quantities, the remaining nine income deciles varied little in their daily intake. Age didn't seem to matter either: adults and children ate bread at exactly the same rate. Only gender seemed to differentiate bread eaters: women, forbidden the staff of life by many popular diets of the time, ate the least, while men and boys, associating bread with bodybuilding strength, ate the most.[44]

During World War II, bread consumption, driven by the rationing of other staples, accounted for as much as 40 percent of all calories consumed in the country daily. After the war, Americans could have abandoned bread, just as they traded ration books for TV dinners. Instead, the proportion of calories derived from bread settled in at 25–30 percent and then, despite the absolute certainty with which food economists and baking industry specialists predicted rapid declines in consumption, hovered around the same point through the mid-1960s. Studies remarked the high percentage of daily vitamins, iron, and protein consumers derived from the much-derided staff of life.

Why did postwar consumers continue to eat so much industrial bread, despite widespread popular condemnation of its flavor and texture? Americans could have abandoned bread as a staple, as many worried bakers feared they would. They didn't. Nor did they choose other kinds of bread in large quantities. When, from time to time, big baking companies attempted to launch lines of whole wheat bread, they invariably fell flat. And despite the continued survival of small specialty bakeries, especially in cities, rye, whole wheat, and other "ethnic" loaves offered little competition, accounting for only 8–12 percent of bread consumption during the postwar period.[45]

Part of the reason Americans stuck to gummy white bread lay in the way wartime enrichment campaigns had cemented a sense that industrial white bread built strength for individual and national defense. Despite their diverse complaints about store-bought bread, Rockfordians agreed on one thing: depending on the year, 96 or 100 percent of the USDA bread study's sample responded that their bread was highly nutritious.[46]

Legions of industrial white bread critics still voiced opposition during the age of Wonder bread, but as the 1950s advanced, scientific consensus turned against them. In 1958 *Consumer Reports* declared that it had reversed its long-standing objection to white bread, citing "an accumulation of evidence" and a particularly convincing experiment carried out in the ruins of postwar Germany by the former white bread critic R. A. McCance. In that 1946 experiment, published in 1954 and widely cited by champions of the new consensus, McCance and his partner, E. M. Woddowson, conducted a feeding trial on 250 orphans in Duisberg and Wuppertal. The researchers had divided the orphans into five groups and fed each group a diet consisting almost entirely of one of five different types of bread (enriched white, various grades of high-extraction dark white flour, and whole wheat). "To the surprise of Dr. McCance and his associates," *Consumer Reports* informed readers, "no appreciable differences whatsoever showed up in the growth of the groups of children. All grew equally well." In another widely publicized study of enriched bread's impacts on child health, researchers in Newfoundland claimed that fortified loaves had given bursting energy to formerly lethargic children, increased child survival rates, and ended adult listlessness, without any increase in total calories consumed.[47]

Health experts, food writers, and ordinary bread eaters who still felt that there was just something wrong with industrial loaves would have to find a different language other than nutrition science to express their doubts. Aesthetic and epicurean arguments, which had played a surprisingly minor role in earlier battles over the staff of life, offered the only way forward. As white-bread critic Clarence Woodbury wrote begrudgingly in *Reader's Digest,* industrial white bread exceeded homemade whole wheat bread in almost every arena except one—taste. "[White bread] is, undoubtedly, pure, sanitary, wholesome, nutritious, clean, white, and beautiful—but it is utterly tasteless."[48]

This aesthetic appeal often rang hollow against the muscle-bound science of enriched white bread advocates. Take, for example, Lee Anderson's tirade, "Busted Staff of Life," which appeared in the *Atlantic Monthly* in 1947. "Modern bread may well be more digestible than the bread our mothers and grandmothers used to bake each week-end, more nourishing, more scientifically pure, more enriched with those essential substances which make hair grow, eyes see better, bones get harder," Anderson conceded. "But Grandma's bread was bread . . . and if Grandpa had to wear 'specs' at sixty-five and lost all his teeth at eighty because his diet was deficient in vitamins, no one ever complained that the bread was at fault."[49]

With friends like these, critics of industrial white bread needed no enemies. Enriched bread might taste like a "doughy mass of chemicals,"[50] but at least you kept your teeth and eyesight. Children kept their competitive edge, and the nation as a whole was stronger. Driven by the security imperative of hot and cold wars, synthetic vitamin enrichment was deeply entrenched in the American dietary consciousness.

LOOK, MOM, IT'S LOADED!

Bakers didn't create the association between enriched white bread and fighting vigor, but during the early Cold War, they worked hard to reinforce it. As fighting ended in the Pacific, bakers hoped to capitalize on the buoyant success of enrichment, but they had to wait. Famine had staked its claim on the immediate postwar period. With bad winters in Europe and crop failures throughout Asia, 1946 and 1947 were desperate years of worldwide grain shortage and mass starvation. In the United States, Truman, struggling to free up wheat for overseas relief, called on consumers to eat less bread and contemplated rationing the staple, something the country had avoided even in the darkest days of the war. Bakers reluctantly postponed their plans for a massive postwar advertising blitz focused on the health-building benefits of enriched bread and aimed at consumers, medical professionals, and nutritionists.[51]

Then in 1948 and 1949, with the immediate global food crisis over, bakers mobilized to pick up where they had left off during the war. Advertising images of war industry workers and soldiers segued smoothly into images of children—mostly boys—engaged in competitive striving for physical and mental superiority. In these ads, boys lunged at fleeing girls, wrestled each other, triumphantly waved straight-A report cards, supported enormous weights, and grew bones, teeth, muscle, and brain cells at explosive rates. Mrs. Bohnet's

Bread in San Antonio helped a skinny boy drive railroad spikes with a toy hammer while burly tracklayers looked on in amazement. Holsum enriched bread gave "Johnny" the energy to swing from chandeliers over his listless, non-bread-eating sister, and a Town Talk bread poster showed a tiny bruiser tackling his grandfather on the football field. Even the Schneider Baking Company's "Little Miss Sunbeam" reminded consumers that Uncle Sam wanted them to "reach for energy-packed bread."

Sometimes ads made the competitive message painfully clear—"Winners Eat Ward's" and ads featuring running races come to mind. Other times it was less obvious, as in the widespread presence of scientific-looking charts and graphs against which parents could measure their child's growth achievements against others'. "Most youngsters today are taller, healthier than children were a generation ago. . . . What about your children?" asked a Jane Parker ad from 1954.

The message that bread was a weapons delivery system grew less explicit after the war, but it was still there. Under the title "Reach! Mom . . . It's loaded!" a 1953 ad for Jane Parker enriched white bread, portraying a cowboy-hat-wearing, pistol-wielding boy reminded readers that bread was "loaded." Most bread companies, it seemed, wanted to have their loaves associated with gunslinging cowboys in some way. Wonder, Wheatty, Merita, Jaeger, and Bond, to name a few, all hawked bread with images of Western action. Bread was for fighting, as one of the very last ad series in this genre—a 1970 Wonder bread ad featuring a discouraged boy with a black eye—made clear. That ad packed a stiff punch with the text "Bigger than Kevin. That's how big I want to be" over the head of the beaten boy.

With the country's burgeoning fertility rates, the shift in focus from soldiers and war workers to children made sense. Baking industry advertising had focused on children in the past, of course. Before the war, however, it typically portrayed them as innocents to be protected through scientific hygiene, as cuddly objects symbolizing purity and wholesomeness, or as fragile objects of care. What changed after World War II was not the focus on children in bread advertising; it was the ubiquitous language of competitive striving used in that effort.

Baby boomer nostalgia paints early Cold War childhood as an age of play and plenty. And it was, for many Americans, at least.[52] But anxiety and competition underpinned play and plenty. Boys' toys took an emphatically bellicose form and the new media of television served up a steady stream of aggressive masculinity and Manichean struggle. Of the top twenty-five TV shows in the late 1950s, nearly half featured cowboys. "In an era marked by anxiety over masculinity and intense hostility toward homosexuality, boy culture emphasized toughness and aggression," the renowned historian of childhood Steven Mintz argues. And this could not be separated from the larger political culture: "During the Cold War there was a symbolic connection between the struggle with the Soviet Union and the battles boys acted out at recess and in backyards."[53]

By 1948, the jubilant optimism felt after V-J Day had been battered by one crisis after another, and was about to disappear for good. Although historians disagree avidly about just how actively afraid ordinary folks felt as they went about their daily business in the late 1940s and early 1950s, a strong current of anxiety clearly flowed beneath the shiny surfaces of the time. George Kennan defined the moment in his 1946 Long Telegram, which clearly and unflinchingly introduced the country to a world organized around two antagonistic, irreconcilable poles, with freedom, justice, free enterprise, and the American way hanging in the balance. Again.[54]

Wonder bread rolled out its iconic "Builds a Body 8 Ways" ad campaign in the thick of the Berlin Airlift and, during its first year, it would have shared newspaper space with the first Soviet atomic bomb test, the first major FBI report on Communist subversives in Hollywood, the creation of the German Democratic Republic, the declaration of the People's Republic of China, rising tensions on the Korean peninsula, and the last bloody gasps of the Greek civil war. Indeed, Wonder bread's infamous campaign—which would later run afoul of the FTC for its extreme claims about bread's ability to boost children's performance—mapped fairly neatly onto the peak years of the Red Scare. Regardless of how scared Americans actually felt while slathering oleo on their morning toast and reading the paper, the promise of peace had been shattered and replaced by a commitment to perpetual readiness.[55]

Atomic-age civil defense planners knew how important bread was. Reflecting back on the London Blitz and Berlin Airlift from the vantage of the early 1950s, civil defense experts noted that "under such conditions the consumption of bread rose to twice the usual level. Bread, the staff of life, apparently becomes all the more a staple food in times of severe stress." After a nuclear attack, they concluded in numerous reports, bread would probably be the main source of food for the affected population. The USDA and other government agencies mobilized bakers to prepare for attacks and put the public on notice to expect a "bread and water diet when [the] A-bomb strikes." In 1951, the popular science and technology magazine *Science News Letter* urged New Yorkers to keep a good supply of spreads like jam and peanut butter on hand to perk up their bread and water diet in anything "short of a complete disaster." Even if keeping peanut butter and jelly on hand for nuclear holocaust lunches wasn't at the top of most housewives' to-do lists, kitchens were still battlegrounds. The invisible germs and swarthy immigrants that threatened domestic hygiene and national vitality in the early twentieth century had given way to the Communist menace.[56]

As in previous periods of national emergency, Cold War popular culture consistently depicted mothers as both the country's first line of defense against invisible enemies—and, potentially, its weakest link. According to the emergent logic of permanent readiness, mothers would oversee the creation of warm, protective havens for the country's future Cold Warriors, while guarding against maternal instincts that might produce overly soft "mamma's boys."[57]

In the heat of the early Cold War, mothers made sure their families ate for victory, but not just so that they could fight in faraway lands. Cold Warriors would have to compete on multiple seemingly mundane fronts. As K. A. Cuordileone observed in his history of postwar manhood, competition on the high school football field, in the national marketplace, and in the international arms and science races blurred together into one critical effort aimed at demonstrating the superiority of the American way. Competitive spirit in the pursuit of individual happiness represented America's secret weapon against the powerful machine of Soviet command and control.[58]

In this context, health and vigor sold bread far more than taste or freshness. As the frequent *Colliers* contributor Robert Froman lamented in 1951, it grieved most bakers "that their bread is often judged not chiefly for its taste and appetite appeal, as are other foods, but for its nutritional values."[59]

The postwar association between industrial white bread and competitive vigor could easily have been reversed. After all, driven by consumers' mistaken idea that softer bread meant fresher bread, the baking industry had begun using a witch's brew of chemical dough conditioners to pump the standard white balloon loaf from its already fairly soft prewar seven cubic centimeters per ounce to its ethereal postwar ten cubic centimeters per ounce. If the country feared soft boys, why feed children history's softest bread? Warren E. Siegmond, an heir to H. L. Mencken's contrarian conservatism, took aim at white bread using just this argument. Writing in the *American Mercury* in 1958, he dared fathers to test the wisdom of their wives' supermarket selection: "Make this simple test. Take a piece of white bread and tear out the center. Now roll it into a ball until the whole thing is a doughy mass of chemicals. Bounce it on the floor; it rivals rubber! Is this food that will see your child through an active school day?"[60]

Christian Science Monitor critic Horace Reynolds made an even scarier observation about soft bread: "Modern industrialism has ruined American bread. . . . It's so soft and spongy you can contract it with your hands, mold it any shape you've a mind to. . . . The soft, fluffy center is like a mouthful of powder puff. The more you eat the hungrier you get. This is what America's staff of life has come to. It's a pretty soft staff. The Russians are leaning on something more substantial. . . . What America needs is bread with crust to exercise the teeth and stick to the ribs, ribs to strengthen the heart for the tasks which lie ahead."[61]

A few took the warnings seriously: for a period, the New York public school system replaced its students' standard white bread with a loaf based on McCay's high-protein "Do-Good" defense bread, and the U.S. Congress convened long hearings about the safety of bread softeners. But the war-trained habit of associating white bread with vitamins, strength, and readiness survived those attacks. In fact, it deepened. While bread manufacturers lured moms with advertising images of tough boys doing tough things, a new scientific and public health consensus formed around the surprising idea that America's pillowy soft bread measured up as sturdily, if not more sturdily, than the bread of any other land. By the end of the 1950s, even industrial bread's most ardent critics would concede this point.

AFTERMATHS OF ENRICHMENT

Synthetic enrichment transformed the way America thought about and ate bread. Thanks to the imperative of building a strong national defense, it did so in a way that was relatively egalitarian. National health was too important to be left to the whims and fashions of elite consumers, which seem to drive present-day food movements. And this raises interesting questions for us today. Thinking back on the wartime campaign for enrichment, I can't help but wonder what level of urgency it would take to move present-day America toward a future where everyone, not just elite shoppers, had access to healthy, safe, environmentally and socially responsible food. Perhaps expanding national security to include food security is just what we need.

At the same time we should realize that during World War II, intense concern about nutrition and national defense pushed aside alternative ideas about improving America's most important food, smoothing the way for the triumph of an expedient compromise dominated by mainstream nutrition scientists, industry voices, and government agencies. In the long run, by redeeming sliced white bread in the face of scientific criticism, the association of food and defense brought the country another step closer to the wholesale triumph of chemically infused, Styrofoam-textured white bread. Indeed, without the wartime campaign for enrichment and the government-backed dismissal of nonsynthetically enriched "health breads" that accompanied it, we might not have witnessed the postwar golden age of Wonder bread. Industrial bakers' ability to associate their product with vigorous defense and spirited competition saved sliced white bread from declining consumption. Ultimately it helped lay a foundation for the postwar triumph of processed foods.

Today, local foodies, health food advocates, and anti-obesity crusaders might consider industrial white bread a national security threat, not an asset. But, in some important way, they owe their ability to speak easily about diet and defense to the training Americans received in the WWII-era campaign for synthetic bread enrichment. In this sense, they inherit a language with the power to galvanize rapid change, stir communities into action, and join disparate interests with a common purpose. But they should also know that urgency comes with a price. Even the most well-intentioned food activists might find that playing the national security card facilitates unfortunate coalitions and limits options where they had hoped to open new horizons.

5

WHITE BREAD IMPERIALISM

Dreams of Peace and Security

Bread comes from America and it does not come from Russia.
—Hamilton Fish, 1947

MUNDO BIMBO

Even as anti-immigrant fervor gripped large parts of the United States during the 2000s, one unexpected border crosser was doing quite well in the land of white bread. Since 1996, Mexico's industrial baking giant Grupo Bimbo had been quietly acquiring some of its northern neighbor's most iconic bakery brands. After its takeover of Weston Foods in 2010 and of Sara Lee in 2011, Bimbo poised itself to become the United States' largest industrial bread baker. With almost $10 billion in global sales in 2009, one hundred thousand employees, and operations in eighteen countries from Chile to China, it was already one of the world's biggest. How did a Mexican company get so far baking such a supposedly "American" food? And how did *pan gringo* take hold in the land of corn tortillas anyway?

When I first visited Mexico as a student in 1991, my lower-middle-class host family served *pan Bimbo* for breakfast—every morning for a hundred days: three hundred slices of the softest, whitest bread I had ever eaten. No matter how I begged to eat a more "Mexican" breakfast, no matter how much my host mother smiled and nodded at my pitiful pleading, Bimbo bread always awaited me on the kitchen patio. Perhaps my host mother believed that sliced white bread suited a gringo like me. Maybe it was just cheap and convenient. Twenty years later, sitting in a taxi on my way to Bimbo's headquarters, still trying to unscramble the mystery of those breakfasts, I asked the driver about the appeal of supermarket bread. Mexicans will never give up corn tortillas, he assured me. But there was something "attractive" about Bimbo bread. His family ate it at most breakfasts and some lunches. It wasn't the flavor that drew him to white bread: Bimbo bread tastes like cotton, he confessed with a self-deprecating laugh. "I don't know why we like it so much, but we do."

Understanding the ascendance of sliced white bread in Mexico requires a foray into the politics of what has come to be called "the Mexican Miracle," a thirty-year period from the 1940s to 1970s marked by high levels of economic growth, explosive industrialization, and rapid urbanization. For better and for worse, that miracle rested on a foundation of cheap, "modern" foods like Bimbo—made possible by government subsidies and incredible advances in agricultural productivity. Just as Mexico's industries and cities grew during this period, its farms came to look ever more like factories. Mexico produced unprecedented quantities of food, easily outpacing the country's rapid population growth. And yet, in this new world of industrial food production, more Mexicans went hungry. Modern agriculture facilitated explosive industrial growth and social peace in the cities, but took a toll on rural workers and peasant farmers, forcing millions from the countryside into urban slums. Through all that tumultuous social change, Bimbo bread stood as a kind of promissory note, a graspable piece of a future yet to come.

At the same time, this uniquely Mexican story can be understood only in a much larger context of cheap food, wheat bread, and Cold War geopolitics. Whether they knew it or not, when Lorenzo Servitje and his three Catalonian immigrant collaborators opened the first Bimbo factory in 1945, they formed part of a bigger web of global food politics and superpower struggle that would define the postwar period. As much as the story of Bimbo bread reveals about Mexico, it is also a story about how the United States understood its place—and the place of its industrial food production system—in a dangerous world. It is a story about how a particular approach to growing, processing, and eating industrial food got fused with hopes for world peace and security—and what that has meant for the United States and the world.

This chapter's globe-trotting exploration of Grupo Bimbo's origins provides a glimpse into the making of a particular form of postwar "American alimentary exceptionalism" premised on the universal desirability of industrially grown and processed food. This alimentary exceptionalism did not assume the U.S. industrial food system was gastronomically superior to the rest of the world's foodways, but rather that it offered a unique foundation on which world peace could rest in the uncertain postwar world. Although this vision had deep roots in the United States, we can trace its postwar origins to successful famine relief—mostly in the form of massive shipments of wheat and flour to Europe and Asia—during the first years of the Cold War.

During the early Cold War, shipments of U.S. bread grains to famine-torn Europe and Asia served two purposes: at home, they prevented rural recession by absorbing farm surpluses. Abroad, U.S. grain shipments saved millions from starvation, buttressed friendly governments, and generally served as one of the United States' most effective weapons against the spread of Communism. As the Cold War wore on, U.S. reliance on "food power"—the strategy of using the United States' undisputed dominance in the arenas of industrial agriculture and industrial food processing as a carrot and a stick on the global stage—deepened. Shipments of U.S. grain as food aid continued, becoming a permanent cornerstone of both domestic farm support and foreign policy. At the same time, direct grain shipments were supplemented and eventually superseded by efforts to remake world agriculture in the American image.

This Cold War history has enduring legacies—not just in the form of globally competitive Mexican bakers. As scholars of U.S. "dietary imperialism" have noted, the export of industrial food and industrial agriculture during this period radically changed the way the world ate. Less noticed is that the exercise of food power also left a deep impression on the way Americans themselves emotionally connect with industrial food: every time a chemical manufacturer tells PBS viewers that its newest high-yield seeds are needed to fight poverty in some conflict-ridden country, every time a grain industry spokesperson warns that only industrial agriculture can keep famine and food riots at bay, every time some environmentalist excuses the social and ecological consequences of new biotechnologies out of fear that population growth will outstrip food supplies, they are deploying a dream forged in the crucible of Cold War anxiety.[1] Understanding that historical context—tracing it through its origins in the European famine of 1946–48 to key laboratories like occupied Japan, Main Street 1950s America and, of course, postwar Mexico—won't resolve decades-old debates about poverty and food, but it will highlight hidden cultural assumptions and unacknowledged shortcomings in the dream of peace and security achieved through industrial eating. The story of bread and the Cold War reminds us that, even when couched in a language of humanitarianism and world peace, the present-day eliding of industrial food production and global security establishes a state of emergency in which the enormous social, economic, environmental, and health costs of industrial food production must be accepted without question or critique.

IF BREAD DOESN'T COME, BOMBS WILL

During the winter of 1945–46, while the United States celebrated peace by consuming three thousand calories a day per person and singing, "Let it snow! Let it snow! Let it snow!" with Vaughn Monroe, severe weather nearly destroyed Europe's entire bread grains crop. Historic drought that summer followed by another bad winter finished the job. In a region where most people got 40–55 percent of their daily calories from bread, nearly 125 million Europeans faced starvation.[2] Bread riots rocked France, which had seen its worst wheat harvest in 132 years. Italy's flour stocks dwindled, and Britain reported that its bread situation was worse than in the darkest days of the war. Wheat stocks were so low in the U.K. that government officials were forced to extend and deepen wartime bread rationing, despite fierce popular opposition. Winston Churchill called the decision "one of the gravest announcements [he] had ever heard in the House in time of peace."[3]

Things looked even more dire in Asia. China faced a massive rice crisis, famine gripped Korea, and millions of conquered Japanese survived on 520 calories per day. In total, the United States estimated, 500 million people—one in five people on the planet—faced famine conditions between 1946 and 1948.

Some relief supplies shipped to Asia, but for racial and geopolitical reasons Truman's attention—and the country's—was riveted on Europe. Making use of his bully pulpit, grain exporters' eagerness to exploit new markets, and almost every Liberty ship in the U.S. Navy, Truman mobilized the largest movement of wheat and flour in world history—almost 900 million bushels between 1946 and 1947, enough to bake, conservatively, 70 billion loaves of white bread.

The United States' role as the postwar world's most important source of bread did not take policy makers by surprise. Even before Pearl Harbor, military strategists commonly argued that food "would win the war and write the peace," and agriculture officials planned for that peace even as they mobilized to fight. Most importantly, they wanted to make sure that the country avoided a devastating rural recession like the one triggered after WWI when war-stimulated grain production collided with a large postwar drop in demand for U.S. wheat. This time around, the country would use its agricultural advantage strategically, killing two birds with one stone: supporting farmers at home while projecting food power into the uncertain political terrain of the future. The fact that the United States emerged from the war as the only power in the world with its agricultural system not only unscathed but in peak form did not surprise the Truman administration. What shook Washington was just how quickly America's responsibilities as the most important player in the world food system thrust themselves on the country.

To free up wheat for the world, Truman called on the country to voluntarily conserve bread, prohibited the use of wheat in alcohol production, and mandated a higher extraction rate for white flour. When Americans complained about the new, supposedly "gray" high-extraction loaves, Truman scolded them, saying that not getting "exactly the kind of bread that many prefer" was a tiny price to pay for saving lives and establishing lasting peace.[4] Publications like *Life, Look, Parents' Magazine, Time,* and *American Home* backed the president, running heart-wrenching stories of hunger in Europe and offering readers advice on how to conserve wheat. Thousands of women signed pledges to conserve bread in their households, and food magazines went back on a war footing, publishing tips and recipes for saving bread.

While Americans felt generally sympathetic toward humanitarian efforts aimed at allies and even former enemies in Europe, public support for wheat conservation, high-extraction loaves, and possible bread rations was short-lived.[5] Letters to newspaper editors reveal widespread skepticism about Americans' willingness to suffer bread restrictions for altruistic reasons. Instead, humanitarian concern for starving European children segued into self-interested thinking about wheat exports and national security. As *Consumers' Guide* assured readers, when they "cast [their] bread on the waters," it would return "in the form of preventing a generation of rickety European children from growing into a sickly, embittered and grasping people bent on war. It will, in other words, return to us in the form of the better chances of peace and security in our own homes which only a healthy and peaceful Europe can assure."[6]

An August 10, 1947, article in the *Los Angeles Times* summed up the new attitude in the headline "Bread: It Is the First Concern of a Hungry World. Trouble Looms for the Nations Which Cannot Provide It." If bread doesn't come, the article continued, "bombs—in one form or another—will." The *Farm Journal,* which, granted, had its own interest in food exports, put the matter bluntly: "Better to win friends now with flour, than have to face their guns later." H. R. Baukhage, a nationally syndicated D.C. pundit and popular radio personality, made the case even more explicit in his Associated Press column: "The history of Europe since the war is that every government falls when the bread ration is reduced. . . . The free world is at stake." The only thing that can "save Europe for democracy," he continued, is "the American farmer."[7]

The news from France appeared particularly grave. The country's 1947–48 wheat harvest was as disastrous as the previous year's, and even with emergency shipments from France's North African colonies, the government could not maintain its basic bread ration at 300 grams per person. Foreign Agricultural Service field officers in France wrote urgent telegrams to the State Department in Washington warning officials to expect a general breakdown of the French food distribution system by the end of May 1948 if even larger U.S. wheat shipments weren't forthcoming. This would likely trigger widespread protests and strikes, as it had in 1946 and 1947, but the situation might get even worse. Opposition groups were already using the country's puny bread ration as a central wedge issue. French Communists, in particular, had made impressive political hay out of a single five-thousand-ton wheat shipment from Russia, and U.S. officials complained that the country didn't seem to appreciate the United States' far greater contributions. If bad harvests forced the government to lower the bread ration to 250 grams, they predicted, it might tip France's delicate political balance toward Communist forces.[8]

In Paris, the May Day parade that year featured a contingent of workers carrying placards reading, "Give us a slice of bread." Meanwhile, back in the United States, syndicated columnists Joseph and Stewart Alsop warned readers that "if France starved, it would go Communist. . . . If France goes to the Communists . . . the great struggle for Europe between the Soviet and western political systems will almost certainly be ended in Russia's favor." The fate of Europe seemed to hang on French bread rations.[9]

Whether those fears were reasonable or not, the United States responded with stepped-up wheat shipments. On May 10, 1948, after two years and nine hundred shiploads of stopgap aid to France, the Liberty ship *John H. Quick* docked at the Port of Bordeaux bearing the first official Marshall Plan wheat. Lavishly praising the United States for its help, government officials announced that the bread ration could be maintained. This averted full-fledged crisis in France, although bread-related protests and political instability would continue into the 1950s.

In Iran, another quickly emerging Cold War battleground, U.S. and Soviet strategists mobilized bread grains in the fight for control over oil. Through the late 1940s, with bad wheat harvests in Iran's Azerbaijan breadbasket triggering bread riots throughout the country, Soviet propaganda spread rumors that Tehran was selling scarce wheat to the United States to pay for arms. U.S. officials worried even more about the Soviets' promise to provide Iran with one hundred thousand tons of wheat in 1949. Luckily for U.S. strategists, however, the Soviet wheat traveling overland trickled into the country, while American Liberty ships filled with wheat arrived with great fanfare.[10]

Bread and flour shipments were also credited with undermining Communist forces in Greece where, in 1948, 96 percent of the nation's staple was made from U.S. flour or wheat.[11] Turkey followed a similar pattern. And the Berlin blockade, for its part, confirmed policy makers' sense of the strategic importance of fresh bread, giving

civil defense experts a firsthand glimpse of the effects of bread deprivation on civilian populations. Although it would have made more
sense to airlift light, nutrient-dense foods instead of heavy flour and
the heavier fuels needed to bake it, officials observing the situation in
Berlin quickly concluded that, in times of crisis, "ample freshly baked
bread . . . was essential to civilian morale." Later, they would apply
this lesson to U.S. civil defense planning, which stressed the importance of bread supplies.[12]

Things did not go as well in Czechoslovakia. In 1948, Truman's
failure to extend bread grain shipments to East-leaning Czechoslovakia was credited with pushing the country definitively into the Soviet
camp, and the president publicly vowed never to allow something like
that to happen again. In a watershed speech, the president demanded
quick passage of the Marshall Plan, which at first consisted largely of
stepped-up bread grain shipments. In the same speech, the president
called for universal peacetime military training and the reestablish-
ment of the Selective Service system. With bread grains leading the
way, the country was going to (cold) war.[13]

SOMETHING BETTER

In a June 1952 commencement address, President Eisenhower, de-
spairing at the country's decline into Red-baiting and book ban-
ning, implored Dartmouth College graduates "to fight Communism
with something better." But, as Secretary of State John Foster Dulles
noted, increasingly visible poverty and racial tensions were "ruining"
the United States' image abroad. The country's Cold War propaganda
machine was struggling to speak convincingly of America's lofty ideals. It was getting harder and harder to point, concretely, to what
"something better" America could offer the world.[14]

To make matters worse, by the end of the 1950s, the United States
appeared to be losing ground to the Soviets in almost every arena
that mattered—education, science, technology, weapons. Every
arena except consumer goods and food production, that is. In this
context, visions of domestic consumer affluence displaced Freedom
and Equality as the most important weapon in U.S. propaganda
efforts.[15]

U.S. efforts to combat the appeal of Communist "workers' paradise" with glamorous images of life in a "consumers' paradise" filled with sleek Chevrolets, color TVs, automatic dishwashers, and Populuxe living room sets have been well documented.[16] The important role that industrial food played in creating the image of America as the land of plenty is less well known, and it is unclear how much U.S. food-related propaganda affected target audiences in the USSR, Western Europe, Asia, and Latin America. It did seem to work on *Americans:* even as confidence in the superiority of U.S. military readiness, technology, and education wavered at home and abroad, Americans picked up on the idea that their ability to produce and consume abundant food set them apart. Industrially produced food was "something better" the United States could offer a hungry world.

During the 1959 American National Exhibition in Moscow, where Vice President Richard Nixon famously accused Nikita Khrushchev of making lousy dishwashers, U.S. newspaper headlines across the country positively crowed over the way American food "dazzle[d] Ivan." Modern food processing was "our secret weapon"—"the newest weapon in America's fight against communism."[17] "Johnny" might not be able to read as well as "Ivan," as Rudolf Flesch warned in his best-selling attack on the U.S. educational system, but few Americans doubted that Johnny could eat better than his Soviet counterpart. Speaking at a U.S. Information Agency symposium on food and the Cold War, Campbell's Soup Company president William B. Murphy captured this spirit: "The best example of the American dream of plenty is in food. . . . Communism is utterly incompatible with the production of food."[18]

To be sure, U.S. food propaganda typically focused on more glamorous modern food concoctions—TV dinners and ready-mix cakes— but industrial bread was basic and U.S. industrial foodways were often juxtaposed with the Communist world's scarce "dark bread." A 1946 *Woman's Home Companion* feature on "life behind the iron curtain," for example, held white bread up as a key example of the *pruducti* Russian people craved, but only America could provide. While some critics of fluffy American bread praised hearty Soviet loaves, they generally conceded that the U.S. baking system was still better at providing affordable abundance. Even as the United States fretted about its own soaring bread prices, the *Los Angeles Times* could proudly declare that "a Soviet worker must work half a day or longer to earn enough money to buy a kilogram of rye bread, while an American needs to work only 12 minutes."[19]

From Gaston, North Carolina ("Reds Stand in Breadlines"), to Lima, Ohio ("Bread Scarce in Soviet Cupboards"), the U.S. press triumphed in stories of Soviet bread shortages.[20] Accounts of daring escapes from the Soviet bloc run frequently by popular magazines during the early 1950s invariably mentioned bread prices and bread lines as a motivating factor in the flight from Communism. And even when American reporters in Russia observed abundant high-quality and nutritious dark bread, industrial white bread was still a symbol of U.S. superiority: the Russian food system was so inefficient, they argued, consumers had few other options and could afford little else beyond dark bread. Finally, with Soviet military technology advancing at frightening speeds, newspapers could still reassure readers that bread shortages periodically brought the Red Army to a screeching halt.[21]

In this way, abundant modern food, including industrial white bread, constituted one of the Cold War's most reassuring dreams: the idea of alimentary affluence in the West and dark Soviet bread lines in the East. In industrial bread, U.S. policy makers, manufacturers, and consumers had definitively fused the assumed universality of their foodways with the imperatives of national security.

This wasn't just an East-West comparison. By the mid-1950s, Americans could increasingly compare their supermarket bread to the golden products of Western European bakeries. Subsidized by Marshall Plan money, U.S. tourists had begun traveling to France in record numbers. And they returned from those tours with stories of astonishingly good bread, sparking a fad for French bread in the United States.[22]

Not everyone in the United States had access to French bread, which began appearing in big-city stores, or would want to pay the hefty premium price, but anyone who read could form an opinion about the difference between American white bread and its European counterparts. Nearly every newspaper and lifestyle magazine ran stories about the French bread craze during the mid-1950s, and a complicated message emerged from those articles. All agreed that

French bread tasted divine. Its arrival in America was something to celebrate. At the same time, there was something off about French bread: the very hedonistic qualities that made it popular also made it suspect. American industrial bread might taste like doughy hot air compared to a good baguette, but American bread embodied strength and fortitude in a way that the French stuff didn't. And for better or worse, in a dangerous world, system and fortitude had to trump taste.

The once-pressing question of whether France's bread had, as one woman remarked in a letter to the *Los Angeles Times,* caused the country to "lose vim and vigor" in the face of Nazi invasion didn't concern U.S. observers so much anymore.[23] Rather, it was the whole French food *system* that seemed off. As articles in *Time* and other national publications concluded, the French baking industry had too many inefficient subsidies, lax sanitation regulations, archaic distribution networks, and monopolistic guilds. France needed industrial baking and American-style competition.

When ergotism, a rare form of hallucination-inducing poisoning caused by fungus-infected rye, sickened two hundred residents of the small village of Pont-Saint-Esprit during the summer of 1951, U.S. media reveled disproportionately in the sensational story. Tellingly, almost every story on the outbreak instructed U.S. readers that ergotism was a medieval disease, a remnant of a scarier age before industrial baking, and all congratulated American industrial bakers for single-handedly eradicating ergotism through vitamin enrichment. These claims were not exactly true on several levels—but that didn't matter: Tales of bread-poisoned peasants, convinced they were jet planes, leaping from windows and rumors that "the village idiot had hexed the baker" seemed to confirm the larger sense of French baking: it was irrational and archaic. French foodways were "charming" and something to "keep . . . happily in mind while we survey most of the other half of mankind," one observer noted, but certainly no model for global security.[24]

This attitude didn't just emanate from Francophobes. Francophiles also replicated the divide between taste and security, pleasure and fortitude. An article by *New York Times* food editor Janet Nickerson exemplified this trend. Pitting American white bread against its European counterparts, Nickerson argued that opposition to American white bread divided into two camps, one based on health and the other on flavor. The epicurean critics held a special place in her heart; indeed, they were incontrovertibly correct. Fluffy, limp-crusted, and bland industrial white bread couldn't hold a candle to crisp, nutty-flavored French and Italian breads. Alas—and one can almost hear her sigh echoing across the decades—"health values deal with *fact* while flavor considerations deal with *opinion*." Thus, in the end, readers were better off buying industrial white bread, for their family's health.[25]

Armed with this confident and urgent vision of good food, America set out to transform the world's bread, sometimes literally, sometimes figuratively. U.S. corporations, with government support, built American-style industrial bakeries in Iran and struggled (without much success) for similar footholds in Western Europe. But what happened when the iron triangle of wheat, industrial baking, and global security set down in countries where bread was not the staple food? The results were far more complicated than both proponents and critics of American industrial foodways acknowledge, as the case of Japan reveals.

RATIONALIZING RICE EATERS

In the early 1950s, U.S.-trained public health officials and agribusiness representatives combined forces to spread the gospel of white bread to the conquered rice eaters of Japan. Their efforts—particularly the targeting of Japanese schoolchildren's palates through school lunch programs—are frequently held up as the ultimate example of U.S-backed agribusiness forcing its industrial foods on defenseless populations, of the premeditated destruction of healthy, "holistic" eating.[26] But the story is quite a bit more complicated than that, not least because the Japanese taste for white bread long predates the end of WWII. Indeed, occupation officials under the Supreme Commander of the Allied Powers (SCAP) faced an imperial conundrum: Japan welcomed white bread and industrial baking technology with open arms, but fiercely resisted cultural assumptions about the nutritional and political superiority of a white bread diet.[27] This two-sided response divided occupation officials, creating room for debate about white bread's role in securing the Asian front against Communism.

While some officials argued for rebuilding Japan on a foundation of rice and fish protein, others insisted on bread and milk.

Japan had been home to a small but flourishing baking industry since the late nineteenth century, with white bread serving as a popular novelty food and sometimes status symbol.[28] Indeed, occupation officials quickly discovered that the most forceful complaint levied by the Japanese against U.S.-supplied bread was that it was *not white enough.* As one fifty-year-old housewife polled by SCAP sociologists in 1950 recalled, "We have always liked bread before the war, and always ate it on Sundays. So we can get used to it [as a new staple], but if it is not white bread we will be very unhappy about it."[29]

After the devastation of war, however, bread of any color was nothing to scoff at. The final years of the war had been a nutritional disaster for the islands' population, as Japan lost control over food-producing territories abroad. The average weight of Japanese children plummeted and even affluent children suffered marked deficiencies of vitamins B, C, and D. After the war, the United States had far greater sympathy for starving white Europeans than it did for the Japanese, and the great food aid machinery doled out stingy rations to the East until the crisis in Europe was resolved. Thus, early school lunch programs consisted of less than an ounce of dry milk per child, thin miso broth, scavenged military surplus rations, and whatever vegetables parents could provide. Schools struggled to meet their goal of five hundred calories per child.[30]

When, in 1949, officials could finally announce, "Owing to the goodwill of SCAP, the complete lunch program will be carried out by providing each child with pure white bread and butter," one hundred grams of bread per child twenty days a month at a heavily subsidized price looked extremely good. Children protested at the "odious flavor" of many SCAP-imported foods—especially dry milk, which students flat out refused to drink—but white bread was popular. Students and parents overwhelmingly praised the school lunch program and lobbied for its continuation.[31]

At the same time, Japanese consumers balked at the idea that bread could sustain a nation, despite the fact that, even before the war, Japanese leaders had tried to connect wheat diets with modernization and military might.[32] Sounding not unlike a European American complaining about sushi, one housewife spelled out the problem: "With a bread diet, one becomes hungry immediately; with a rice diet it lasts longer." "With bread alone," another housewife bemoaned, "people like my husband, who does carpentry work, get tired." Although, thanks to subsidized ration coupons, 93 percent of the islands' population ate bread once a day and the majority told pollsters that they enjoyed it, few would choose bread over rice if given a choice.[33]

This attitude generated debate among occupation officials, public health officers, and agribusiness representatives. From early on in the occupation, public health officials—whose cultural understandings of what constituted a "real meal" had a tendency to mix freely with their understanding of scientific nutrition—saw the occupation as a watershed chance to "rationalize" and "improve" the Japanese by liberating them from their polished rice staple. Officials' frustration and disappointment are palpable in documents complaining of the inability to provide a "complete" or "real" lunch for Japanese schoolchildren—by which they meant that they could not provide bread and butter along with what they recognized as a more culturally appropriate table of miso stew, fish protein, and vegetables.[34]

Only when school districts finally had the flour, baking facilities, and cooking fuel to produce bread would they deem their program a true success—the school lunch program had much loftier goals than mere calorie distribution. Its larger mission was to "correct" the Japanese diet while fostering "the scientification of the Japanese kitchen; [and the] permeating of democratic thought." "Democratic spirit," SCAP headquarters insisted, could be nurtured in school cafeterias through the "substitution of reason and scientific practices in place of local customs and superstitions regarding cooking practices."[35] Propagating American meals was part of a strategy of forging civilized citizens, and without bread—the perceived core of a civilized diet—a local school official complained, how can we teach these lessons to our children?[36]

In 1950, J.L. Locke, a U.S. milling industry representative, summed up these cultural assumptions in an appeal to "improv[e] the health and attitude of the Japanese people by supplementing their diet with enriched white bread": "There is some reason to believe that a change in diet might so change the health and attitude of that warlike people that we could live with them in improved peace and harmony." Locke's self-interested motives were transparent, and occupation officials, hoping to develop a domestic milling industry in Japan, roundly rejected the U.S. milling industry's appeals.[37] But in many ways they accepted the basic premise of Locke's argument. The occupation offered a historic opportunity to transition Japan toward wheat, and this, in turn, had important political ramifications. As SCAP commander general Douglas MacArthur wrote in 1950, finding a reliable substitute (that is, wheat) for rice was a key to "block[ing] the rapacious encroachment of Communism" in the region.[38] In 1958 Secretary of Agriculture Ezra Taft Benson visited Japanese schools, where he reported seeing "kiddies at their desks—each kiddie . . . with a big wheat roll made of American-grown wheat." In Benson's account of the trip, Japanese schoolchildren eating wheat wasn't merely a gift for U.S. farmers. It was a good sign for world peace.[39]

An age-old belief in the moral and physiological superiority of wheat bread had found a new home in Cold War rhetoric: the conservative columnist George Sokolsky, for example, worried that rice would not fortify Asia against Communist incursions, and urged the government to deploy America's genius for advertising in the service of shifting Japan toward more vital foods. To support this idea, Sokolsky pointed to the popular radio adventure character Jack Armstrong, "the All American Boy," who so effectively cemented connections between fortitude and Wheaties in the 1930s.[40] This, in turn, might have reminded readers of the central plotline of many Jack Armstrong shows: the handsome, wheat-fueled All-American Boy travels to an exotic, non-Western land where he accomplishes heroic feats unimaginable to the natives.

Reporting on an eleven-fold increase in Japanese wheat consumption during the occupation, a widely reprinted 1957 news story gave this plot a new twist: thanks to the presence of bread in Japanese school lunches, "Japan's youth is literally outgrowing and outweighing its parents." This effect could also be observed in Japanese beauty pageants, where bread was producing "long-limbed beauties."[41]

Although white bread remained popular, most Japanese were not so convinced that they owed their improved lives to it. U.S.-sponsored bread subsidies, school lunch programs, bread festivals, baking classes, advertising campaigns, and sandwich recipe contests had only marginal impact. Bread production increased dramatically during the 1950s, but the association of bread with vigor and civilization did not stick. Even the founder of one of the country's largest postwar bakeries—a pioneering force behind the Americanization of Japanese baking—complained in 1967, "I find myself the only one in my family who stubbornly sticks to eating bread. . . . My children, who went off to study overseas, have come home and now won't touch anything but rice. What's a father to do?"[42]

Officials connected with the USDA and farm lobby continued to present wheat exports and bread habits as central to peace, but others wavered. By the 1960s, talk of transitioning Japan to a wheat diet had faded, and rice supplies topped the list of food security concerns. Wheat exports and American bakery technology transfer continued, but with fewer of the trappings of a civilizing mission. The association between American bread habits and military strength was durable, but not unshakable.[43]

In corn tortilla–eating Mexico, however, a new paradigm for food power was taking shape. It would replace the focus on acute famine relief with a longer-term emphasis on tackling problems of poverty and agricultural productivity. Born out of a specific combination of U.S. and Mexican government interests, the new paradigm would eventually spread throughout the world, helping to cement associations between industrial eating, economic development, and social stability.

REVOLUTIONARY BREAD

One of the most memorable photographic images of the Mexican Revolution depicts Emiliano Zapata and Francisco Villa, surrounded by rough peasant soldiers, eating breakfast at Mexico City's elegant Sanborn's Café. The two leaders have just hammered out a truce and triumphantly occupied the capital. They appear dazzled by camera flashes, and their barefoot troops, accepting service from tuxedoed waiters, evince a mixture of pride and discomfort. Although Zapata and Villa's sojourn at the center of Mexican government lasted less than a year, the image of them sprawled in the capital's most refined palace of aristocratic dining has endured in national memory for almost one hundred years. More than any other single image, it seemed to crystallize the revolution's challenge to class and racial hierarchies. What usually gets forgotten about that famous breakfast, though, is the menu. The generals and their troops didn't eat corn tortillas and beans that December morning in 1914; they ate sweet white rolls.[44]

Although corn tortillas never risked displacement from the center of Mexico's diet, white bread has been a fixture in the country since the earliest days of Spanish conquest. And for just as long, eating it has been an act of social positioning. As historian Jeffrey Pilcher explained, in colonial Mexico "Creole gentlemen . . . paraded their status within New Spain's racial hierarchy by wearing ruffled collars and eating wheat bread. One 18th-century English visitor to the remote southern state of Chiapas even noted that aspiring gentlemen would stand conspicuously in their doorways, 'to see and be seen . . . shaking the crumbs of bread from their clothes.' "[45]

If anything, the status of white wheat bread increased after independence, particularly during the late nineteenth-century dictatorship of Porfirio Díaz. With the regime's governing ideology of white supremacy and avid emulation of European fashions, bread baking boomed under Díaz. The "French-style" *bolillo* roll emerged as an edible incarnation of Mexico's progress. Reflecting on "the Future of the Hispanic American Nations," prominent Porfirian senator Francisco Bulnes gave the old preference for bread a modern spin grounded in the emerging "science" of racial improvement. "The race of wheat is the only truly progressive one . . . maize has been the eternal pacifier of America's indigenous races and the foundation of their refusal to become civilized." While U.S. food reformers inspired by Grahamism tried to suppress enflamed passion with whole wheat diets, Pilcher notes, late nineteenth-century Mexican elites "sought the opposite effect, to ignite vigor in the Indian masses through the consumption of [white] wheat."[46]

The Mexican Revolution of 1910 toppled Porfirio Díaz and challenged the privileges of the country's light-skinned aristocracy, but the social dualism of modern wheat bread and backwards corn tortillas proved more immutable. Intellectuals and artists of the postrevolutionary period like Octavio Paz and Diego Rivera waxed eloquent about corn, casting it as the embodiment of Mexico's authentic, pre-Hispanic cultural essence. But for post-revolutionary rulers and their working-class cadres, wheat still symbolized the country's urban, industrial future.

Robert Weis, a historian of Mexican baking, argues that by 1929, white bread—particularly *bolillos*—had become a key symbol of the revolution's promise to ordinary consumers.[47] Heavily subsidized by the government, white bread baking boomed. Even President Lázaro Cárdenas—who revived the revolutionary spirit of Zapata and Villa between 1934 and 1940 with sweeping land reforms, anti-imperialist rhetoric, and the expropriation of foreign oil companies—preached the superiority of wheat bread.[48]

There was only one problem. Even as World War II ended, Mexico was still very much a peasant country without the capacity to supply a large urban industrial workforce with cheap bread. In the country's traditional wheat-growing regions, overtaxed soils produced meager crops and declining yields. New farmland in the north, opened up for wheat cultivation by ambitious government irrigation projects, offered better prospects, but endemic plant disease—a plague of black stem rust—continued to cripple production.[49]

Meanwhile, in the cities, technology for turning wheat into bread had not advanced much since the eighteenth century. Even the capital city supported only one large industrial bakery—la Panadería Ideal— well into the 1930s, and the Ideal Bakery certainly didn't live up to its name: thanks to antiquated wrapping equipment, Ideal loaves tended to reach customers' hands covered in mold. As a 1939 survey revealed, despite the promises of revolutionary governments, "wheat bread is almost a luxury good in Mexico, destined almost exclusively for the middle and upper classes."[50]

Bad weather and poor corn and wheat harvests between 1943 and 1945 turned everyday grain scarcity into acute crisis. Even with government bread subsidies, prices soared beyond the reach of urban consumers. Roving gangs of frustrated consumers attacked bakeries in Mexico City, and bread riots spread throughout the country. In May 1945, protests against a 100 percent increase in the price of bread shut down the capital city of Veracruz state. That same spring, U.S. ambassador George Messersmith warned Washington that without emergency shipments of corn and wheat, Mexico would "fly a [Communist] red flag in three months time."[51]

U.S. officials responded with a mixture of anxiety and opportunism. A food crisis in Mexico threatened to destabilize a southern neighbor already perceived as unpredictable and prone to anti-imperialist outbursts. At the same time, hunger could also create opportunities for the furthering of U.S interests. The election of right-leaning Manuel Ávila Camacho as president in 1940 had signaled a turn away from Lázaro Cárdenas's radical social reforms and anti-U.S. rhetoric, creating an opening for closer ties with the United States. A friendly display of U.S. food power could help seal that rapprochement.

With war-ravaged Europe absorbing all the grain America could spare, however, the United States could not fight on another food front with exports alone. Rhetoric aside, U.S. farmers could not save the *whole* world. Industrial food power would have to expand to include other weapons beside direct exports of surplus grain. Henry Wallace, FDR's secretary of agriculture and then vice president, understood this challenge as early as 1940. While representing the Roosevelt administration at President Ávila Camacho's inauguration, Wallace observed the country's need for agricultural improvement firsthand and listened to the new leader's plan. Ávila Camacho pledged to steer Mexico away from radical land redistribution and support for peasant farmers. Instead, he would fight hunger and spur urban development through investments in capital-intensive agriculture. On his return to Washington, Wallace set out to convince policy makers that the United States must join in efforts to modernize Mexican agriculture, for the sake of hemispheric security—even if it threatened grain exporters at home.

The Rockefeller Foundation, which had already begun to formulate similar ideas on its own, agreed to the vice president's plea. As the foundation's influential report "The World Food Situation" declared later, "The time is now ripe, in most places possibly over-ripe for sharing some of our technical knowledge with these people." "Agitators from Communist countries," the Rockefeller Foundation warned, were taking advantage of America's failure to share its alimentary abundance. "Appropriate action now," the foundation argued, "may help [Third World countries] to attain by evolution the improvements . . . which otherwise may have to come by revolution."[52]

EL TRIGO DE ROCKEFELLER

What the Rockefeller Foundation proposed had never been tried before: a private U.S. foundation, in collaboration with Washington and a foreign government, would set out to transform the entire agricultural system of another country, from the ground up, in the image of the United States. Maybe U.S. farmers couldn't save the whole world from Communist takeover all on their own, but U.S.-style farming practices might.

In 1943, the Rockefeller Foundation established the Office of Special Studies (later called the Mexican Agricultural Program, or MAP) in collaboration with the Mexican Ministry of Agriculture. Over the next eighteen years, the MAP's twenty U.S. agricultural scientists and one hundred Mexican counterparts would tackle two fundamental priorities: creating high-yield, disease-resistant wheat seeds and raising the productivity of the country's corn farmers. Work on improving vegetables, beans, barley, and sorghum would come later, but the Mexican government and Rockefeller Foundation agreed that wheat and corn were top priorities. Corn covered 65 percent of the country's agricultural land, supplying the cornerstone of the Mexican diet. It was an obvious place to start. Wheat was less prevalent, taking up only 7 percent of the country's farmland, but it was grown primarily by large commercial farmers and consumed by affluent urbanites. It suited the country's modern image of itself—wheat and white bread were aspirational commodities. As a result, wheat received disproportionate attention. The payoff from this work was stunning and quick.

By 1948, the American plant pathologist Norman Borlaug and his team had already developed and begun to distribute wheat strains resistant to Mexican stem rust. Their ultimate success came a few years later. In a series of genetic crosses conducted during the late 1950s and early 1960s, Borlaug successfully brought together the three Holy Grails of Mexican wheat improvement: rust resistance, of course, but also dwarf stature and heightened responsiveness to petroleum-based synthetic fertilizer. While Mexican wheat production couldn't have grown without rust resistance, it was the latter two traits—dwarf stature and input responsiveness—that would truly change the world. On their own, the MAP seeds were only marginally more productive than traditional Mexican varieties. But, unlike traditional varieties, they were specially designed to thrive as part of a larger package of modern inputs—pesticides, intensive irrigation, mechanized harvesting, and, most importantly, large quantities of synthetic fertilizer. Given sufficient water and chemical pest control, the MAP seeds could efficiently convert massive quantities of fertilizer into ever-larger grain heads. This is what made them revolutionary. In fact, the new seeds were so good at converting synthetic nutrients into large grain heads that their stalks tended to collapse under their own weight, making mechanized harvesting impossible. Dwarfism solved that problem. The creation of wheat varieties with thick stalks and squat stature prevented collapse (called "lodging") and ushered in the era of ultra-mechanized, high-yield grain farming.

Of course, the promise of the MAP seeds could be realized only in conjunction with a full package of modern inputs. This was expensive and would have long-term consequences. In the short term, however, backed by subsidized credit, education programs, and infrastructure investment, "el trigo de Rockefeller"—Rockefeller wheat—spread faster than its creators could have imagined. By 1957, 90 percent of all wheat seeds planted in Mexico were the high-yield varieties supported by industrial inputs. Between 1940 and 1960, the index of Mexican fertilizer consumption soared 4,000 percent, while pesticide application increased eight-fold. In the space of just a few years, wheat yields more than doubled, and they would increase 400 percent over the next two decades. Despite the fact that Mexico experienced its highest ever population growth rates during the postwar period, wheat production far outpaced the number of new consumers. Indeed, from 1940 to 1970, thanks in substantial part to the MAP's work, overall *per capita* food production in Mexico increased from 1,991 calories and 54 grams of protein per day to 2,623 calories and 80 grams of protein. Mexico quickly erased its wheat deficits and by the 1960s joined the ranks of exporting nations, at least for a while.[53] So incredible were the results that the MAP model eventually came to be called "the Green Revolution."

THE WHITE REVOLUTION

The first Bimbo Bakery emerged out of the same early-1940s crucible as the Green Revolution. At some inchoate level, the company's founders understood something typically left out of histories of the Green Revolution: in order for Mexico's dreams of modernization and consumer affluence to succeed, someone would have to turn mountains of wheat into inexpensive sliced white bread.

Like nearly all Mexico City bakers, Lorenzo Servitje came from a tight-knit clan of Spanish immigrants. His father was born in Catalonia, and as a young immigrant in turn-of-the-century Mexico City, he worked his way up through a series of Spanish-owned bakeries. In 1928, Lorenzo's father managed to open his own bakery, with support of the Spanish community. He called it el Molino, the Windmill, to evoke images of Don Quixote and the rolling plains of La Mancha. But even amidst all those European influences, young Lorenzo Servitje set his gaze firmly on the north. After taking over el Molino in 1936, he began obsessively studying American-style industrial baking, reading every U.S. trade journal he could find and seeking out U.S.-trained bakery engineers. "I wanted to know every detail of the North American bread industry," he recalled later, "[all] the newest technologies and cutting-edge machinery." Eating U.S.-style industrial loaves, or *pan de caja*, "was not a tradition in Mexico," Lorenzo acknowledged. But he believed he could change that.[54]

Along with three other members of the Spanish baking community, including the first Mexican trained in modern industrial techniques at the American Institute of Baking, Lorenzo began scheming in 1938. Wartime machinery shortages in the United States delayed his plans for Mexico's first American-style bread factory, but in 1945 Bimbo Bakery opened its doors with four bread lines: sliced white sandwich bread, an unsliced white "table" loaf, a soft rye, and packaged toast "for children and the sick."

The sparkling new bakery sported dough-handling machines from American Machinery and Foundry, high-speed mixers from Readco, two Flex-o-Matic seventy-tray ovens from Union Steel, and a temperature-controlled proofing room installed by the Chicago Metallic Corporation. Two of the very latest bread-wrapping machines from Sheboygan, Wisconsin, would ensure that, unlike Ideal bread, Bimbo reached stores mold free. With almost three times more Ford delivery vans than Ideal, Bimbo bread would get there faster, too.

During Bimbo's early years, many Mexican bakers avoided flour made from the new Green Revolution wheat. Modeled after U.S.

wheat varieties and bred with the rigors of industrial processing in mind, flour made from el Trigo de Rockefeller didn't work well with traditional Mexican baking practices. As one small-town baker complained to an anthropologist, "You have to be a chemist" to bake with the new wheat. Bimbo, on the other hand, had scientists on staff, and in keeping with its embrace of all things modern and North American, was the first major bakery in Mexico to embrace the nontraditional wheat varieties. By the mid-1950s, Bimbo had established strong ties with the most modern milling companies in northern Mexico, paving the way for widespread acceptance of the new wheat.[55]

Lorenzo's admiration for the U.S. baking industry also extended to its ingenious use of advertising, and from its first days, Bimbo plastered its name across newspapers, comic strips, and radio. Later, it would be the first Mexican bakery to appreciate the power of television. As a result, the cuddly bear mascot that bore the name Bimbo didn't take long to become one of the most-loved characters in Mexican commercial pop culture. Beyond the bear, Bimbo's campaigns touched all the same themes as early industrial bread advertising in the United States: the hygienic nature of factory bread, the importance of modern bread in building a strong nation, and the ultra-squeezable quality of industrially baked loaves.

There was one thing, however, that Bimbo did better than any North American counterpart, right from the start: distribute its product to the far-flung corners of a rapidly expanding city. Bimbo delivery trucks relentlessly plied the city in search of new sales points, and within a few years soft packaged bread had saturated the nation's capital. In 1947, Bimbo bought twenty-six new trucks and opened routes into nearby cities and state capitals. Photos from the period show Bimbo trucks sharing rutted roads with ox carts and being ferried across rainforest waterways on rafts. Oscar Lewis, in his classic ethnography of a small village outside Mexico City, noted that less than a third of townspeople ate bread in 1940. By 1950, according to Lewis, that had changed completely: almost everyone ate bread regularly.[56]

THE MEXICAN MIRACLE?

As pan Bimbo spread throughout Mexico and the country's first (and only) wheat-export freighters set sail for distant lands in the early

1960s, so too did the Rockefeller-Mexico model. Heralding it as the template for successful agricultural development, U.S. government agencies, foreign governments, the United Nations, and nonprofit organizations such as the Rockefeller and Ford Foundations worked to replicate Mexico's plant research program from India to Algeria. Following similar lines of government–private sector collaboration, researchers also turned their sights on other staples: rice in Asia, potatoes in the Andes, millet in Africa.

Thanks to improved seeds and modern input packages, world per capita food supplies climbed steadily in the postwar decades. In the United States, fears that the world was about to run out of food still enjoyed considerable popularity during the 1960s and 1970s, appearing everywhere from apocalyptic Hollywood movies to best-selling nonfiction, but these Malthusian nightmares never came true. Recognizing the scale of this achievement, in 1970, the Nobel committee awarded Norman Borlaug its Peace Prize. "More than any other single person of this age," the prize's citation read, Norman Borlaug "has helped to provide bread for a hungry world."[57]

Humanitarian causes aside, policy makers in the United States credited the Green Revolution with staving off Red Revolution around the world, and Mexican officials saw it as a stepping-stone to even grander things. For them, rural-development programs held the key to dreams of rapid industrialization.[58] Regardless of its effects on the countryside, Green Revolution wheat would ensure steady flows of cheap food into the country's cities. Since Mexico's growing urban industrial workforce still spent the majority of its wages on food, these flows would, in effect, subsidize factory owners, keeping labor costs low without provoking political unrest. Not having to import wheat would also free up currency that could be channeled to pay for even more direct industry subsidies.

In many ways the Mexican government's gambit worked. Orthodox economists today ridicule Mexican policies of that era, reveling in their inefficiencies and heavy-handed state interventions, but Mexican officials had grasped something important that mainstream U.S. economists often forget: no country in history had ever industrialized through laissez-faire and free trade. Active state intervention was necessary to achieve the promises of modernization. And despite their inefficiencies and limits, the government's cheap food policies, promotion of basic education, investment in infrastructure, and extensive trade protections did, in fact, usher in Mexico's most explosive period of economic growth. Automobile, steel, and electronics factories rose up in what had been a largely rural country. Modern highways, electrical grids, and ports connected its far-flung corners, and Mexicans could, increasingly, buy their own appliances instead of importing them. But the Mexican Miracle had an Achilles' heel: the peasant countryside.

Every member of the U.S. MAP team had been formed in American land grant universities and spent time in the USDA, bastions of industrial agriculture. The scientists brought with them a strong cultural bias toward large-scale projects, and they also faced stiff pressure from the Mexican government to produce dramatic results quickly. As a result, the MAP, and its descendants, often ignored the mandate to improve the lives of peasant corn farmers, focusing attention on the country's few large commercial wheat farms. Rather than design technologies accessible to poor farmers, they pushed packages of expensive inputs. And they got exactly the results you would expect: a water-, machinery-, and chemical-intensive Green Revolution package capable of out-of-this-world yields—with out-of-this-world production costs. To realize the promise of Green Revolution technology, farmers didn't just have to purchase new seeds; they also needed to install modern irrigation equipment, apply heavy doses of synthetic fertilizers, and control pests with chemicals.

Paying these costs required continual access to credit. And in the Mexican countryside, that meant only larger farmers with disposable wealth and close ties to private banks or government bureaucrats could grow Green Revolution wheat over the long haul. Smaller farmers without access to subsidized credit could try, but this meant turning to rapacious moneylenders. So, as much as it increased productivity, the Green Revolution also reinforced rural inequality, creating a new class of wealthy U.S-style industrial farmers, coddled with subsidies, and masses of peasants who couldn't compete in the debt-driven race. Worse still, the new mechanized and chemically dependent commercial farms required less labor—meaning fewer jobs and lower wages for rural workers, and these changes impacted women disproportionately. The few jobs created by the spread of Green Revolution technologies—driving tractors or working with irrigation equipment—tended to be seen as "men's work," while traditional hand labor that women counted on for income shrank. As was the case in many countries adopting the new agricultural model, declines in women's incomes had devastating consequences for family nutrition, health, and opportunities.[59] Taken as a whole, Mexico's efforts to facilitate industrialization and urbanization with Green Revolution seeds and U.S.-style farms resulted in what Harvard-trained biologist turned social scientist John H. Perkins called a "tragic irony": increased hunger in the presence of rapidly growing agricultural productivity.[60]

During the 1950s and 1960s, peasants and landless workers, displaced from the countryside by these forces, streamed into the cities faster than even the country's record economic expansion could create new urban jobs. Mexican industrial policies bear some of the blame for this—they tended to favor more glamorous heavy industries over labor-intensive production, even though the former generated fewer jobs—but the U.S.-style approach to agricultural development exacerbated the problem. The glut of rural refugees—a classic army of surplus labor—kept wages low in cities, despite record increases in industrial productivity. This stymied the creation of a large, self-sustaining society of middle-class consumers.[61]

Recognizing the tragic bias of its past efforts, the MAP initiated a new project in 1970—the Plan Puebla—targeting small-scale peasant corn producers.[62] It had some success, but by that point the association between large-scale industrial agriculture, progress, and national security was too deeply engrained to turn back.

THE PROBLEM WITH MORE FOOD

In India, where the Mexican Green Revolution model was exported first, the results were even more ambiguous. Indeed, the Punjab region—considered a "success story" of South Asian agricultural development—has emerged as the ultimate case study in the failings of a productivity-focused approach to rural poverty. There, Green Revolution wheat programs helped food supplies increase at double the rate of population growth. Yet, as even one pro–Green Revolution scholar acknowledged soberly, "There may have been no improvement at all in human nutrition, in the proportion of poor people, or in the average severity of their poverty." Ardent Green Revolution critic Vandana Shiva put it more bluntly: the introduction of new agricultural technologies in Punjab, she argued, displaced farmers, created intractable rural unemployment, increased the proportion of people living in poverty, and sparked violent conflicts over resources.[63]

By the 1970s, knowledge of the Green Revolution's negative effect on rural equality and its failure to alleviate poverty had become widespread, thanks in large part to work done around the world by the United Nations Research Institute for Social Development.[64] U.S. policy makers, agribusiness, and many development practitioners, however, had a hard time seeing beyond the mantra of higher yields. They saw a world where exploding population growth threatened to outrun food supplies and trigger revolution at every turn. The answer was obvious: the world needed more food to feed more mouths.

What this perspective ignored, however, was the crucial question of food *access*. As the Nobel Prize–winning economist Amartya Sen demonstrated powerfully, it wasn't just the amount of food produced that matters, but whether people could access the bounty. More efficient food production didn't always result in greater food access—particularly when it increased inequality and undercut small farmers' ability to earn a living. All too frequently, hunger and plenty went hand in hand.[65]

Green Revolution technology was not inherently bad. Indeed, a more grassroots approach to biotechnology could achieve important changes in the Third World. But Green Revolution technology *was* hampered by the social and political context in which it was deployed. This was a classic case of a good story gone out of control: accepting the intuitive Malthusian narrative of "Too many mouths, not enough food" proved far more appealing to policy makers than wrestling with the complicated dynamics of rural poverty.[66] A large part of the appeal of dreams of peace through industrial food lay in the fact that the single-minded focus on increasing productivity through industrial agriculture allowed policy makers to ignore sticky questions of power and resource distribution. In theory, as long as food production continued to grow, it didn't matter that a small percentage of the planet controlled most of the world's resources and consumed the vast majority of its calories. The ideology of industrial agriculture held out the attractive fantasy that hunger could be alleviated through purely technical means—without needing to challenge power relations or alter the economic status quo.

HOME TO ROOST

Crowded in with the glass offices of Mexico City's exclusive Santa Fe business district, Grupo Bimbo's white stone headquarters look—there's no getting around it—like a giant loaf of sliced white bread set on its end. As with many places in Mexico, contrasts between rich and poor leap out in Santa Fe. Chauffeured cars slide through the gates of Amgen, IBM, Bancomer, and Kraft, around armed guards who shoo away street vendors. Carlos Slim, one of the world's two or three richest men, lives a couple of miles away, enjoying a fortune built in part by acquiring state-owned companies on the cheap, while more than 15 million Mexicans survive on less than $2 a day. Staggering inequality is a fact of life here, but perhaps more than any other company in Mexico, Grupo Bimbo has thrived because of it.

Not that Bimbo is one of the country's most exploitative companies. In fact, Bimbo's founding family places Catholic social teachings in the company's mission.[67] As a result, Bimbo is regarded by many for its charity work, code of labor ethics, and environmental commitments. Nevertheless, Bimbo owes its ascendance to inequality because, from the very start, it literally fed national dreams of reduced class conflict and upward mobility. To be sure, the company innovated in other ways, but none of that would have amounted to much if Bimbo hadn't offered the country affordable, edible aspiration. By the end of the 1960s, the company had spread this dream to nearly every remote corner of Mexico. Eventually the extraordinary dreams embodied in white bread evolved into the stuff of taxi drivers' humdrum breakfasts. Today, Mexican elites eschew Bimbo for authentic brick-oven-baked European breads—even in Mexico, soft white bread has lost its association with high-class status.

But for Bimbo, the impulse to expand hasn't stopped. During the 1990s, Bimbo expanded to Central America, then Chile, Argentina, Colombia, and Peru. It also looked north, first shipping Mexican-made production to U.S. border states and then, in 1996, buying the company's first U.S. factory in Escondido, California. Having grown accustomed to nearly absolute control over Mexico's packaged bread market, the company was surprised at first by stiff competition in the United States. Lorenzo's son Roberto Servitje reflected that in South America, the challenge was convincing people to eat packaged bread. In the United States, it was "ferocious competition" from "monstrous" companies like Interstate Baking, Sara Lee, and Weston Foods. But Bimbo took enormous risks in the United States, aggressively buying up its competition's routes, factories, and brands.[68] Today, if you buy Arnold bread in the East or Orowheat in the West, Freihofer in Pennsylvania or Mrs. Baird's in Texas, Stroehmann's in the mid-Atlantic or Old Country in Arizona, not to mention Roman-Meal, Sun-Made, and Francisco sourdough, it's Bimbo. White bread imperialism has come home to roost.

On the other hand, the dream of building world peace and security through industrial food production has never left the United States. More than a half century later, even as critiques of industrial food mount from all directions, Cold War–era beliefs about a hungry planet's need for ever-more-industrial food production still seem commonsensical to most Americans. Indeed, this geopolitical urgency often underpins attempts to defend large-scale industrial food production against proponents of slow, local, and organic eating. Viewed through the lens of Cold War Malthusianism, supporters of small-scale nonindustrial food production can be painted as dangerously insular and elitist. Evoking the humanitarian legacies of U.S. food power, supporters of industrial agriculture can pose themselves as heroes of the poor, calling for a "Second Green Revolution" to meet the challenges of the future.[69]

We would do well to not dismiss a Second Green Revolution out of hand, particularly if it could realize its advocates' promises of raising productivity with fewer chemical inputs. But we should also remember the key lesson of the *first* Green Revolution: a technology is only as good as the power relations in which it is deployed. If the seeds and inputs of a Second Green Revolution are monopolized by large chemical companies like Monsanto intent on selling expensive inputs (as they are today), we should brace for many more tragic outcomes.

It's easy to make sport of rich locavores, but we shouldn't forget the myriad ways in which industrial abundance often makes hunger worse, not better. What remains to be seen is whether and how advocates of food system change can counter the deep and potent associations between industrial food and the security-driven urgency of feeding a dangerous, hungry world.

6

HOW WHITE BREAD BECAME WHITE TRASH

Dreams of Resistance and Status

You're scum, you're fucking white bread.

—David Mamet, *Glengarry Glen Ross*

WHITE TRASH REBELLION?

Somewhere between the Cheez Whiz hors d'oeuvres and the looped Jerry Springer clip, it hit me: the "white trash party" trend of the 2000s was a cultural phenomenon best forgotten, and quickly. Sadly, you can't hold back a fad this debauched. Fueled by books like *White Trash Cooking* and *White Trash Etiquette*, White Trash Nation websites, college students' love of Daisy Duke cutoff shorts, and hipsters' apparently innate affection for trucker hats, the trend only grew. And it grew until, in the words of one awestruck journalist, it shined "brighter than a big, fat 'skeeter getting fried on a bug zapper."[1] For all that zap-blue brightness, though, white trash chic turned out to be a decidedly murky affair—starting with the strange bedfellows it attracted.[2]

Reporters, mostly caught up in the pleasure of dabbing the pages of staid venues like *Metropolitan Home* with lines like "Jes' belly up to the trough and dig in," or inflecting *New York Times* style with "shonuffs" and "hons," depicted the trend as a unified phenomenon. In fact, it arose from two very different places. The props were the same for both—a hodgepodge of white bread, processed cheese, southern rock, cheap beer, and pregnant teen costumes. They both reveled in stylized poverty. They both cultivated vulgar ugliness. And both, at some level, attempted to subvert the pretensions of an imagined elite. But the politics and participants were different.

On one hand, urban hipsters chugging Pabst Blue Ribbon beer in upscale dives dreamt of working-class authenticity, rebelling against high-class consumerism with aestheticized poverty. Hipster white trash chic embraced the "simplicity" of mass-produced commodities as an ironic antidote to yuppie consumption. It assembled cool style out of the kitschy trappings of poverty, but in doing so reinforced the line between hipsters and actual low-income consumers.

On the other hand, segments of the white working class—fans of the comedian Jeff Foxworthy's self-mocking "You might be a redneck if . . ." brand of humor—took tongue-in-cheek pride in the iconography of trailer parks, beer bellies, and kissing cousins meant to stereotype *them*.[3] Here the dream was a different kind of resistance: armed with "shit on a shingle" (canned corn beef on white bread) and Confederate flags, white trash parties threw what Foxworthy called "a glorious lack of sophistication" in the face of an imagined enemy of uptight liberal elites.[4] In this vein, white trash parties, for all their carnivalesque hilarity, were deadly serious. They appropriated a demeaning insult, turning it into a celebration of "authentic" white Americans fighting for their rightful place in a culture supposedly poisoned by liberal multiculturalism.

Industrial bread played a key role in both versions of white trash fun. It was both a ubiquitous menu item and a visual stand-in for a whole range of assumptions about low-class consumption. Industrial white bread called up a lack of pretension—unfussy and authentically American—but also irresponsibility and shame. To eat white bread at a white trash party was to proclaim, "I never *really* eat white bread." And of course, as should be clear by now, none of that symbolism would have been possible, even imaginable, for most of the twentieth century.

To make the Wonder bread–laden gags of white trash chic legible, America's "best invention" had to become an icon of poor choices and narrow lives. This historic upending was a relatively recent phenomenon. It played out between the mid-1960s and the mid-1980s, in the cultural trajectory from hippie to yuppie. During that remarkable twenty-year period, "white bread" became an adjective as well as a noun—an adjective with two related but different meanings that still compete with each other today. In the early years of the 1960s counterculture, "white bread" came to signify all that was bland, homogeneous, and suburban. White bread was establishment, plastic, and corporate—everything the counterculture in all its manifestations hoped to destroy. This meaning remains: you know that music described as "white bread" will be funkless pablum. A TV show set "in a white bread cul-de-sac" will deal with life in cookie-cutter tract mansions.

By the early 1980s, however, another usage had emerged. In this case, "white bread" signified almost the opposite: not bland, affluent suburbia, but white trash. In movies and fiction white bread, like broken-down trailers, came to denote poverty of a white and rural kind—the world described by residents of TV's *South Park* as "a quiet, little, white-bread, podunk, white-trash, redneck corner of the U.S.A." The writer James Salter evoked the despair and grim prospects of this kind of white bread life in his story "Dirt." The story turns around a waitress who is young and beautiful now, but beginning to feel the walls of inescapable poverty closing in around her. As Salter sums up her sparse future, "She would be living in the trailer park. . . . Her kids would eat white bread in big soft packages."[5]

This association between white bread and white trash endures, even as African Americans and Latinos make up an ever-larger portion of the market for Wonder bread and pan Bimbo. So how did white bread become white trash? In very much the same way white trash parties work—through a complex play of cultural subversions, rebellious aesthetics, rituals of social status, and protests against mass consumption. The outcomes of this process have been just as ambiguous as any white trash party: in 2009, for the first time in U.S. history, whole wheat bread sales topped white—presumably a healthy development. And yet the same anti-elitist attacks on industrial eating that set that change into motion during the late 1960s had by the 1980s generated new alimentary elites, new forms of social distinction. Dreams of good bread as an antidote to an oppressive and unhealthy social structure became the stuff of ultra-high-end consumption.[6]

FIGHT THE WHITE

In 1954, the legendary industrial designer Raymond Loewy, commissioned to study bread packaging, observed that there was pretty much only one color combination that moved loaves off shelves—red, white, and blue, and maybe golden yellow. Ten years later, a young Catholic nun named Sister Corita with a fast-growing reputation for making edgy pop art, hijacked the classic red, white, blue, and yellow Wonder bread package design for decidedly different purposes. In a series of prints drawing inspiration from the Wonder bread label, Sister Corita proclaimed that radical Christian commensality and social justice could be snatched even from the heart of mass-consumer society. In one of Sister Corita's Wonder bread prints, text from the French existentialist Albert Camus followed the iconic words "Enriched Bread Wonder" like an ingredient list: "Great ideas," it read, "come into the world as gently as doves. Perhaps if we listen attentively, we shall hear, amid the uproar of empires and nations, a first flutter of wings, the gentle stirrings of life and hope. Helps Build a Body Twelve Ways."[7]

In the years that followed, the country saw much uproar of empires and nations—race riots, mechanized slaughter in Vietnam, assassinations, and toxic spills—but also the birth of new social movements, civil rights, feminism, environmentalism, farm workers' rights: the gentle, and not so gentle, stirrings of life and hope. Amidst all that roar and counter-roar, however, it was increasingly difficult, if not impossible, to associate industrial bread with anything living or hopeful—even as a subversive jest. Store-bought white bread combined the two most hated motifs of the era: industrial origins and whiteness. As food historian Warren Belasco wrote, "For Theodore Roszak, who popularized the word 'counterculture' in his 1969 bestseller, white bread was a perfect metaphor for the regime of experts and technocrats who, for the sake of efficiency and order, threatened to rob us of all effort, thought, and independence." "Only in *Amerika* could people want their food bleached . . . all bleached to match the bleached-out mentality of white supremacy," another counterculture writer proclaimed.[8] Good food was rustic, unrefined, and brown, ideally with roots in peasant society. "Don't eat white; eat right," the saying went, and Dr. Clark's 1920s-era ditty, "The whiter your bread, the quicker you're dead," experienced a dramatic revival.

The counterculture—itself a diverse collection of movements, philosophies, impulses, and ideals—strained against the homogeneous, the artificial, and the mechanical in myriad ways. Factions and subgroups often spent more time denouncing each other's shortcomings than they did fighting the Man, but they could all agree about one thing: white bread. It was, for the counterculture, an instructive commodity—a familiar, accessible way to comprehend any of the binaries that gave shape to the movement and animated revolt: authentic vs. artificial, natural vs. chemical, brown vs. white, healthy vs. poisonous, real vs. plastic, peaceful vs. militaristic. As a 1973 essay in the Minnesota counterculture magazine *North Country Alternatives* explained, "Bread is a good focal point because its story, from grain grown on giant factory farms to technologically-produced Wonder Bread, is a very clear illustration of where power lies, and how it is used against us."[9] The sterile, chemically laced, and homogeneous substance of white bread could stand in as a synecdoche for social conformism, the environmental costs of industrialism, racism, bland suburbia, or cultural imperialism abroad. Establishment archenemies such as Robert McNamara or Earl Butz weren't *like* white bread, they *were* white bread.[10]

This political allegory had deep roots in American culture, and 1960s counterculture drew heavily on earlier food reform movements. Rumblings of the countercultural revolt against white bread could even be felt during the 1950s golden age of industrial eating. Most consumers happily ate six slices of industrial white bread a day during the 1950s, but sporadic and short-lived waves of anxiety were not uncommon. During those outbursts, fanned by popular radio health advisors like Carleton Fredricks, the FDA or USDA received thousands of letters decrying "unnatural" chemical additives in bread.[11] Congress responded through the 1950s with hearings on the makeup of industrial bread and the safety of chemical emulsifiers, dough conditioners, softeners, and other additives. In 1951, for example, Congress gathered seventeen thousand pages of testimony on the bread question and headlines across the country asked, "Are We Eating Poisoned Bread?"[12]

Nevertheless, 1950s-era concerns about bread were different from those that would emerge later. In the 1950s, consumers and officials expressed their dismay at the state of bread in a language of public health, corrupt baking trusts, and adulteration that would have been immediately familiar to any food reformer of the Progressive Era. "Change the national food habits and we can still [have] a virile nation," read one typical letter to the FDA about bread. It could have come straight out of the century's first decades.[13] In the 1960s and 1970s counterculture, food reformers clearly drew on these Progressive Era roots, but they also created a new language for talking about the problems of diet. Rejecting the dream of public health expertise and government regulation in the service of national virility, the counterculture imagined individual eating itself as a form of activism.

Food choices had already begun to factor into civil rights and early antiwar activism. Lunch counter sit-ins, political fasts, and the UFW grape boycott all linked sustenance and social change. The act of eating (or not eating) could draw attention to demands for rights and recognition. But none of those late-1950s and early-1960s movements believed that social change could be achieved solely by eating the right food. Bread's role in these movements was indicative: to the extent that it factored into their struggles, bread served generically as a symbol of Christian commensality posed against worldly injustice, as in the *Wonder Bread* seriographs of Sister Corita, Daniel Berrigan's antiwar poetry (*And the Risen Bread*), or Thomas Merton's socially engaged spiritual teachings (*Bread in the Wilderness* and *The Living Bread*). For these purposes, any bread would do, and social movements saw little reason to focus their attentions specifically on the evils of processed food. When Martin Luther King Jr. called for a boycott of Wonder bread in Memphis, for example, it was unfair hiring practices, not chemical additives, that concerned him.[14]

With the emergence of the "hippie" counterculture, however, food wasn't just a tactic in the theater of social change. Changing diets had become an arena of politics in its own right—perhaps *the* arena. As Crescent Dragonwagon, author of the popular *Commune Cookbook*, declared, the ecology of human diet united all struggles against oppression, from black and women's liberation to antiwar movements. Again, bread was indicative. As influential whole foods guru Beatrice Trum Hunter proclaimed, bread baking constituted "a revolt against plastic food in a plastic culture. The free-form loaf is but another aspect of the revolt against the mechanization of life."[15]

Mostly middle-class, white, and buoyed by an upbeat economy, flower children and whole foods advocates exuded an optimistic sense that changing one's lifestyle could change the world. Utopian dreams of leisure, freedom from oppressive experts, the pursuit of pleasure, and self-actualization flourished. Although segments of the counterculture would harden considerably after the upheavals of 1968 and into the grim recessions of the 1970s, much of it was as joyous and raucous as earlier generations of civil rights activists had been earnest and disciplined.[16]

Counterculture cooks threw off the heavy hand of home economics, dispensing with recipes and reveling in chance, experimentation, and imperfection. Counterculture cookbooks—often self-published—mocked their own authority, encouraging readers to distrust instructions found in cookbooks. Precise directions and exact measurements were oppressive vestiges of an inhuman system. Readers should "learn to feel for themselves through experience and experimentation," as *Tassajara Bread Book* author Edward Espe Brown urged. Instructions in *Mother Earth News* for baking bread captured this new outlook perfectly, directing would-be bakers to knead until the dough "springs like a plump baby's bottom," and then enjoining them to "take this opportunity to grease the cans and light a joint."[17]

During the first half of the twentieth century, experts from home economics and the baking industry had so thoroughly convinced Americans that only lab-coated professionals could succeed at the cryptic science of bread baking that counterculture food gurus took distinct pride in liberating it for the untrained masses. "Anyone can do this" and "Baking is easy" were constant refrains in counterculture cookbooks. Buddhist monk Edward Espe Brown, whose *Tassajara Bread Book* taught a generation to bake, went even further: the precise outcome of bread making didn't matter. Instead, he counseled readers to understand baking as a deeply sensual spiritual practice, independent of attachment to perfect final products.[18]

The freeform revolt against culinary expertise could seem frivolous and self-involved at times. Mo Willet's *Vegetarian Gothic,* for example, offered this dietary advice: "You should eat when you're hungry, feast when you're joyful, fast to get high, and sing of love all the time." "Fill your bread with wholesome foods and lots of love and you'll find yourself feeling good all over," Willet glowed.[19] But there was method in the revelry. Just as industrial white bread stood for larger systems of oppression, upending decades of dietary expertise challenged all forms of authoritarian control. For Crescent Dragon-wagon, encouraging imperfect cooking undermined "antinatural" uniformity in other realms, from the beauty myths of femininity to the lockstep war machine. Women, she argued, experienced cooking as an oppressive burden because generations of food experts had turned it into an overcontrolled, rationalized, and deadening imposition. Thus, treating cooking as a "creative, expressive art" undermined larger systems of gendered oppression.[20]

Similarly, her short stint as professional baker taught her the larger lesson that *"capitalism can't work."* After struggling to produce affordable bread without sacrificing ingredient quality or wholesome process, she concluded, "It's impossible to make good, healthy bread at any kind of profit. Her reasoning was insightful, quite possibly true, and certainly revealing of the larger dream of "good bread" animating the counterculture. It's worth quoting at length.

> If you got [your ingredients] in bulk enough to make it sizably cheaper, you'd be doing so much business, probably, that you would be shipping the breads all over the place—and then you'd have to add preservatives or have stale bread! I really believe the answer lies in small communities. But—and this is what brought all this to mind—it's interesting that good bread, the symbol of the American dream (or rather, one of many symbols) cannot be produced within it now. I don't consider myself, really, in it. I don't mean that as arrogantly as it sounds—I just mean that I and the people I live with are surely not typical of Americans, and the bread we bake we don't "produce." Some people and their narrow definition of politics! Baking a loaf of brown bread in this society is revolutionary, if you know why you're doing it. It is for us.[21]

Invocations of bread politics like this were standard fare in the counterculture, but Dragonwagon's take was both intelligent and influential. The statement begins with a concise gloss on the pressures of capitalist baking—the constraints of efficiency and scale in a competitive, profit-driven context. Then, like so many critics in the American agrarian tradition, she offers small communities as an antidote. The statement never clarifies exactly how small communities baking their own bread might sidestep the capitalist system—historically they rarely have, even on the remote frontier—but it was a powerful vision. And it attached a feeling of profound agency to the simple act of baking one's own bread. To bake was to stand apart from the system. With this elegant argument, Crescent Dragonwagon repositioned cooking as an act of resistance, turning domestic binds into the stuff of liberation.

And yet, for all its radical anti-capitalist trappings, this dream of good bread also aligned Dragonwagon and the counterculture in general with a deeply conservative lineage. The countercultural dream of good bread challenged authority and expertise, stood against capitalist agribusiness, and sought to remake relations among people and between nature and society. Yet it also rested on rather orthodox myths of American individualism and independence. "Homemade bread," Dragonwagon observed wryly, "is a symbolic thing. It's American— it goes with pioneers and beginnings and family."[22]

In this evocation of frontier independence and its foodways as the bedrock of good society, the counterculture drew heavily on Grahamism. Perhaps more surprisingly, given the counterculture's disdain for regimen, the dream of good bread also gave new life to the ideologies of Physical Culture: sickness, both individual and social, was, in large part, traced back to weak, duped individuals' descent into an unnatural diet. Sickness might not have been a sin, but it did arise from individual irresponsibility. To be sure, this was a more politically conscious vision than MacFadden's. Dragonwagon and her comrades believed that individual irresponsibility could only be understood in the context of a poisonous, corrupt System in need of radical change. But, like MacFadden, they didn't reflect much on what values and assumptions got smuggled in with their utopia of self-defense through good food. At the very least, they failed to recognize how easily their vision of good bread and good society could be recast in accordance with entirely capitalist and individualistic values.

DOMESTICATING THE COUNTERCULTURE

On October 23, 1969, the United States celebrated its first National Day of Bread, sponsored by the country's millers, bakers, and grocers and enshrined by congressional resolution.[23] Most Americans missed it, though. There were a few other things going on in the country. The National Day of Bread fell in the midst of Chicago's Days of Rage and only a week after hundreds of thousands of Americans mobilized across the country in the first National Moratorium Day of antiwar protests. It came after a long summer that saw the Stonewall uprising, Manson murders, Woodstock, stepped-up nuclear testing by the Soviet Union, and the beginning of U.S. troop withdrawals from Vietnam. Two extraordinary events—the moon landing and the '69 Mets' underdog World Series victory—brought the country together a bit that summer. But mostly it felt like things were coming apart at the seams. In other words, for anyone threatened by social turmoil and political upheaval, it was a good time for a National Day of Bread. Celebrating bread allowed besieged conservatives to talk about family, Christianity, and old-fashioned values. What little press coverage the National Day of Bread received unanimously featured churches and happy families—quite different from the images of upheaval and bloodshed shown on nightly TV.

During the summer and fall of 1969, arguments about Vietnam, long hair, and tofu might have turned many kitchen tables into war zones. But not bread. At a time when Abby Hoffman purportedly urged kids to kill their parents, homemade, whole wheat, and multigrain breads were an easy piece of the counterculture for outsiders to swallow. A few social conservatives and hardliners within the baking industry rallied against dark loaves peddled by "food faddists," "scaremongers," and "anti-Americans," but mostly people embraced countercultural bread. In a stirring 1968 editorial, even E. J. Pyler, the elder statesman of baking science and publisher of the industry's leading trade magazine, urged his fellow bakers to "fight conformity."[24]

By the late 1970s, whole wheat bread consumption had soared, industrial white bread sales had plummeted, and the country was experiencing an unprecedented revival of home baking. For the first time in decades, overall bread consumption inched upwards, and "health breads" with roots in the counterculture led the way.[25] Three factors accounted for this epochal shift. First, as already suggested, countercultural critiques of industrial baking drew on a social dreamworld of conservative nostalgia that was easy to appreciate on Main Street and in suburbia. Second, stripped of its emphasis on community and social transformation, the counterculture's love of natural whole grains translated fluidly into the consumer-driven health food and self-actualization trends of the 1970s. Finally, high-value whole grain health breads offered a desperately needed source of profit and enhanced public image for industrial bakers crippled by declining sales and food safety scandals. Let's look at each of these factors more closely.

• • •

In 1970 Richard Pryor stormed off stage in the middle of his popular nightclub act at Las Vegas's Aladdin Theater, refusing to do another minute of "white bread humor." This was a pivotal moment in the comedian's career. He fled to Berkeley, California, where he immersed himself in drugs and the teachings of Malcolm X, only to emerge a few years later as a bigger, much edgier star.[26] It was also the first widely cited use of "white bread" as an adjective. The phrase spoke to soaring racial tensions and a mounting sense of despair over white Americans' unwillingness to compromise even a little on their investment in the political, cultural, and economic institutions of white privilege. Strangely though, "white bread" America seemed quite ready to adopt brown bread as a symbol of its values.

Brown breads of various sorts—mostly highly sweetened whole wheat loaves—were rare in the postwar United States, but they were not unknown. Rather, they were fixtures of particular times and places: church bake sales, family gatherings, and quaint country inns. Although many still doubted whole wheat breads' digestibility and questioned whether they were appropriate for daily consumption, in limited venues they were treasured delicacies. Father and the kids might have grumbled about brown bread's "sawdust" texture, but the loaves were also esteemed as symbols of old-fashioned feminine care and rural fortitude. So, in the late 1960s and early 1970s, when barefoot girls in peasant skirts made home baking cool, hippie brown bread would have seemed less of a threat to "American" tastes and values than other counterculture staples.

The decidedly uncountercultural global milling and food-processing conglomerate International Multifoods captured this affinity perfectly in a 1970 pamphlet, *Naturally Good Baking*. The recipe book could be read simultaneously as an attempt to appropriate counterculture chic and as a rebuke of youth rebellion. Illustrated with drawings of pioneer life, the booklet addressed itself to modern homemakers who had recently come to appreciate the value of whole wheat breads and desserts, but who long ago lost "Grandma's cookbook." According to International Multifoods, recapturing the aroma of fresh-baked bread could return families to the days when Grandma "cared about what her family ate and spent hours in the kitchen" to provide it.[27] With a few deft words and drawings, the recipe book repositioned the origins of 1970s interest in whole grain goodness—away from unwashed, rebellious youth and into the sanitized territory of "how things used to be."

Counterculture food gurus and activists had different takes on this kind of nostalgia. Some groups actively resisted it. Worker-owned cooperatives like Seattle's Little Bread Company and Chicago's Bread Shop, for example, dwelled less on the past and more on community organizing, job creation, and providing good low-cost bread. Even the moral superiority of whole wheat bread was not always a given. Particularly in more socialist-leaning bakeries, for example, members argued over whether to value white bread, with its low-cost, working-class appeal, alongside brown.[28]

Other counterculture figures approached sentimentality in a more conflicted manner. For Crescent Dragonwagon, homemade food cemented the foundations of an alternative social structure. And yet, at times, Dragonwagon seemed aware that her alternative might not be so alternative: *The Commune Cookbook* expressed an extraordinary faith in the ability of its idea of "good food" to appeal to people across differences of class and race, but it also acknowledged the way visions of good food could divide groups. On paper, Dragonwagon's dream of a new way of relating to food resonates with her desire for women's rights. In practice, though, she realized that renewed emphasis on women's place in the kitchen smacked of old-fashioned patriarchy and ran the risk of creating yet another burden women must bear.

Carol Flinders, coauthor of the popular *Laurel's Kitchen,* for her part, understood this tension but didn't appear worried. For Flinders, kitchens were women's "most effective front for social change." "I'm not saying that women shouldn't take jobs," she claimed in the introduction to *Laurel's Kitchen,* just that the place "where [women's] efforts will count the most is not in business or professions . . . but in the home and community."[29] These were "the most effective front[s] for social change." But the fact that Flinders didn't apply the same logic to men was telling: for Flinders, women, not men, made social change from the kitchen outward because women were naturally and innately positioned to make the world whole through caring labor.[30] In *Laurel's Kitchen* bread making exemplified a feminine ethic of care, and learning to make bread served as a, if not *the,* crucial rite of passage into that ideal. Reconnecting with women's innate goodness and transformative potential required reconnecting with the innate goodness of whole grain, something that had been lost when machines began making bread.

At the same time, Flinders clearly saw how closely her feminine ideal allied her with generations of constrictive patriarchic tradition. Her solution to this conundrum was to imagine a bygone era of empowered domesticity that could be revived in the modern world. *Laurel's Kitchen* unfolds around the character of Flinders's coauthor Laurel Robertson, a friend with "natural wisdom" who dedicated herself single-mindedly to caring for her hearth and family. Robertson epitomized Flinders's feminine ideal. She was a woman who didn't betray her innate value as a mother or true place in the political life of her community by seeking a place in men's unnatural, externally focused world.

It would have been hard to read *Laurel's Kitchen* as anything but conservative, written as it was in the era of Gloria Steinem, Equal Rights Amendment battles, expanding definitions of family, and the first sparks of the gay rights movement. And yet Flinders's picture of the content, hearth-centered life available to women was so beautifully drawn, so sensual and full of love, that it couldn't help but appeal, even to many feminists.

Thirty years later, the same tension still haunts the alternative food movement. In 2010, *New York Times* columnist Peggy Orenstein identified the newest incarnation of this recurring conundrum as "the femivore's dilemna." Femivores, she observed, were "highly educated women who left the workforce to care for kith and kin," and then carved out a space of meaning and agency in the home by devoting themselves to politically conscious food provision. In this way, femivores redefined "traditional" domestic labor—cooking from scratch, canning, gardening, raising chickens, and even shopping—as an arena of "self-sufficiency, autonomy and personal fulfillment"— the very principles that, according to Orenstein, had led women to the workforce in the first place.[31]

Orenstein's article sparked a predictable debate. Many critics focused on a contradiction that even Orenstein acknowledged: the "tomato-canning feminists'" realm of self-sufficiency and autonomy assumed an income-earning spouse somewhere just outside the picture frame. How could "autonomy" be premised on financial dependence? As Orenstein wrote, "If a woman is not careful, it seems, chicken wire can coop her up as surely as any gilded cage."[32] Other critics dug into the more hidden assumptions of Orenstein's piece: while feminists might disagree on whether femivore life was a cage or not, it was most definitely gilded. To suffer the femivore's dilemma one must be relatively affluent. Like "the omnivore's dilemma," the femivore's dilemma emerges out of the highly privileged position of having almost limitless life options, something that most women— and men—in contemporary America don't experience.

This brings us back to *Laurel's Kitchen*. For, while critics in the 1970s and today have noted the gendered contradictions of nostalgia for the lost days of Grandma's cooking, less has been said about the vision of America smuggled in with the aroma of fresh bread. When counterculture food gurus like Flinders imagined the American past, they saw a halcyon world of independent cabins filled with nuclear families. Grandma didn't slave in cotton fields or garment factories, nor did she struggle to save the farm from creditors. She didn't campaign for suffrage or march for workers' rights on May Day. Home was not a migrant farmhand's wagon. Great Depressions only increased the "realness" of American food. And when immigrants or people of color appeared in this America, they were scrubbed of actual history, eagerly waiting to share exotic new ingredients or a bit of ancient wisdom with their white audience. This was a romanticized past.

In the enchanted broccoli forest of best-selling counterculture cookbooks, however, at least one author offered a glimmer of perspective. Mollie Katzen, perhaps the most influential cookbook author of the era, honestly admitted, "It is difficult to talk about bread-baking without lapsing into sentimentality." "One is tempted to go on and on about how exhilarated and connected to the universe one feels, about how the kitchen atmosphere acquires sublime soulfulness, about how born-again breadmakers are magical, charismatic individuals," she confessed. "[But] it is not my place to promise you a transformed existence. What I offer is one with more bread recipes. The rest is what you make of it."[33]

By the late 1970s, however, it was clear that Americans were hooked on self-transformation. Even more than through their appeal to conservative nostalgia, counterculture bread tastes spread to mainstream America via the quest for perfect health.[34] Healthy eating had, of course, been one important component of the counterculture since the mid-1960s, but by the mid-1970s it had been elevated to a supreme position in American life. Stripped of its political and social critiques, the counterculture's fixation on wellness easily morphed into an individual-centered, consumer-driven bodily project. Health food stores, yoga studios, and exercise fads flourished across the country, permanently changing the way Americans thought about wellness. Bernarr MacFadden would have been proud: the counterculture's search for bodily harmony had found its love match in 1970s self-actualization.

During the 1960s and early 1970s, counterculture food rebels believed that if Americans only knew about the dangers of industrial food and the goodness of healthy eating, they would change their diet. Changing the country's relation to food would, in turn, bring about swift changes in economic and political relations. By the late 1970s, counterculture food gurus saw part of their dream fulfilled: more Americans knew about the dangers of industrial eating and aspired to counterculture visions of healthy eating than at any other point in the past century. By the early 1980s, a study revealed that six out of ten young singles thought that white bread was unhealthy and

to be avoided.[35] But it was also becoming clear that this consciousness wouldn't necessarily set in motion the larger structural changes
counterculture food activists had hoped for. In fact, the industrial
food system could almost effortlessly assimilate health consciousness.
The fixation on wellness emerging across large swathes of the U.S.
population in the late 1970s could serve as a much-needed new engine
for profit in the industrial food system.

This was clearly the case in the baking industry. The perceived
moral and bodily goodness of whole wheat bread had helped lead
the country toward health food, and the baking industry was ready
to share in the bounty. In fact, the 1970s health craze couldn't have
come at a better time for the industry. Through the late 1960s and
early 1970s, industrial bakers labored under low profits and a tattered
image. After the great chemistry- and engineering-driven advances of
the 1950s and early 1960s, even industry insiders conceded that their
business had fallen into a state of torpor. Market studies revealed that
bread itself had become so homogeneous that consumers had trouble
distinguishing one brand from another. What little profits could be
squeezed out of cheap white bread came mostly from mergers and
oligopoly power, rather than innovation. A handful of companies—
many the descendants of William Ward's Bread Trust—jockeyed for
market position using brute force instead of quality product. Constant investigations into price fixing by dominant firms marked the
period, as market concentration increased.[36] When wheat prices, and
by extension bread prices, soared in the mid-1970s as a result of high
oil prices and large sales of surplus grain to the USSR, it only heightened consumers' sense that bakers were taking advantage of them.

Meanwhile, the public embrace of health foods and environmentalism exposed industrial baking practices to more condemnation.
And the locus of this opprobrium had shifted from counterculture to
mainstream, from Haight-Ashbury to Capitol Hill. In 1971, Ralph
Nader launched a new round of Senate hearings on the baking industry and spurred the Federal Trade Commission to take action against
misleading health claims in Wonder bread advertising.[37]

Accounts of early twentieth-century experiments feeding rats a
white bread–only diet resurfaced, migrating from their traditional
place on the mimeographed pages of alternative weeklies to the

science sections of major newspapers.[38] Even mainstream nutrition scientists, long reluctant to question the place of white bread in a balanced diet, joined in. As Hilda Swenerton, California state nutrition expert for the university extension service, admitted in the *Los Angeles Times*, "We've been so busy pointing out how the faddists are all wrong that we've failed to recognize some of the good faddists have done."[39]

In 1977 the Senate Select Committee on Nutrition and Human Needs, backed by a stable of mainstream scientists, issued its landmark *Dietary Goals for the United States*. The report put a government seal on a set of recommendations not all that different from those found in Frances Moore Lappé's radical 1971 *Diet for a Small Planet*: Americans should dramatically increase consumption of whole grains, fruits, and vegetables, while cutting back on meat, dairy, and refined sugars.[40] Even more importantly, mainstream nutrition science had discovered the paramount importance of fiber. Starting in 1975, scores of books, magazine articles, and news items touted the lifesaving benefits of roughage, ushering in "the fiber era" in American nutrition.[41]

While some in the baking industry fought back against this dietary heresy, most treated it as an opportunity. Two companies had already shown that health bread could be mass-produced with industrial methods at a high profit. Both begun out of Connecticut homes decades earlier, Pepperidge Farms and Arnold Bakers exemplified the way industrial producers could appeal to a health-obsessed nation without sacrificing scale and efficiency. By the late 1960s, Margaret Rudkin, founder of Pepperidge Farms, had built the company into a multimillion-dollar industry leader, but its origin was classic American health foodism.[42] In the 1930s, asthma crippled Rudkin's youngest son and doctors could offer little assistance. Convinced that diet played a role in the boy's affliction, Rudkin set out to cure him with a diet of whole wheat bread, baked from her Irish grandmother's recipe. It worked well enough to attract interest in the community. The boy's doctor requested loaves for his other patients and demand grew from there. Soon Rudkin had, with the help of two servants, started a small bakery in the family's home kitchen.

The wife of a wealthy financier, Rudkin raised money to open one real bread factory, and then others. By the late 1950s, Pepperidge Farms baked more than a million loaves a week in its cutting-edge bakeries. Despite its dependence on high-tech production, however, the company's advertising was self-consciously old-fashioned—even by baking industry standards. The combination was unbeatable. With its cutting-edge technology and homey image, the company soon dominated national markets for health bread, even though its loaves sold for more than double the price of regular bread. In 1961 the Campbell's Soup Company bought Pepperidge Farms, and Rudkin died in 1967, but the company kept pace with the country's emerging interest in counterculture food.

So did Arnold Bakers, a second multimillion-dollar company built on dark, dense loaves.[43] Paul Dean Arnold had founded that company in 1940 out of his garage after quitting work at a Nabisco plant. Touting products like "Bran-Nola Bread," the company had grown to more than $200 million in annual sales by the time of Arnold's death in 1985. The Arnold "Health Loaf Natural," a highly sweetened light brown mixture of stone ground whole wheat and unbleached white flour, was, in many ways, the iconic health bread of its time.

Through the 1970s, ingredients that seemed drawn straight from a commune kitchen—sprouted wheat, unsulfured molasses, raisin juice, and wheat germ—gave Pepperidge Farms and Arnold loaves exotic appeal. They were Woodstock in cellophane. Other companies quickly followed suit, and soon health breads were the fastest-growing segment of the entire baking industry. Between 1967 and 1982, white bread consumption plummeted 30 percent—but overall bread consumption, led by high-fiber brown loaves, actually increased.[44]

The advent of industrial health bread was not without hiccups. Few of the country's major bread conglomerates shared Rudkin's and Arnold's attachment to the spirit of health food doctrines. Theirs was a purely instrumental embrace. If loaves could be made to *look* like brown health loaves by adding caramel color, it was fine. And why not rack up impressive amounts of fiber at a low cost by adding cheap wood pulp to industrial loaves? Wonder bread's parent company, ITT Continental, advertised that its Fresh Horizons loaf, filled with "powdered cellulous" (aka wood pulp), had 400 percent more fiber than white bread, but "the same great taste." Consumers didn't buy it. Fresh Horizons and other wood pulp fiber breads earned a spot on the *New York Times*'s list of the worst foods of 1976—just under Tube-A-Goo, syringes filled with brightly colored syrup that looked and smelled "exactly like hair waving lotion."[45]

In the end, consumer outrage and concerted action by government regulators reined in the early excesses of industrial health bread. Unfortunately, that didn't stop many of the new mass-market health breads from tasting a bit like Tube-A-Goo. In order to achieve extended shelf life without the use of chemical preservatives, bakers jammed health loaves full of moisture-retaining natural sweeteners. The result, as *New York Times* food writer Mimi Sheraton noted, was sometimes less than pleasant: "cloying sweetness" and "a limp, wet texture."[46]

Still, the baking industry pressed on. By the late 1970s, health breads weren't just a lucrative niche market—they were the essential element of the industry's battle against resurgent home baking.

REVOLT IN THE KITCHEN AND THE RISE OF YUPPIE BREAD

Thanks to the counterculture, conservative nostalgia, and spreading concern about wellness, home baking was more popular than at any time in the previous century. Guided by *Laurel's Kitchen, The Tassajara Bread Book,* and James Beard's *Beard on Bread,* millions of Americans were experimenting with their own doughs for the first time. And these were definitely experiments. Uncertain how to parse competing ideas about which new grain was the purest and most salubrious, 1970s home bakers crammed every grain they could get into their bread. The age of the whole-wheat-spelt-oat-amaranth-brown rice-millet-buckwheat-barley loaf was born. For good measure, 1970s bakers also threw in zucchini, olives, carrots, bananas, sunflower seeds, soya, whey, carob, and dates. Meanwhile, large doses of honey and molasses eased the unfamiliar taste and texture of whole grains onto the American palate.

Between 1973 and 1979, nearly every major newspaper, home magazine, and cooking monthly ran stories noting the boom in home baking and offering tips to first timers. John Hess, writing in the *New York Times,* called it a "kitchen revolt."[47] Bread making was in vogue. In fact, it was in *Vogue:* the style magazine's April 1979 issue touted homemade bread as an easy way its readers could ensure less sugar and more fulfillment in their lives.[48] That home bread making had made it from the food section to the fashion pages said something to the baking industry. It seemed as if the country's bakers had to fight a small version of the early twentieth-century battle against home baking all over again.

In the 1900s bakers undercut home baking with fears of impurity and contagion, buttressed by a charismatic sheen of scientific authority. By the 1970s, however, counterculture gurus had effectively associated charismatic food science with hubris and destruction. A new strategy was needed. So, in the 1980s, the baking industry took back terrain from home baking with niche marketing and appeals to upscale chic.

This approach reflected larger shifts in the U.S. economy. Rocked by recessions, oil crises, and de-industrialization, the U.S. economy began to take on a new form in the 1970s. Manufacturing no longer served as the country's driving engine. Financial services—making money from money—had begun to take their place at the center of the economy.

After steadily rising through the postwar period, real wages for most Americans began to decline. Even forty years later, average wages adjusted for cost of living still wouldn't have returned to their pre-1970s level, but the financialization of the U.S. economy did produce enormous wealth for urban professionals. Wealth distribution in the country became, and remained, more polarized than at any other period since the Roaring Twenties. Affluent singles and childless couples reveled in unprecedented disposable incomes, giving rise to a world of "yuppie" consumption. And yet, across the country, households that could afford to maintain Carol Flinders's dream of a dedicated homemaker were growing increasingly rare.[49]

These trends would have a marked effect on the very nature of consumption. During the postwar era of rising wages and decreasing inequality, consumption largely took the form of standardized, one-size-fits-all, mass-market commodities. As with enriched white breads on supermarket shelves, differences among competing commodities were relatively small. During the 1980s, however, fueled by

the rapid segmentation of American society, consumer life diversi-
fied into ever-more precise niche markets. Massive department stores
lost ground to boutique chains catering to narrow bands of consumers, who increasingly began to tie their identities to specific niche
markets.[50]

Along with advances in transportation and packaging, this had a
profound effect on the American diet. No longer would everyone eat
the same iceberg lettuce. Increasingly, shoppers could choose the style
of lettuce—shipped in from Mexico, if needed—that fit their status
aspirations exactly. To survive, bakers would have to embrace real
product diversification. And in this area, upstarts outpaced industry
leaders. Small bakeries sprouted up across the country in record numbers during the 1980s. By the 1990s, some of them had grown into
chains, "vying to become the 'Starbucks' of bread."[51] Au Bon Pain,
La Vie de France, Great Harvest, the St. Louis Bread Company, and
Breadsmith clones spread through suburban malls and city streets.

Many of the resurgent small bakeries paid the rent with sweets
and sandwiches, not bread. Nevertheless, by the early 1990s, observers could point to a "new bread mystique" seducing the country.
Like the new consumer economy in general, the small-bakery revival
of the 1980s and 1990s targeted specific class and status groups. Su-
permarkets still sold industrial white bread, of course, but demand
for fluffy loaves increasingly concentrated in lower-income brackets.
By the end of the 1970s, people buying supermarket white bread almost universally ranked low price as their top consideration in food
purchasing. Middle- and upper-class consumers were increasingly
willing to pay more for distinctive bread. Now "we can sell Cadillacs
along with the Fords," a *Bakery Magazine* writer beamed.[52]

Catering to middle- and upper-class consumers interested in health
and charmed by novelty, supermarket chains opened in-store bakeries
that made high-value specialty breads from scratch or "baked off"
partially cooked loaves from central distribution centers. Comfortable suburbanites switched to health breads like Arnold and Orowheat and flocked to strip-mall chain bakeries.

Meanwhile, urban elites could select from a growing array of
high-end bread bakeries—often with roots in the counterculture. In
1977, Mimi Sheraton had eulogized urban ethnic bakeries, lost to

gentrification and suburbanization. According to Sheraton, San Francisco sourdough had become "practically extinct."[53] Within a decade, however, the situation had changed dramatically. On the West Coast, young urban professionals—yuppies—discovered the pleasures of European-style artisan loaves at Nancy Silverton's La Brea Bakery or Steve Sullivan's Acme Bread. In New York, the late 1980s and early 1990s saw the opening of soon-to-be-institutions like Amy's Bakery, Tom Cat Bakery, and the Sullivan Street Bakery.

Multiple forces drove this explosion of high-end bread bakeries: choosing healthy grain foods had become closely associated with ideas of personal responsibility and successful self-image; yuppie consumers craved distinctive gourmet foods, especially ones with ties to Europe or California; and, perhaps most importantly, high-quality bread appealed to a new consumer dream. Market researchers called it "neo-traditionalism," and it combined nostalgia for 1950s-vintage family values with a cash-charged belief in the possibility of achieving self-actualization through consumer choice. Artisanal bread offered a perfect neo-traditionalist symbol, self-consciously old-fashioned and yet decidedly upscale.[54]

European-style breads as gourmet status symbols were not new, at least in New York. As early as 1962, the year Eero Saarinen's bird-like TWA terminal swooped down at what was still called Idlewild International Airport, a subsidiary of Pepperidge Farms was airlifting Parisian baguettes into Manhattan. By 1963, affluent New Yorkers could buy the "astronomically priced" 85-cent bread at 250 outlets, including Bloomingdales. Baked overnight in a prestigious Paris *boulangerie* and on New York shelves by noon, the loaves' thirty-six hundred "food miles" were something to brag about.[55]

By the 1980s European bread was spreading west into the country's heartland. Meanwhile, the isolation of *Lactobacillus sanfrancisco*—the bacteria responsible for San Francisco sourdough's tang—set off a craze for sourdough that marched east across the country.

High-status bread inspired legions of imitators, some crude and some creative. On the crude side, bakeries interested in scale and efficiency could substitute "natural sourdough flavor" for costly slow, cool fermentation. Often, as one bakery scientist acknowledged, the all-important *look* of artisan authenticity could be achieved without sacrificing industrial efficiency. "We developed our technology to produce perfectly regular looking loaves. It's not that hard to program them to make perfectly irregular ones," he confessed.[56] Like rustic faux-Italian tiles and factory-scratched "vintage" furniture, which give a patina of history and character to fifteen-minute-old McMansions, artfully mutilated bread promised a mini respite from the soulless world of modern commodity production—even though it was still fast food.

On the more creative side, La Brea Bakery in Los Angeles went from one-room bakeshop to multibillion-dollar global conglomerate by pioneering artisan-industrial technology: loaves shaped by gentle robots and factory assembly lines adapted to the same kind of slow, careful procedures used by small bakeries. The result was a true hybrid, combining a bit of the artisan spirit with a bit of the industrial method.

Whether through small, unfranchised bakeries, strip-mall chains, or industrial artisans like La Brea, the dream of good bread, European-style, was no longer confined to coastal cities. By the turn of the millennium, it had reached consumers in every corner of "the United States of Arugula." With this delicious bread, of course, came new dreams about society.

OH, YOU POOR THING

A mile from the heart of Berkeley's Gourmet Ghetto, Steve Sullivan's Acme bakery is a good place to observe the artisan bread revolution in its highest form. This is the real deal: a small, unfranchised neighborhood bakery producing slow-fermented, handcrafted bread. It doesn't sell sandwiches. It doesn't sell coffee or cookies. It sells bread.

On a spring morning two years ago, I queued in a convivial crush outside Acme's clacking screen door. When my turn came to squeeze into the hot, floury shop, I paid $8 for an Italian bâtard and the best walnut levain in the Western Hemisphere. The levain wouldn't make it home uneaten—that much I knew—so I thought I might as well sit down with a cup of coffee from Alice Waters's Café Fanny next door while I tore through its malty mix of chewy crumb and toasted nuts.

Acme's walnut levain—organic flour, natural starter, malted barley, water, walnuts, and salt—has only a quarter of the ingredients found in Wonder bread. Its crumb's intense, almost beery flavor comes from the unrushed work of microbes—the slow artistry of *Saccharomyces* and *Lactobacilli*. Its dark, almost scorched crust gives a smoky, nutty counterpoint to the crumb's tang. Considering that, when stripped of fats, sweeteners, and added flavorings, most of bread's taste comes from browning reactions in the crust, we Americans eat our bread far too pale. Steve Sullivan knew better.

In 1983, fresh from a stint at Chez Panisse—what was then, and still is, the epicenter of California cuisine—Steve Sullivan opened Acme with a loan from Doobie Brothers guitarist Patrick Simmons. Acme now has a wholesale bakery making loaves for local restaurants and three retail outlets, including one in San Francisco's ultra-high-end Embarcadero Market. But Sullivan has resisted expansion beyond that, focusing instead on community, quality, and craft. The payoff has been a fierce continued attention to flavor and the jovial community feeling surrounding the bakery.

These are big ideas in small loaves: dreams of pleasure, community, and authenticity, a glimpse into the possibility of a different kind of food system. But, after shelling out $8 for a couple of pounds of bread, I was painfully aware that these are also exclusive dreams.

In *The Commune Cookbook*, Crescent Dragonwagon railed against the "elitist thinking" behind America's taste for industrial white bread. The introduction of inexpensive refined flours in the nineteenth century had allowed the country to share in aspirational dreams of high-class living embodied in light, white loaves. Dark breads, she observed perceptively, had become more and more associated with social inferiority.[57] Today, however, thanks to the convergence of counterculture and industry, we live in a world that presents a mirror image of Dragonwagon's.

A *Washington Post* article commemorating the moment in 2009 when whole wheat bread sales surpassed white for the first time in U.S. history explained this reversal. Growing awareness of the importance of the fiber and nutrients found in whole grains played a role, but so did status aspirations. Today, the article observed, whole wheat bread "signifies the sophistication of your palate, your appreciation for texture and variety. . . . The grainier you like it, the more refined your sensibilities. The darker it is, the greater your chance for enlightenment."[58] Industrial white bread has completed its two-hundred-year trajectory from modern marvel to low-class item. As the spokeswoman for a food industry–affiliated nonprofit nutrition policy organization concluded, "It used to be, 'Oh, you poor thing, you have that nasty brown bread.' . . . Now it's, 'Oh, you poor thing. You have that nasty white bread.' "[59]

White bread still sells—Americans bought 1.5 billion loaves of it in 2009—but its consumer profile has changed, settling into the lower classes. And while references to nutrition facts give distaste for white bread a patina of scientific truth, elites' feelings toward people who choose to eat "unhealthy" bread are anything but objective. Just as in the 1920s, disdain for difference can come cloaked in seemingly neutral discussions of healthy eating and responsible choices.

Given the country's post-1970s preoccupation with fitness and body image, we could take the *Post*'s analysis a step further. Caring about health and social status are not separate matters. Today, showing interest in healthy eating is an essential piece of the performance of eliteness. Maintaining a fit-looking body, keeping abreast of new health food trends, and at least paying lip service to scientific nutrition advice proclaim one's superior virtue and self-control to the world. In this way, concern with health and fitness helps tacitly justify social inequality: a person's elite status and fit body may, in fact, have arisen from destructive behavior—like insider trading and bulimia—or just some lucky inheritance, but the visual spectacle of an affluent healthism declares, "I earned my wealth through discipline, self-sacrifice, and hard work, just like I earned this body."

Thus, something as simple as bread choice is an act of social positioning. Bread choice stakes a claim to a particular identity, but also opens one up to others' ideas about what that selection means. Some manifestations of the white trash revival try to reclaim white bread eating as a virtuous cultural celebration, an authentic piece of southern regional foodways, as Ernst Matthew Mickler's *White Trash Cookbook* contends. African Americans join in this, as well, touting Wonder bread's place in traditional soul food. Even an article in the haute cuisine magazine *Saveur* admitted, "Sopping up [Kansas City barbeque] may well be the only legitimate use for spongy, store-bought white bread."[60]

Industrial white bread may also serve as an edible emblem of class solidarity. "I've wanted to scream this for so long / There is no shame in the trailer park / or white bread, or government cheese / There is no shame on the victims of poverty," the hard-core band Crimson Spectre thrashed out in its "White Trash Manifesto."[61] But all those acts of positive self-positioning face a grim association between white bread, failure, and irresponsibility. "White Trash Momma," a song by another heavy metal band, expressed this connection even more brutally. In it, a woman "raised on white bread" slides into crack use and prostitution, sealing her "white trash fate."[62]

In the end, there's something sad about the way counterculture dreams of building good society through good bread morphed into reinforced social distinctions. Nevertheless, this wasn't an intended or inevitable outcome of counterculture food activism: large-scale and unexpected shifts in both how Americans thought about health and the very nature of the U.S. economy sealed hippie brown bread's fate (in a fancy wrapper with a high price tag). Certainly the world is better because of counterculture efforts to raise awareness about the politics of eating. And we gained an artisanal bread revolution along the way.

The social dreams embodied in that artisanal revolution may sometimes seem precious and far removed from the daily grind of poverty evoked in white trash rhetoric. But this doesn't mean that they should be abandoned. I, for one, crave the world of community, cultural vibrancy, environmental responsibility, and alimentary diversity embodied in a fresh-baked loaf of local artisanal bread. But if the story of white bread's journey from modern marvel to low-class symbol teaches anything, it is that food dreamers must be ready to modify their vision if it does more to reinforce social stratification than to build a better world.

CONCLUSION: BEYOND GOOD BREAD

There is so much fog around the moral high ground.

—Peter Carey

BEGINNINGS

There is a seven-inch crack in the ceramic bowl I use to make bread most weeks. I never wash the bowl, just give it a quick rinse and a wipe. It's not hygienic. Millions of leftover microbes colonize the cruddy fissure. A slurry of flour and water begins to bubble with life when sealed in the bowl overnight, and after two days, it stinks of overripe fruit. What had been a clean white paste now looks like the surface of an uninhabitable swamp planet. It's easy to imagine why, before microscopes, people turned to theories of spontaneous generation to explain yeasty effervescence. Today, plagued and blessed by our acute awareness of invisible life, we associate the change in my bowl with rogue microbial colonies and it makes us squirm. "Shouldn't you use some bleach on that bowl?" a friend asks.

These days, playing with microbes at home is generally considered improper behavior. My fermentation experiments are pretty tame; my wife's raw milk cheeses are a littler edgier. Then there's this from the "wild fermentation" activist Sandor Katz: "After a goat slaughter, I fermented some of the meat for a couple weeks. I placed the meat in a gallon jar, then filled it with a mixture of all the other live ferments I had around: wine, vinegar, miso, yogurt, and sauerkraut juice. I covered the jar and left in an unobtrusive corner of our basement [for two weeks]. It bubbled and smelled good. . . . [Later], as it cooked, an overwhelming odor enveloped the kitchen . . . there was some swooning and near fainting."[1]

It's not hygienic, but I can't help but wonder whether this kind of "improper handling"—the creative contagion of yeasty fermentation—might offer a model for challenging the chauvinisms and exclusions wrapped up in quests for "good bread." Fermentation is my own food dream, and I know that's problematic. But one thing should be clear by now: food is so central to how we think about social life that we'll probably never be able to completely avoid dreams of good food and their attendant risks. Nor should we. Utopian dreams of good food inspire people to make the world better. I wouldn't want to lose that passion. We can, however, be a lot more reflective about the politics, assumptions, and absences contained in our visions of changing the world through food. Ultimately, it is possible, and eminently practical, to strive for *both* eager optimism about social change *and* self-critical pessimism about the costs of our actions. One without the other is dangerous, either overly naïve or debilitatingly negative. In this book, I've offered a lot of the latter—critique abounds in the preceding chapters. So, by way of conclusion, here is my self-consciously optimistic dream of political fermentation.[2]

First, what fermentation is not. Throughout this book, five seductive dreams come up over and over again. They touch a deep chord in consumers' relation to food, and yet have underpinned many of the most ambiguous outcomes of well-meaning efforts to change the way the country eats. They are the dreams of purity, naturalness, scientific control, perfect health, and national security and vitality. Each of these dreams rose to prominence because it crystallized deep currents of longing and anxiety—and thus galvanized action. All five dreams endowed eating with seductive moral clarity: some foods were obviously good and some were clearly evil. On the surface, at least, who could possibly disagree with wanting purer food, more natural food, more abundant food made possible by science, healthier food that fought disease and weakness, or food that made the world a little safer and less hungry? And yet, we've seen that each of these rousing visions of improvement framed the problems of society and the food system in dubious ways.

The dream of *purity* animated important food safety activism, but also drove industrial and anti-industrial food reformers alike to exclude and divide groups of people in the name of sanitation. Quests for purity created an enduring bridge between concerns about healthy diet and attempts to police against social "contagions" (like unwanted immigrants or alien ideas about health and nutrition).

Visions of *naturalness,* for their part, facilitated important critiques of industrial hubris and giant oligopoly food producers, as seen in the 1960s counterculture. But fears that the country had grown estranged from nature also enveloped food reform movements in nostalgia for an American Eden of independent, white, property-owning farmers. That nostalgia idealized female domesticity and local communities, glossing over the power disparities that always marked those realms. In the process, sentimental dreams of naturalness made it harder for well-meaning people to address inequalities in the fields, factories, and kitchens of industrial food production.

Narratives of *scientific control* typically stood opposed to the quest for natural harmony, but they were no less utopian in appeal. Large-scale food producers and ordinary consumers leaned breathlessly toward a future of abundance, leisure, and harmony made possible by speed, efficiency, and the conquest of nature. In the 1920s and 1950s, this dream blinded many Americans to the hubris and shortsightedness of scientific control. In exchange for spectacles of efficiency, abundance, and control, people harnessed their sustenance to greedy corporations, embraced bread infused with chemicals additives, lost sight of heterogeneous pleasure, cheered the remaking of world wheat farming into a petroleum-fueled factory system, and ignored the destruction of small-scale bakers.

The dream of *perfect health* seeks something that is hard to dislike: life extension and bodily improvement. Nevertheless, even those achievements come at a cost. As seen in food movements from Grahamism to gluten free, the quest for perfectly tuned bodies individualized and medicalized problems that might have been better addressed through social and political means. The quest for perfect health has also come with psychological costs for those who participate in it. With its fantasies of bodily control comes a relentless fear of deterioration and a sense that imperfect health reflects character weakness or moral failing.

Finally, dreams of food and *national security and vitality* help produce an anxious, Manichean geography. At times the perceived need
to fortify "us" against "them" has legitimated attention to marginal-
ized people's demands for better bread, whether through wartime
enrichment campaigns or postwar Food for Peace. But it has also nurtured an emergency mentality that propelled ill-conceived changes in
the American diet and made alternative ways of organizing the food
system appear dangerous and unpatriotic.

In sum, these five big dreams of food and society roused Americans to change their diets and food system, but often at great cost.
At root, each one of the five gave us the idea that good eating was
a form of combat. We manned the barricades against impurity and
contagion and fought to defend the borders of an imagined state of
natural harmony. We mobilized science to conquer and tame that
same nature, used food to arm ourselves against bodily decay, and
rallied to defend the nation by eating right. We fought this combat
in the name of protecting our health and the health of society—good
things. But our alimentary trench war often had grave consequences
for people on the margins or excluded from society. The urgency of
defending purity against contagion, nature against artifice, health
against weakness, and us against them helped proliferate other social
divides.

This is why I like fermentation. Unruly to its core, fermentation
defies boundary making and combat mentality. It blurs lines between
nature and society and suggests that true security may lie in conscien-
tious impurity, not coerced purity. And it does this from a moral low
ground: dreams of purity, naturalness, control, perfect health, and
security evoke precise borders and confident certainties, but fermentation can't. It requires acceptance of constant flux and perpetual
reconsidering.

Let me explain. The dominant strain in my cracked bowl is probably *Saccharomyces cerevisiae,* the planet's most common baking
and brewing yeast. One of its ancestors may have been the first living species domesticated by humanity, our first biotechnology.[3] Of
course, by helping humans produce beer, bread, and cheese—the
first manufactured foods and the foundations of settled life—yeasts
domesticated us as much as we domesticated them.

Although contemporary bioscience hotly debates the origins and ecology of *Saccharomyces cerevisiae,* baking yeasts have not been "wild" or "natural" in any meaningful way for as long as humans have made food. Contrary to popular belief, *Saccharomyces cerevisiae* exists in relatively low levels in the so-called natural environment—even if we include orchards and vineyards in this category. The "natural" habitat of this creature culture is not fields or forests, but rather the artisanal-industrial environment of wineries, breweries, and bakeries. It is the crack in my bowl, the countertop where I knead, the walls of the hundred-plus wineries in my town, the world under my fingernails.[4]

For a long time, I prized an heirloom starter inoculated with the must of some particularly prestigious organic tempranillo grapes. The romantic in me—the part of me that would have been at home in Grahamism or the 1960s counterculture—clung to the idea of "wild" yeast. Like artisan bakers around the world, I coveted the powdery must coating grapes, apples, and certain other fruits as a source of wild yeast, and imagined that making a bread starter was something like hunting untamed beasts. There is something comforting about these natural origin stories. Who really wants to hear that the microbes rising in their *pain au levain* come from underneath someone's fingernails? But the natural origin story probably has it backwards: the life forms colonizing my tempranillo grape starter almost certainly came *from* the nooks and crannies of a winery, carried *to* the surface of the fruit on the tools, hands, and containers of the people who handled it. The ecology of *Saccharomyces cerevisiae* is a human ecology, just as certainly as human civilization is, in turn, very much a product of fermentation.

Despite the mystique ascribed to old heirloom starters with noble bloodlines, yeasts also defy human nostalgia. *Saccharomyces* are famed for their genetic volatility, swapping DNA with abandon, constantly morphing and changing. Whether we like it or not, the ecology of old starters is constantly changing.[5] A group of microbiologists has shown that even "pure" commercial strains employed by industrial beer makers are riddled with genetic material from different species, the result of enthusiastic promiscuity in the brewing environment.[6]

The dream of naturalness runs strong in food movements, and many avid fermenters cling to visions of authentic connection to nature and the past. Slow Food writer Dominique Fournier concludes, "Whether in domestic rituals or public codes, people use fermented foods to maintain a harmonious relationship with Nature and, more generally, all that is transcendental."[7] From this perspective, fermentation offers a pathway back to "authentic" and "natural" life. What I see instead is a more complex companion-species relationship, continually remade in the present.[8] This is not a warm fuzzy relationship. When I gaze affectionately at jars of *Saccharomyces cerevisiae* imprisoned in my fridge, *Saccharomyces cerevisiae* does not wag its ascospores at me. Sometimes it refuses to help me bake bread when I need to, and I am aware that any ideas of control or conquest I might have are illusions. I negotiate with the invisible world, trying to cultivate an advantageous ecology; but I don't control it. Even when a batch of starter gets too weak or too sour and I flush it down the toilet, irrepressible *Saccharomyces cerevisiae* has already begun to recolonize my kitchen. It is an agent in my life.

In a similar way, fermentation breeds acceptance of compromise and contradiction. Fermentation rebels against an ultra-pasteurized food system and our culture's obsession with anti-bacterial, hand-sanitizing, border-guarding purity.[9] As a growing body of research on probiotic foods suggests, cultivating a diverse and beneficial bodily ecology may protect our health as much as building ever-tougher barriers against all microbial life. Fermentation teaches us to live with impurity, not against it. But it also teaches the importance of hygiene and cleanliness. Nothing tastes worse than an off-fermented item, and fermentation frequently reminds me that sometimes I *do* need bleach, not to mention clean water, antibiotics, and protection from food-borne pathogens—the fruits of humanity's combat approach to microbes.

In other words, fermentation requires openness to ambiguity, acceptance of impurity, and the courage to redefine preconceived boundaries between "good" and "bad." This is a dream of good food, and thus loaded with unintended assumptions and complicities that I can't yet see. But unlike the other dreams of good bread presented here, fermentation is not a utopian end state like purity or naturalness. It is a utopian process of intelligent action followed by constant self-questioning, reassessment, revision, and more action. Always negotiated, relational, and changing, fermentation contains an appealing built-in safeguard against hubris.

To be clear, I am not suggesting, like some counterculture guru, that just by making fermented foods we undermine social domination and nurture a more inclusive world. Rather, since it's so apparent that people and social movements think politically through metaphors of good food, I'm offering my own: how would adopting the mindset of fermentation change the way we view the social world, the way we think about food politics?

At the very least it would undermine unhelpful dreams of purity and naturalness. Perhaps it would change the way we relate with one another across seemingly dangerous borders. Certainly it would ask us to abandon the false clarity of moral high grounds and find footing on the harsher slopes of open dialogue. To return to a metaphor used at the beginning of the book, an orientation toward fermentation tells food reformers to begin not by generously inviting others to sit at a table they have already laid according to their vision of "good food," but by courageously inviting others to join a discussion of how the table should be set in the first place.

All this discussion of critical self-questioning and acceptance of ambiguity might sound terribly risky and impractical. Indeed, it may well be more effective to stick with familiar dreams of purity, naturalness, scientific control, perfect health, and national security. In the end, I'm inclined to feel generous toward any effort to change the food system using whatever dream, as long as it strains against injustices in the status quo more than it reinforces them. Nevertheless, I fear that the combat-minded dreams outlined in this history mostly lead back to the mistakes of the past. Perhaps trying a new dream—fermentation or something else—would help, although it too would have to be examined carefully. The important thing is that food movements keep in mind the recurring paradox of efforts to produce "good bread." Whether in their early twentieth-century high-modern aspirations or their late twentieth-century anti-modern guises, they both reflect incisive social critique—desires for purer foods and promises of social improvement—and reinforce social hierarchies by (to hearken back to Diana Vreeland) separating those who dream from those who don't. In a time when open disdain for "unhealthy" eaters and discrimination on the basis of dietary habits grow increasingly acceptable, we might do well to spend more time thinking about how we relate to others through food and less about what exactly to eat.

ACKNOWLEDGMENTS

A long time ago I realized that I wanted to write a book about U.S. bread politics. As someone trained in subjects like Latin American history and anthropology and the political economy of Third World agriculture, however, I had no idea what that might mean. Figuring it out has taken lots of help from many people.

Special thanks go to Melanie DuPuis, Susanne Freidberg, and Julie Guthman. My thoughts about food politics emerged out of numerous conversations with them, and all three offered valuable comments on parts of the book at different stages. I also owe a great debt to Paul Apostolidis, Jennifer Boyden, Rachel Hope Cleves, and Johanna Stoberock. Their critiques of an early version of the manuscript proved to be a turning point in the process of writing this book.

Many other people offered comments, suggestions, support, and inspiration along the way. I'd particularly like to thank Warren Belasco, Charlotte Biltekoff, Carolyn de la Peña, Julia Ireland, Jake Kosek, Heather Paxson, Jason Pribilsky, Gary Rollefson, William Rubel, Nathan Sayre, Lynn Sharp, Kyla Wazana Tompkins, Helen Veit, Dan Vernon, and Robert Weis. Members of several groups provided useful feedback on portions of the book: the BFP Collective; the University of California at Irvine Humanities Research Institute Working Group on Food and Race; the University of California Multicampus Research Program on Food and the Body; the University of Minnesota Agrifood Group; and the Yale Agrarian Studies Seminar.

I'm also grateful to folks who extended a hand in my many far-flung research sites: Jon Davis at La Brea Bakeries; Tom Lehman, Kirk O'Donnell, Tim Sieloff, and especially Tammy Popejoy at the American Institute of Baking; Catherine Stortz-Ripley at the *Chillicothe Constitution-Tribune;* and Monica Bretón Salazar at Grupo

Bimbo. I wrote much of this book at the Colville Street Patisserie in Walla Walla and am grateful to David, Tiffany, and their staff for keeping me going with encouragement and cookies.

At Whitman College, Robin Lewis, Rhadika McCormick, and Justine Pope provided exceptional research assistance. Several generations of students in my "Whitman in the Global Food System" course served as sounding boards for the ideas that became this book. Generous funding from the Dean of Faculty's Office, Abshire Research Scholar Award, Louis B. Perry Research Award, and Robert Y. Fluno Research Fellowship made the project possible. At the Penrose Library, Jen Johnson waved her magic wand and made even the most obscure sources appear almost overnight. Lee Keane came up with a key piece of reference assistance. Finally, my colleagues in the politics department offered unwavering support, even if they secretly wondered why their Latin Americanist was writing a book about white bread.

I'm grateful to Sam Stoloff for seeing something in white bread and to Matt McGowan for helping me turn that something into a book. Matt has been an adept guide to the world of writing and publishing outside academia. Likewise, getting to work with Alexis Rizzuto at Beacon made the final stages of the project pleasurable. She understood the tensions inherent in writing for academic and nonacademic audiences, and knew how to keep me on track with a deft editorial touch.

Finally, I owe a tremendous debt to my family. My parents, Charles R. Strain and Dianne Hanau-Strain, beautifully mixed unqualified enthusiasm with critical feedback. As early civil rights and antiwar activists, they also shared insights into the 1960s and 1970s counterculture. My brother, Daniel Strain, offered a science writer's critical ear, particularly on matters relating to yeast microbiology. My grandmother Ruth F. Strain and uncle Paul F. Strain helped out with Farrell family lore. Carol Blue and Ken Bobrow, my in-laws, also deserve significant credit: I wouldn't have been able to write this book without their willingness to help with child care. And to the "We demand baguettes" crew itself, I send much love and many thanks: Hana and Sam appreciated even my worst bread experiments and endured many absences as I researched this book. Nine-year-old Hana's great questions ended up influencing chapters 1 and 2, while reading "chapter books" aloud to Sam for hours and hours undoubtedly improved my writing.

I dedicate this book to Kate Bobrow-Strain, my companion, bread of my existence, who has walked with me in food politics since Tucson and the days of Red the cow. Thank you for your unstinting support, and for always trying to make me explain myself more clearly.

NOTES

PREFACE

1. Eleanor Bang, "World in a Loaf of Bread," *Independent Woman,* October 1951, 287.

INTRODUCTION. BREAD AND POWER

1. The phrase "the bread question" was widely employed by journalists and pundits in the nineteenth century. Depending on the context, it referred to debates about the production of bread, to literal bread supplies or prices, to the state of food supplies more generally, to cost of living, or to workers' wages. Particularly before the decline of bread consumption in the late twentieth century, bread (as in loaves) and bread (as in sustenance) were so connected that it is sometimes difficult to distinguish between literal and figurative uses.

2. Anna Revedin et al., "Thirty-Thousand-Year-Old Evidence of Plant Food Processing," *Proceedings of the National Association of Science* 44, no. 107 (2010): 18815–19; Biancamaria Aranguren, Roberto Becattini, Marta Mariotti Lippi, and Anna Revedin, "Grinding Flour in Upper Paleolithic Europe (25,000 Years BP)," *Antiquity* 81 (2007): 845–55; Daniel Zohary and Maria Hopf, *Domestication of Plants in the Old World: The Origin and Spread of Cultivated Plants in West Asia, Europe, and the Nile Valley* (Oxford, UK: Oxford University Press, 2000).

3. David Waines, "Cereals, Bread and Society: An Essay on the Staff of Life in Medieval Iraq," *Journal of the Economic and Social History of the Orient* 30, no. 3 (1987): 255–85; Jean Bottéro, André Finet, Bertrand Lafont, Georges Roux, and Antonia Nevill, *Everyday Life in Ancient Mesopotamia* (Baltimore: Johns Hopkins University Press, 2001); Karen Rhea Nemet-Nejat, *Daily Life in Ancient Mesopotamia* (Westport, CT: Greenwood, 1998); Heinrich Eduard Jacob, *Six Thousand Years of Bread: Its Holy and Unholy History* (New York: Skyhorse, 2007); John

Merchant and Joan Alcock, *Bread: A Slice of History* (London: History Press, 2008).

4. I. J. Gelb, "The Ancient Mesopotamian Ration System," *Journal of Near Eastern Studies* 24, no. 3 (1965): 230–43; Rosemary Ellison, "Some Thoughts on the Diet of Mesopotamia from c. 3,000–600 B.C.," *Iraq* 45, no. 1 (1982): 146–50; Kasia Maria Szpakowska, *Daily Life in Ancient Egypt: Recreating Lahun* (Malden, MA: Blackwell, 2008); Jacob, *Six Thousand Years of Bread*; Merchant and Alcock, *Bread*.

5. Christopher Dyer, "Changes in Diet in the Late Middle Ages: The Case of Harvest Workers," *Agricultural History Review* 36, no. 1 (1988): 21–37; Kathy L. Pearson, "Nutrition and the Early-Medieval Diet," *Speculum* 72, no. 1 (1997): 1–32.

6. Fernand Braudel, *The Structures of Everyday Life: The Limits of the Possible; Civilization and Capitalism, 15th–18th Century* (New York: Harper & Row, 1981); League of Nations, "Rural Dietaries in Europe. Annex: Report on Bread," August 26, 1939, Foreign Agricultural Service Correspondence, RG 166, "France 1950–1954," box 152, National Archives II, College Park, MD (hereafter FAS-NA).

7. Eighteenth- and nineteenth-century Americans generally preferred the taste of wheat loaves, but corn, rye, oat, and barley breads often predominated thanks to their lower production costs. Waverley Lewis Root and Richard De Rochemont, *Eating in America: A History* (New York: Ecco, 1981).

8. U.S. bread consumption statistics from "Boost for Bread," *Business Week,* February 28, 1948; Marguerite C. Burke, "Pounds and Percentages," in *Food: The Yearbook of Agriculture, 1959,* ed. United States Department of Agriculture (Washington, DC: U.S. Government Printing Office, 1959); William G. Panschar, *Baking in America*, vol. 1 (Evanston, IL: Northwestern University Press, 1956); Esther F. Phipard, "Changes in the Bread You Buy," in *Crops in Peace and War: The Yearbook of Agriculture, 1950–1951,* ed. United States Department of Agriculture (Washington, DC: U.S. Government Printing Office, 1951); Richard G. Walsh and Bert M. Evans, *Economics of Change in Market Structure, Conduct, and Performance: The Baking Industry, 1947–1958* (Lincoln: University of Nebraska Studies, 1963); M. L. Way and H. B. McCoy, *Establishing a Retail Bakery* (Washington, DC: United States Department of Commerce, 1946); Ronald L. Wirtz, "Grain, Baking, and Sourdough Bread: A Brief Historical Panorama," in *Handbook of Dough Fermentation,* eds. Karel Kulp and Klaus Lorenz (New York: CRC, 2003).

9. Christopher Hibbert, *The Days of the French Revolution* (New York: Morrow, 1980); Darlene Gay Levy and Harriet Branson Applewhite, "Women and Political Revolution in Paris," in *Becoming Visible: Women in European History,* eds. Renate Bridenthal, Susan Mosher

Stuard, and Merry E. Wiesner (Boston: Houghton Mifflin, 1998); Donald Sutherland, *The French Revolution and Empire: The Quest for a Civic Order* (Malden, MA: Blackwell, 2003).

10. Merchant and Alcock, *Bread*.

11. USDA Economic Research Service, "100 Years of Eating in America," February 18, 2010, http://www.ers.usda.gov/Features/Centennial/.

12. Some examples include E. Melanie DuPuis, *Nature's Perfect Food: How Milk Became America's Drink* (New York: New York University Press, 2002); Roger Horowitz, *Putting Meat on the American Table: Taste, Technology, Transformation* (Baltimore: Johns Hopkins University Press, 2006); Sidney W. Mintz, *Sweetness and Power: The Place of Sugar in Modern History* (New York: Viking, 1985); Jeffrey M. Pilcher, *¡Qué Vivan los Tamales!: Food and the Making of Mexican Identity* (Albuquerque: University of New Mexico Press, 1998).

13. Chapters 1 and 2 expand on this idea.

14. Plato, *The Republic* (Cambridge, UK: Cambridge University Press, 2000), section 372a–d.

15. I use the phrase "alternative food movement" with some hesitation. Although it provides a useful shorthand, the label also ascribes a false sense of unity and coherence to what is really a diverse collection of actors and political visions. Writing on the contemporary U.S. alternative food movement has been as diverse as the movement itself. A number of key scholarly analyses shaped my thinking about U.S. food activism: Patricia Allen, *Together at the Table: Sustainability and Sustenance in the American Agrifood System* (University Park: Pennsylvania State University Press, 2004); Patricia Allen, Margaret FitzSimmons, Michael Goodman, and Keith Warner, "Shifting Plates in the Agrifood Landscape: The Tectonics of Alternative Agrifood Initiatives in California," *Journal of Rural Studies* 19, no. 1 (2003): 61–75; Alison Blay-Palmer, *Food Fears: From Industrial to Sustainable Food Systems* (Aldershot, UK: Ashgate, 2008); E. Melanie DuPuis and David Goodman, "Should We Go 'Home' to Eat?: Toward a Reflective Politics of Localism," *Journal of Rural Studies* 21, no. 3 (2005): 359–71; Julie Guthman, *Agrarian Dreams: The Paradox of Organic Farming in California* (Berkeley: University of California Press, 2004); Julie Guthman, "Bringing Good Food to Others: Investigating the Subjects of Alternative Food Practice," *Cultural Geographies* 15, no. 4 (2008): 431–47; Jonathan Murdoch and Mara Miele, "A New Aesthetic of Food? Relational Reflexivity in the 'Alternative' Food Movement," in *Qualities of Food*, eds. Mark Harvey, Andrew McMeekin, and Alan Warde (Manchester, UK: Manchester University Press, 2004); Hugh Campbell, "Breaking New Ground in Food Regime Theory: Corporate Environmentalism, Ecological Feedbacks and the 'Food from Somewhere' Regime?" *Agriculture and Human Values* 26, no. 4

(2009): 309–19; Christie McCullen, "The White Farm Imaginary: How One Farmers Market Refetishizes the Production of Food and Limits Food Politics," in *Food as Communication: Communication as Food*, eds. Janet M. Cramer, Carlnita P. Greene, and Lynn Walters (New York: Peter Lang, 2010); Carolyn de la Peña, *Empty Pleasures: The Story of Artificial Sweeteners from Saccharin to Splenda* (Chapel Hill: University of North Carolina Press, 2010); Richard R. Wilk, *Fast Food/Slow Food: The Cultural Economy of the Global Food System* (Lanham, MD: Altamira, 2006). Important popular accounts that give a sense of the variety of approaches to food activism include David Kamp, *The United States of Arugula: The Sun Dried, Cold Pressed, Dark Roasted, Extra Virgin Story of the American Food Revolution* (New York: Broadway Books, 2007); Sandor Ellix Katz, *The Revolution Will Not Be Microwaved: Inside America's Underground Food Movements* (White River Junction, VT: Chelsea Green, 2006); Michael Pollan, *The Omnivore's Dilemma: A Natural History of Four Meals* (New York: Penguin, 2006); Mark Winne, *Food Rebels, Guerrilla Gardeners, and Smart-Cookin' Mamas: Fighting Back in an Age of Industrial Agriculture* (Boston: Beacon, 2010).

16. Jonathan Fox and Libby Haight, eds., *Subsidizing Inequality: Mexican Corn Policy since Nafta* (Washington, DC: Woodrow Wilson International Center for Scholars, 2010); Gisele Henriques and Raj Patel, *Policy Brief No. 7: Agricultural Trade Liberalization and Mexico* (Oakland, CA: Food First: The Institute for Food and Development Policy, 2003).

17. Kamp, *The United States of Arugula.*

18. Julie Guthman, " 'If They Only Knew': Color Blindness and Universalism in California Alternative Food Institutions," *Professional Geographer* 60, no. 3 (2008): 387–97.

19. This dynamic can sometimes be flipped: the food of one's own group can be seen as "bad," while that of other groups is "good" (i.e., "exotic" or "different"). Although this changes the location of approval/disapproval, it maintains the overarching idea of clear-cut divides between "us" and "them," "good" and "bad." In more theoretical terms, we can think of diet as an arena of Foucaultian biopolitics. Because visions of good food link individual preferences to the overall health of society, straying from the norm has real consequences. We ascribe social virtue to people who share our vision of good food. And when a person or group fails to embrace our dream of good food, it isn't seen as an innocent difference—it represents a potential threat to the health of society. For a reading of Foucault through the lens of diet, see Aaron Bobrow-Strain, "White Bread Bio-politics: Purity, Health, and the Triumph of Industrial Baking," *Cultural Geographies* 15, no. 1 (2008): 19–40.

20. See chapter 3 for an extended discussion of this moment. Also Charles E.

Rosenberg, *The Cholera Years: The United States in 1832, 1849, and 1866* (Chicago: University of Chicago Press, 1987); James C. Whorton, *Crusaders for Fitness: The History of American Health Reformers* (Princeton, NJ: Princeton University Press, 1982).

CHAPTER 1. UNTOUCHED BY HUMAN HANDS

1. Daniel Block, "Purity, Economy, and Social Welfare in the Progressive Era Pure Milk Movement," *Journal for the Study of Food and Society* 3, no. 1 (1999): 20–27; DuPuis, *Nature's Perfect Food*; Susanne Freidberg, *Fresh: A Perishable History* (Cambridge, MA: Belknap Press of Harvard University Press, 2009).

2. James Harvey Young, *Pure Food: Securing the Federal Food and Drugs Act of 1906* (Princeton, NJ: Princeton University Press, 1999); Clayton A. Coppin and Jack C. High, *The Politics of Purity: Harvey Washington Wiley and the Origins of Federal Food Policy* (Ann Arbor: University of Michigan Press, 1999); Lorine Swainston Goodwin, *The Pure Food, Drink, and Drug Crusaders, 1879–1914* (Jefferson, NC: McFarland, 1999); Eric Schlosser, *Fast Food Nation: The Dark Side of the All-American Meal* (Boston: Houghton Mifflin, 2001).

3. Coppin and High, *The Politics of Purity*; Goodwin, *The Pure Food, Drink, and Drug Crusaders*; Young, *Pure Food*.

4. Estimated by comparing Ward Bakery production figures with New York City consumption statistics. New York consumption figures from "Greatest Egg and Bread Eating City," *Olean* (NY) *Evening Times*, August 5, 1910, 3.

5. "Farm Boy's Opportunities," *Iowa Homestead*, June 9, 1910; "Table and Kitchen," *Evening News*, September 18, 1900, 8.

6. Robert H. Wiebe, *The Search for Order, 1877–1920* (Westport, CT: Greenwood, 1980).

7. Ibid.

8. Michael McGerr, *A Fierce Discontent: The Rise and Fall of the Progressive Movement in America, 1870–1920* (Oxford, UK: Oxford University Press, 2005); Wiebe, *The Search for Order*; Steven J. Diner, *A Very Different Age: Americans of the Progressive Era* (New York: Hill & Wang, 1998); Nell Irvin Painter, *Standing at Armageddon: A Grassroots History of the Progressive Era* (New York: Norton, 2008).

9. Wiebe, *The Search for Order*.

10. National Association of Master Bakers, *Proceedings of the Eighteenth Convention of the National Association of Master Bakers* (Chicago: National Association of Master Bakers, 1915). Data on bread production in the preceding paragraphs calculated from Panschar, *Baking in America*; Donald R. Stabile, "Bakery Products," in *Manufacturing: A*

Historiographical and Bibliographical Guide, eds. David O. Whitten and Bessie Emeric Whitten (Westport, CT: Greenwood, 1990); "Flavor of Today's Bread Is Much Better Than Many Critics Are Willing to Admit," *Western Baker,* January 1937, 21–22; "The Story of American Efficiency," *U.S. News,* October 31, 1938; T. E. King, "Largest and Most Wonderful Bakery in the World," *Baker's Helper,* September 1, 1925, 497. On Perry County baking history, see Saxon Lutheran Memorial, *Heritage of Cooking: A Collection of Recipes from East Perry County, Missouri* (Frohna, MO: Saxon Lutheran Memorial, 1965).

11. On the idea of "fresh" food and its role in the industrialization of eating, see Freidberg, *Fresh.*

12. My discussion of the Ward Baking Company draws from Carl Alsberg, *Combination in the American Bread-Baking Industry* (Stanford, CA: Stanford University Press, 1926); the Edward L. Bernays Papers, MSS 12534, "Ward Baking," box 1:401, Library of Congress, Washington, DC; "Big Bread Concern Formed," *New York Times,* April 1, 1909, 1; "The Story of an American Business Success" (advertisement), *New York Times,* November 8, 1911, 5; "$30,000,000 Baking Company Formed," *New York Times,* June 22, 1912, 17; F. C. Lane, "Famous Magnates of the Federal League: R. B. Ward, the Master Baker," *Baseball Magazine,* September 1915, 24–33; J. C. Jenkins, "The Bread We Eat," *National Magazine,* June 1916, 665–83; Stuart Bruce Kaufman, *A Vision of Unity: The History of the Bakery and Confectionery Workers International Union* (Kensington, NY: Bakery, Confectionery, and Tobacco Workers International Union, 1986); Stabile, "Bakery Products"; George S. Ward, "The Public Responsibility of the Baker of Bread," *McClure's,* June 1925, 86–99; "Bread Takes Its Place among Great Industries," *New York Times,* October 11, 1925, 10; "Ask an Inquiry into 'Bread Trust,' " *New York Times,* December 9, 1925, 21; "Government Opens Bread Inquiry Here," *New York Times,* February 9, 1926, 2; "Suit Is Filed to Halt Baking Merger," *New York Times,* February 9, 1926, 1; "Congress Takes up Big Baking Merger," *New York Times,* February 2, 1926, 1; "Baking Concerns Hit Congress," *New York Times,* July 1, 1926, 13; "W. B. Ward Named in $4,260,000 Suit," *New York Times,* February 16, 1929, 13.

13. "Bread Takes Its Place among Great Industries."

14. "Big Bread Concern Formed."

15. Ward, "The Public Responsibility of the Baker of Bread"; Julia M. Sample, MSS. 1801 (1938), Manuscript Division, WPA Federal Writers' Project Collection, Library of Congress, Washington, DC.

16. Quote from Truman Pierson, "A Layman's View of Baker's Bread," *American Baker,* January 26, 1927, 344. On the allure of novel foods in the early twentieth-century American diet, see Freidberg, *Fresh;* Har-

vey A. Levenstein, *Revolution at the Table: The Transformation of the American Diet* (Berkeley: University of California Press, 2003). On widespread fears of declining consumption, see Panschar, *Baking in America;* Phipard, "Changes in the Bread You Buy"; Alfredo de Matteis, *The Human Side of Bread* (New York: n.p., 1936).

17. Burke, "Pounds and Percentages"; L. Wolfe, "The Growth of Bread Production," *Baking Industry,* April 12, 1952, 122. Some of this increase can be accounted for by southerners switching from corn bread to white wheat bread, which also speaks to the modern allure of white bread.

18. Catharine Esther Beecher and Harriet Beecher Stowe, *The American Woman's Home; or, Principles of Domestic Science* (New York: J.B. Ford, 1869), 170, 173.

19. Burton J. Bledstein, *The Culture of Professionalism: The Middle Class and the Development of Higher Education in America* (New York: Norton, 1976). This section also draws from Rima D. Apple, *Perfect Motherhood: Science and Childrearing in America* (New Brunswick, NJ: Rutgers University Press, 2006); Megan J. Elias, *Stir It Up: Home Economics in American Culture* (Philadelphia: University of Pennsylvania Press, 2008); Elizabeth Murphy, "Expertise and Forms of Knowledge in the Government of Families," *Sociological Review* 51, no. 4 (2003): 433–62; Nancy Tomes, "Spreading the Germ Theory: Sanitary Science and Home Economics, 1880–1930," in *Rethinking Home Economics,* eds. S. Stage and V. Vicenti (Ithaca, NY: Cornell University Press, 1997); Nancy Tomes, *The Gospel of Germs: Men, Women, and the Microbe in American Life* (Cambridge, MA: Harvard University Press, 1998); Whorton, *Crusaders for Fitness;* Barbara Ehrenreich and Deirdre English, *For Her Own Good: Two Centuries of the Experts' Advice to Women* (New York: Anchor Books, 2005).

20. "Science in Households," *Chicago Daily Tribune,* October 15, 1891, 6.

21. Ellen Swallow Richards, *Euthenics: The Science of Controllable Environment* (Boston: Whitcomb & Barrows, 1910).

22. Tomes, *The Gospel of Germs;* Suellen M. Hoy, *Chasing Dirt: The American Pursuit of Cleanliness* (New York: Oxford University Press, 1995).

23. Adrian Forty, *Objects of Desire* (New York: Pantheon Books, 1986), 169.

24. W. R. C. Latson, "The Times Answers by Experts: On Health Reform," *Los Angeles Times,* December 23, 1902, A4. Or, as a reader of *Good Housekeeping* insisted, "Take care of the digestive organs and the heart and brain and soul of humanity will as a rule take care of themselves. Improper nourishment, indigestion, and an illy sustained body are factors in crime, while content and prosperity are promoted by a health diet." Harry Douglas, letter to the editor, *Good Housekeeping,* September 1894, 132.

25. Levenstein, *Revolution at the Table*, 86; Whorton, *Crusaders for Fitness*. On the Pure Foods Movement, see Goodwin, *The Pure Food, Drink, and Drug Crusaders*; Young, *Pure Food*.

26. Young, *Pure Food*.

27. Howard Markel and Alexandra Minna Stern, "The Foreignness of Germs: The Persistent Association of Immigrants and Disease in American Society," *Milbank Quarterly* 80, no. 4 (2002): 757–88. See also Nancy Tomes, "The Making of a Germ Panic, Then and Now," *Public Health* 90, no. 2 (2000): 191–99.

28. Jacob A. Riis, *How the Other Half Lives: Studies among the Tenements of New York* (New York: Charles Scribner's Sons, 1890), 172–73.

29. "Bread Does Not Advance," *New York Times*, August 25, 1897; Howard B. Rock, "The Perils of Laissez-Faire: The Aftermath of the New York Bakers' Strike of 1801," *Labor History* 17, no. 3 (1976): 372–87.

30. "A Bread Riot in Newark," *Cedar Rapids Evening News*, July 28, 1903; "Dough Dumped into Gutters by Strikers," *Evening Record*, August 10, 1903, 1; Kaufman, *A Vision of Unity*; Rock, "The Perils of Laissez-Faire"; "$250,00 for Hospital," *New York Times*, November 23, 1925, 23; "Ward Fund Gives Million to Help the Poor," *New York Times*, January 11, 1926, 1. A cynical reader might also note the fact that Ward's most sensational charity donation occurred at almost exactly the same time as the formation of the Ward Food Products Corporation.

31. Michael Williams, "Fletcherizing with Fletcher," *Good Housekeeping*, May 1907, 505.

32. For example, a 1903 domestic advice column presented home-baked bread as self-evidently more sanitary than "dark, dingy cellar bakeries." "Domestic Science," *Chicago Daily Tribune*, September 13, 1903, 53.

33. Quoted in Kaufman, *A Vision of Unity*, 1.

34. Ibid.

35. "Inspectors Find Foul Bakeshops," *Chicago Daily Tribune*, July 3, 1906, 2. This account of the Chicago bakery sanitation movement also draws from "Disease-Breeding Bread," *Chicago Daily Tribune*, December 6, 1894, 6; "Chicago Licensing Bakeries for Sanitation," *New York Evening Post*, June 2, 1895; "Dirty Dough in Bakeries," *Chicago Daily Tribune*, September 14, 1907, 1; "Clean Up the Bakeries," *Chicago Daily Tribune*, September 22, 1907, B4; "Sanitary Inspection," *Chicago Daily Tribune*, January 6, 1907; "City Makes War on Spoiled Food," *Chicago Daily Tribune*, December 9, 1907, 5; "In 1,000 Bakeries Only 30 Get 'O.K.,'" *Chicago Daily Tribune*, May 31, 1908, 2; National Association of Master Bakers, *Proceedings of the Eighteenth Convention of the National Association of Master Bakers*; "Making Daily Bread of Chicago," *Chicago Daily Tribune*, July 11, 1909, E3; "Evans Fights for New Bakers' Law," *Chicago Daily Tribune*, December 11, 1909, 3; "Cellar Bakeries Raided," *Chicago Daily Tribune*, January 14, 1913, 1.

36. "In 1,000 Bakeries Only 30 Get 'O.K.'"

37. *Minutes of the Hearings of the New York State Factory Investigating Committee* (New York: New York State Factory Investigating Committee, 1911); "Bakeshops Menace Health in the City," *New York Times,* November 15, 1911.

38. "Cellar Bakeries Anti-trust Issue," *New York Times,* December 4, 1912, 10.

39. "I Want to Know Where My Bread Comes From!" (advertisement), *Charleston (WV) Daily Mail,* January 11, 1929, 8; "Warning: State Health Authorities Condemn Unwrapped Bread" (advertisement), *Fort Wayne Journal-Gazette,* April 2, 1912, 24.

40. "A Perfect Loaf of Bread" (advertisement), *New York Times,* November 10, 1911; "Clean Bread Has Come to New York" (advertisement), *New York Times,* November 9, 1911, 9; "Our Physician Guards Your Interests" (advertisement), *New York Times,* November 24, 1911, 10; "Behind the Scenes in New York" (advertisement), *The New York Times,* December 1, 1911, 8; "Warning: State Health Authorities Condemn Unwrapped Bread" (advertisement); "Bakeries Here Are Now Models of Cleanliness," *Atlanta Constitution,* November 7, 1914, 9; "The Clean Bakery" (advertisement), *Lima (OH) Times-Democrat,* October 11, 1916; "We Look upon Our Bread Factory as a Civic Institution" (advertisement), *Oakland Tribune,* April 20, 1924, 2-B; "Wholesome Bread Is Healthy" (advertisement), *Emporia (KS) Daily Gazette,* March 25, 1927, 12. See also Harry Barnard, "Sanitation in Bakeries," *American Journal of Public Health* 11, no. 5 (1921): 407–9; Nels August Bengston and Donee Griffith, *The Wheat Industry, for Use in Schools* (New York: Macmillan, 1915).

41. "The Clean Bakery" (advertisement). Examples of widespread public interest in sanitary bread can be found in numerous letters received by Pure Foods crusader Harvey W. Wiley (Harvey W. Wiley Papers, MSS 416, "General Correspondence," box 163, Library of Congress, Washington, DC) as well as in the messages of praise from public officials collected by the Ward Baking Company for its seventy-fifth anniversary celebration (Bernays Papers, MSS 12534, "Ward Baking," box 1:401).

42. Helen Christine Bennet, "Cleaning up the American City," *American Magazine,* September 1913, 48.

43. "Bakeries in Ogden Are Praised by Expert," *Ogden (UT) Standard,* July 2, 1915, 6.

44. "Some Potent Curatives and Preventives of Disease," *Chautauquan,* March 1895, 763–70.

45. "Disease-Breeding Bread"; Ellen Richards, *The Chemistry of Cooking and Cleaning: A Manual for Housekeepers* (Boston: Estes & Lauriat, 1882).

46. J. Thompson Gill, *The Complete Bread, Cake, and Cracker Baker* (Chicago: J. Thompson Gill, 1881), 27.

47. Quoted in "Uncooked Foods," *Good Housekeeping*, July 1913, 98.

48. C. H. Routh, *Infant Feeding and Its Influences on Life; or, The Causes of Infant Mortality* (New York: William Wood, 1879); A. Cressy Morrison, *The Baking Powder Controversy* (New York: American Baking Powder Association, 1907).

49. Reprinted in "School Lunches," *Fitchburg (MA) Daily Sentinel,* January 22, 1916, 7.

50. "On Filthy Food War Is Declared," *Atlanta Constitution,* August 26, 1909, 2.

51. Harry Barnard, "The One Objection to Baker's Bread," *Good Housekeeping,* May 1913, 694; Harvey Wiley, "Returns from the *Good Housekeeping* Food and Drug Ballot," *Good Housekeeping,* March 1913, 398. For an example of the many newspapers reprinting the *Journal of the American Medical Association*'s statement, see "Unwrapped Bread" (advertisement), *Oshkosh Daily Northwestern,* November 28, 1914, 7.

52. For examples of the struggle over bread wrapping, see "Asheville to Have Wrapped Bread," *Lumberton (NC) Robesonian,* March 25, 1915, 7; Mrs. Harvey Wiley, "Why Bread Should Be Wrapped," *Syracuse Herald,* April 10, 1912; "Would Buy Wrapped Bread," *Washington Post,* March 2, 1914, 4; "Assert Bread Wrapping Is Trust Scheme," *San Antonio Light,* July 31, 1914, 5; "Warning: State Health Authorities Condemn Unwrapped Bread" (advertisement); "State Authorities Condemn Unwrapped Bread" (advertisement), *Fort Wayne Sentinel,* April 3, 1911; "Read What the *Ladies Home Journal* Says about Unwrapped Bread" (advertisement), *Fort Wayne Sentinel,* June 3, 1919; "Bread Wrapping: Its History and Development," *Baking Industry,* August 24, 1968, 51–56.

53. "State Authorities Condemn Unwrapped Bread" (advertisement).

54. These messages are collected in Bernays Papers, MSS 12534, "Ward Baking," box 1:401.

55. Calculated from Department of the Census, United States Department of Commerce, *Biennial Census of Manufacturing* (Washington, DC: U.S. Government Printing Office, 1927 and 1935). See also Panschar, *Baking in America.*

56. "Modern Bread-Baking: The Loaf Untouched by Human Hands in the Process of Making," *Scientific American,* March 11, 1916, 282–83; "The Butter-Krust Bread Girl Keeps Being a Powerful Magnet," *New Castle (PA) News,* October 6, 1914, 11; "Bakeries Here Are Now Models of Cleanliness."

57. Richards, *The Chemistry of Cooking and Cleaning,* 45.

58. On food consumption and social hierarchy, see Pierre Bourdieu, *Distinc-*

tion: A Social Critique of the Judgment of Taste (Cambridge, MA: Harvard University Press, 2007).

59. For an accessible overview of key issues raised here, see *Grist*'s forum on food safety reform: http://www.grist.org/article/food-2010–11–05-food-safety-modernization-act.

60. Schlosser, *Fast Food Nation*.

61. Elysa Batista, "Modern-Day Slavery Was Focus of Group's Tour of Immokalee," *Naples News* website, March 17, 2009, http://www.naplesnews.com/news/2009/mar/04/modern-day-slavery-was-focus-groups-tour-immokalee/.

62. "If you're not worried, you should be." Douglass argues, "Think about where these illegals work, like chicken factories, fast-food restaurants, and other places where they handle your food." William Campbell Douglass, "8 Ways Illegal Immigrants Are Making You Sick," *The Douglass Report,* February 14, 2008, http://douglassreport.com. See also William Campbell Douglass, "Put Down That Drumstick," *The Douglass Report,* n.d., http://douglassreport.com; Lourdes Gouveia and Arunas Juska, "Taming Nature, Taming Workers: Constructing the Separation between Meat Consumption and Meat Production in the U.S.," *Sociologia Ruralis* 42, no. 4 (2000): 370–90.

CHAPTER 2. THE INVENTION OF SLICED BREAD

1. Julia Moskin, "Taking the Artisan out of Artisanal," *New York Times,* March 10, 2004, F1.

2. Rachel Dowd, "Dough Pros Rise Up," *Daily Variety,* March 10, 2006, V1. For more on La Brea's development, see the company's webpage and Moskin, "Taking the Artisan out of Artisanal"; L. Joshua Sosland, "Prodigious Success," *Milling and Baking News,* March 2007.

3. My account of the "invention of sliced bread" draws from "Sliced Bread Is Made Here: Chillicothe Baking Co. the First Bakers in the World to Sell This Product to the Public," *Chillicothe (MO) Constitution-Tribune,* July 6, 1928, 1; "Frank Bench Put First Sliced Bread on Market in Chillicothe," *Chillicothe Constitution-Tribune,* January 13, 1939, 1; "Sliced Bread on the Market Today," *Chillicothe Constitution-Tribune,* March 9, 1943, 1; Catherine Storz-Ripley, "A Slice of History," *Chillicothe Constitution-Tribune,* August 21, 2003, 1–2; J.M. Albright, "How the Bakers and Equipment Manufacturers Cooperated to Build Better Bread Baking Machinery," *Baking Industry,* April 12, 1952; editorial, *Baker's Helper,* September 28, 1928, 57.

4. "Sliced Bread Is Made Here."

5. Peter Pirrie, "What the Engineers Say about Sliced Bread," *Bakers' Weekly,* October 5, 1929, 70; Bernard Kilgore, "Sliced," *Today,* Sep-

tember 5, 1936, 15; H. A. Haring, "The Baker Slices His Bread and Cuts a Melon," *Canadian Baker & Confectioner,* September 1930, 23–24; Gordon Darnell, "Darnell Talks on Sliced Bread," *Western Baker,* November 1929, 9–10; "Comments on Sliced Bread," *National Grocers Bulletin,* September 19, 1929, 62; editorial.

6. W. H. Colson, "Building by Slicing," *Bakers' Weekly,* August 8, 1931, 43–44.

7. Kilgore, "Sliced."

8. Haring, "The Baker Slices His Bread and Cuts a Melon"; Darnell, "Darnell Talks on Sliced Bread"; Colson, "Building by Slicing"; "Comments on Sliced Bread."

9. Haring, "The Baker Slices His Bread and Cuts a Melon," 23.

10. Darnell, "Darnell Talks on Sliced Bread"; "Bread Softness vs. Flavor," *Baker's Digest,* April 17, 1953; "Consumers Prefer Home Baked Taste in Bread, Institute Study Shows," *Food Field Reporter,* January 19, 1948.

11. Victor Marx, "A New Development in Sliced Bread," *Baker's Helper,* September 1929, 60–61.

12. Christina Cogdell, *Eugenic Design: Streamlining America in the 1930s* (Philadelphia: University of Pennsylvania Press, 2004), 108.

13. "Skinny Bread Here to Stay," *Hagerstown (MD) Daily Mail,* April 22, 1937, 11; "It's Smart Because It's Streamlined" (advertisement), *Dunkirk (NY) Evening Observer,* August 11, 1937, 14; "Look for the Streamline Wrapped Bread Products" (advertisement), *Charleston Gazette,* September 5, 1937, 2. Thanks go to John F. Varty for suggesting this connection between industrial bread and modern design. John F. Varty, "On Wonder: Why Mass-Produced Bread Looks a Little Like Bauhaus Furniture" (paper presented at the Society for the History of Technology, Minneapolis, November 3–6, 2005).

14. "1939 Gasco Food Institute Opens Three Day Affair," *Zanesville (OH) Signal,* October 19, 1938, 6.

15. In the 1890s, only the Bible sold more copies than *Looking Backward.* Edward Bellamy, *Looking Backward, 2000–1887* (Boston: Bedford Books of St. Martin's Press, 1995); Jean Pfaelzer, *The Utopian Novel in America, 1886–1899: The Politics of Form* (Pittsburgh: University of Pittsburgh Press, 1988).

16. Beecher and Stowe, *The American Woman's Home,* 131.

17. Ibid., 134.

18. Mary D. Warren, "Science of Oven Management," *Ladies' Home Journal,* May 1923, 150–51.

19. Bengston and Griffith, *The Wheat Industry,* 184.

20. L. A. Rumsey, "Progress of Education in Making Bread," *Baking Technology,* April 12, 1952, 126. Also see the American Institute of Baking's account of its history: www.aibonline.org/about/history/.

21. National Association of Master Bakers, *Proceedings of the Eighteenth Convention of the National Association of Master Bakers;* National Association of Master Bakers, *Proceedings of the Nineteenth Convention of the National Association of Master Bakers* (Salt Lake City: National Association of Master Bakers, 1916).

22. National Association of Master Bakers, *Proceedings of the Eighteenth Convention of the National Association of Master Bakers,* 22.

23. H. W. Zinmaster, "The 10 Cent Loaf" (paper presented at the the the Nineteenth Convention of the National Association of Master Bakers, Salt Lake City, August 7–11, 1916), 58.

24. "As Mother Used to Make It," *New York Times,* July 24, 1904, SM9.

25. "How Illinois Farm Homemakers Have Made Adjustments to Present Conditions," *Journal of Home Economics* 24, no. 3 (1932): 240–43; May Van Asdale and May Monroe, "Some Other Experiments on the Comparative Cost of Homemade and Baker's Bread," *Journal of Home Economics* 8, no. 7 (1916): 380–83; David Samuel Snedden, *Vocational Home-making Education: Illustrative Projects* (New York: Teachers College of Columbia University Press, 1921); Frances Stern and Gertrude T. Spitz, *Food for the Worker* (Boston: Whitcomb & Barrows, 1917); Panschar, *Baking in America.*

26. "The Butter-Krust Bread Girl Keeps Being a Powerful Magnet."

27. Mrs. Alice Norton, "Bread Is Still the Test," *Des Moines News,* February 1, 1915, 5.

28. Marx, "A New Development in Sliced Bread"; Charles Oliver, "Building a Loaf to Slice," *Northwestern Miller and American Baker,* June 25, 1930.

29. For an example discussing white milk, see DuPuis, *Nature's Perfect Food.*

30. Woods Hutchinson, "The Conduct of the Physical Life," *American Magazine,* February 1913, 94–99. On the social history of white and whitewash, see Forty, *Objects of Desire;* Mark Wigley, *White Walls, Designer Dresses: The Fashioning of Modern Architecture* (Cambridge, MA: MIT Press, 1995).

31. Alfred Watterson McCann, *The Science of Eating: How to Insure Stamina, Endurance, Vigor, Strength and Health in Infancy, Youth and Age* (New York: Truth, 1921), 398.

32. "Peroxide Also Bleaches Cereals," *Scientific American,* August 1929, 183.

33. Harvey Wiley, "Fooling with Flour: The Nation's Bread Is in Danger," *Good Housekeeping,* January 1914, 118–19; Harvey Wiley, "The End of the Bleached Flour Case," *Good Housekeeping,* June 1914, 832; Harvey Wiley, "Our Wheaten and Breakfast Foods," *Good Housekeeping,* March 1913, 393–94; Wiley Papers, MSS 416, "Bleached Flour," boxes 115, 129, 132, 199.

34. "USDA Notice of Judgment No. 2549, Supplement to Notice of Judgment No. 722, Alleged Adulteration and Misbranding of Bleached Flour," October 18, 1913, in Wiley Papers, MSS 416, "Bleached Flour Case," box 199.

35. Ibid.; United States of America v. Lexington Mill & Elevator Company, 232 U.S. 399 (1914).

36. *Lexington Mill & Elevator Company.*

37. Ibid. On the ruling's legacy, see Kirsten S. Beaudoin, "Comment: On Tonight's Menu: Toasted Cornbread with Firefly Genes? Adapting Food Labelling Law to Consumer Protection Needs in the Biotech Century," *Marquette Law Review* (Fall 1999): 237–78; Peter Burton Hutt, "The Dietary Supplement Health and Education Act: Regulation at a Crossroads: Article: FDA Statutory Authority to Regulate the Safety of Dietary Supplements," *American Journal of Law and Medicine* (June 22, 2005): 155–74; James T. O'Reilly, "Losing Deference in the FDA's Second Century: Judicial Review, Politics, and a Diminished Legacy of Expertise," *Cornell Law Review* (July 2008): 939–79.

38. Harvey W. Wiley to Mr. V. L. Clark, March 31, 1922, in Wiley Papers, MSS 416, "Bleached Flour Case," box 199.

39. Ibid.; Harvey W. Wiley to Hon. John H. Smithwick, March 2, 1921, in Wiley Papers, MSS 416, "Bleached Flour Case," box 199; Wiley, "Fooling with Flour"; Wiley, "The End of the Bleached Flour Case," 832.

40. Harvey W. Wiley to Hon. John H. Smithwick, March 2, 1921.

41. "Enzyme Bleaching Flour," *Scientific American,* May 1930, 408.

42. Harvey W. Wiley to Hon. John H. Smithwick, March 2, 1921.

43. William J. Orchard, "The John C. Baker Do-Maker Process," *Baking Industry,* April 23, 1953, 42.

44. "Continuous Mixed Bread Launched in Southeastern New England," *Bakers' Weekly,* April 11, 1955, 32; Orchard, "The John C. Baker Do-Maker Process"; "Baldridge's Introduces Do-Maker to Texas," *Southwestern Baker,* October 1959, 25; Thomas Spooner, "Continuous Mixing," *Modern Miller and Baker News,* October 31, 1959, 32; Hugh Parker, "Up-to-the-Minute Report on the John C. Baker Continuous Do-Maker," n.d., Ruth Emerson Library, American Institute of Baking, Manhattan, Kansas; K. L. Fortmann, "Technology of Continuous Dough Processing," *Cereal Science Today,* December 1959, 290–92.

45. USDA Economic Research Service, *Adoption of the Continuous Mix Process in Bread Baking (Ers-329)* (Washington, DC: USDA, January 1967).

46. "Continuous Mixed Bread Launched in Southeastern New England"; Parker, "Up-to-the-Minute Report on the John C. Baker Continuous Do-Maker."

47. These bakers, for example, worried that the industry's emphasis on bread's appearance and obsession with speed would eventually backfire: M. A. Gray, "Launching a Counter Offensive against Declining Consumption," *Northwestern Miller and American Baker*, February 5, 1936, 1; William Owen, "Flavor—The Lacking Element in Modern Bread," *New South Baker*, April 1938, 15–30.

48. James E. McWilliams, *Just Food: Where Locavores Get It Wrong and How We Can Truly Eat Responsibly* (New York: Little, Brown, 2009). See also Robert Paarlberg, *Food Politics: What Everyone Needs to Know* (New York: Oxford University Press, 2010).

49. Ruth Schwartz Cowan, *More Work for Mother: The Ironies of Household Technology from the Open Hearth to the Microwave* (New York: Basic Books, 1983).

50. For example, "Members Urge That Citizens Patronize Home Industries and Services," *New Castle News*, March 14, 1929, 14; "Factory Made Bread vs. Home Bakery Bread: The Bread Factories Reap Where They Sow Not" (advertisement), *Spirit Lake* (IA) *Beacon* , June 18, 1931, 1.

51. "White Bread: Criminals Are Made by the Food They Eat as Children," *New York Evening Graphic Magazine*, June 1, 1929.

CHAPTER 3. THE STAFF OF DEATH

1. Sarah W. Staber, "Christian Vande Velde's Secret?" *VeloNews*, May 11, 2009, 1–2; Vanessa Gregory, "How a Gluten-Free Diet Powers On the Best Cycling Teams in the World—and How It Can Help You Perform Better and Recover Faster," *Men's Journal*, March 2010, 1–2.

2. Gregory, "How a Gluten-Free Diet Powers On the Best Cycling Teams in the World."

3. Packaged Facts, *The Gluten-Free Food and Beverage Market: Trends and Developments Worldwide* (Rockville, MD: Packaged Facts, 2009); Caroline Scott-Thomas, "Gluten-Free Trend Could Fall Like 'a House of Cards,'" FoodNavigator-USA.com, 2010, http://www.foodnavigator-usa.com/Financial-Industry/Gluten-free-trend-could-fall-like-a-house-of-cards.

4. Information on celiac disease is drawn from R. J. Presutti, J. R. Cangemi, H. D. Cassidy, and D. A. Hill, "Celiac Disease," *American Family Physician* 76, no. 12 (2007): 1795–1802. See also "The Squishy Science of Food Allergies," *New York Times*, May 16, 2010; Gina Kolata, "Doubt Is Cast on Many Reports of Food Allergies," *New York Times*, May 11, 2010. My thinking on this topic has been shaped by the work of several authors writing about the cultural politics of health: Marc Chrysanthou, "Transparency and Selfhood: Utopia and the Informed Body," *Social Science and Medicine* 54, no. 3 (2002): 469–79; Mark Jackson,

Allergy: The History of a Modern Malady (London: Reaktion, 2006); Ann Kerr, Brian Woods, Sarah Nettleton, and Roger Burrows, "Testing for Food Intolerance: New Markets in the Age of Biocapital," *BioSocieties* 4 (2009): 3–24; Sarah Nettleton, Brian Woods, Roger Burrows, and Ann Kerr, "Food Allergy and Food Intolerance: Towards a Sociological Agenda," *Health* (London) 13, no. 6 (2009): 647–64.

5. See, for example, Chrysanthou, "Transparency and Selfhood"; E. Melanie DuPuis and Julie Guthman, "Embodying Neoliberalism: Economy, Culture, and the Politics of Fat," *Environment and Planning D: Society and Space* 24, no. 3 (2006): 427–48.

6. The phrase "think outside the celiac box" comes from Allison St. Sure, "Think Outside the Celiac Box," *Sure Foods Living*, April 14, 2009, http://surefoodsliving.com/2009/04/think-outside-the-celiac-box/. Another author refers to the "celiac iceberg," arguing that celiac disease is just the most visible form of a much more widespread problem: Sayer Ji, "The Dark Side of Wheat: New Perspectives on Celiac Disease and Wheat Intolerance," July 7, 2009, *GreenMedInfo*, http://www.greenmedinfo.com/page/dark-side-wheat-new-perspectives-celiac-disease-wheat-intolerance-sayer-ji.

7. Kerr et al., "Testing for Food Intolerance."

8. See Jackson, *Allergy;* Nettleton et al., "Food Allergy and Food Intolerance."

9. The Weston A. Price Foundation (http://westonaprice.org) is a key source for this kind of analysis.

10. Some natural foods proponents contend that people with celiac or gluten intolerance are better able to tolerate bread made with slow sourdough fermentation. One 2004 study is often cited in support of this theory: M. De Angelis, R. Di Cagno, S. Auricchio, L. Greco, C. Clarke, M. De Vincenzi, C. Giovannini, M. D'Archivio, F. Landolfo, G. Parrilli, F. Minervini, E. Arendt , and M. Gobbetti, "Sourdough Bread Made from Wheat and Nontoxic Flours and Started with Selected Lactobacilli Is Tolerated in Celiac Sprue Patients," *Applied and Environmental Microbiology* 70, no. 2 (2004): 1088–96.

11. In the same way, gluten-free proponents also drew energy from very real concerns about the U.S. health care system. It made sense to preemptively defend your body by going gluten free, they argued, because mainstream medicine was too conservative and narrow minded to perceive the silent damages of a modern diet. Under pressure from insurance companies to speed through patients, even doctors who cared couldn't take the time for the long, slow diagnosis process needed to identify low-grade chronic food intolerances.

12. I'm indebted to Melanie DuPuis for suggesting the phrase "Not in my body."

13. Thomas Tryon, *The Way to Health, Long Life and Happiness; or, A Discourse of Temperance and the Particular Nature of All Things Requisit for the Life of Man* (London: A. Sowle, 1683); Plato, *The Republic.*

14. C.B. Morrison, "Some Anti-fat Breads," *Baking Technology,* October 1924, 304–6.

15. The "graham cracker" was invented by Graham's followers. Its unleavened form draws inspiration from Graham's collaborator William Alcott, who opposed the use of yeast. In my discussion of Graham and his time, I draw gratefully on the following secondary sources: Catherine L. Albanese, *Nature Religion in America: From the Algonkian Indians to the New Age* (Chicago: University of Chicago Press, 1990); Ruth C. Engs, *Clean Living Movements: American Cycles of Health Reform* (Westport, CT: Praeger, 2000); R. Marie Griffith, *Born Again Bodies: Flesh and Spirit in American Christianity* (Berkeley: University of California Press, 2004); Daniel Walker Howe, *What Hath God Wrought: The Transformation of America, 1815–1848* (New York: Oxford University Press, 2007); Karen Iacobbo and Michael Iacobbo, *Vegetarian America: A History* (Westport, CT: Praeger, 2004); Stephen Nissenbaum, *Sex, Diet, and Debility in Jacksonian America: Sylvester Graham and Health Reform* (Westport, CT: Greenwood, 1980); Kyla Wazana Tompkins, *Racial Indigestion: Eating Bodies in the Nineteenth Century* (New York: New York University Press, forthcoming); James C. Whorton, *Inner Hygiene: Constipation and the Pursuit of Health in Modern Society* (Oxford, UK: Oxford University Press, 2000); James C. Whorton, *Nature Cures: The History of Alternative Medicine in America* (Oxford, UK: Oxford University Press, 2002).

16. Albanese, *Nature Religion in America.*

17. Quoted in Whorton, *Nature Cures,* 87.

18. Sylvester Graham, *Lecture to Young Men on Chastity* (Boston: George W. Light, 1838), 194.

19. The following paragraphs draw on Rosenberg, *The Cholera Years.*

20. Albanese, *Nature Religion in America,* 126.

21. Sylvester Graham, *Treatise on Bread and Bread Making* (Boston: Light & Stearns, 1837), 40.

22. Ibid., 34.

23. Louisa May Alcott, "Transcendental Wild Oats," in *Bronson Alcott's Fruitlands,* eds. Clara Endicott Sears and Louisa May Alcott (Boston: Houghton Mifflin, 1915).

24. Sarah Josepha Hale, *The Good Housekeeper* (Boston: Weeks & Jordon, 1839), 17.

25. "Vegetarian Festival," *New York Daily Times,* September 5, 1853, 1; "College Rebellions," *New York Daily Times,* January 8, 1854, 4.

26. "Vegetarian Festival."

27. Albanese, *Nature Religion in America,* 117.

28. "Quackery, Deceptics, and Humbug of the Age," *Wisconsin Herald and Grant County Advertiser,* September 20, 1845, 1; "Humor," *Chicago Daily Tribune,* January 20, 1875, 3.

29. Quoted in Iacobbo and Iacobbo, *Vegetarian America,* 54.

30. Reprinted in William Mathews, *Hours with Men and Books* (Chicago: S. C. Griggs, 1877).

31. Iacobbo and Iacobbo, *Vegetarian America;* Richard W. Schwarz, *John Harvey Kellogg, M.D.: Pioneering Health Reformer* (Hagerstown, MD: Review and Herald, 2006). On the connection to 1960s counterculture, see Warren James Belasco, *Appetite for Change: How the Counterculture Took On the Food Industry* (Ithaca, NY: Cornell University Press, 2007).

32. Tompkins, *Racial Indigestion.*

33. Dugan's Baking Company, *Dugan's Fiftieth Anniversary* (Brooklyn, NY: Dugan's Baking Company, 1953).

34. Little has been written on McCann's food crusades, although several books address his involvement in debates about evolution and creationism. This section draws primarily on his newspaper columns and books, including Alfred Watterson McCann, *The Science of Keeping Young* (New York: George H. Doran, 1926); Alfred Watterson McCann, *Starving America* (Cleveland: F. M. Barton, 1913); McCann, *The Science of Eating.* Also "Medicine Man McCann," *Time,* January 14, 1924.

35. McCann, *The Science of Eating,* 203.

36. McCann, *Starving America,* 64.

37. Quoted in Harvey A. Levenstein, *Paradox of Plenty: A Social History of Eating in Modern America* (Berkeley: University of California Press, 2003), 13.

38. McCann, *The Science of Eating.*

39. My discussion of MacFadden and Physical Culture draws gratefully on these secondary sources: Susan Currell, "Eugenic Decline and Recovery in Self-Improvement Literature of the Thirties," in *Popular Eugenics: National Efficiency and American Mass Culture in the 1930s,* eds. Susan Currell and Christina Cogdell (Athens: Ohio University Press, 2006); Robert Ernst, *Weakness Is a Crime: The Life of Bernarr Macfadden* (Syracuse, NY: Syracuse University Press, 1991); Griffith, *Born Again Bodies;* Carolyn de la Peña, *The Body Electric: How Strange Machines Built the Modern American* (New York: New York University Press, 2003). See also www.bernarrmacfadden.com.

40. Bernarr MacFadden, *Strength from Eating: How and What to Eat and Drink to Develop the Highest Degree of Health and Strength* (New York: Physical Culture Publishing, 1901), 133.

41. Bernarr MacFadden, *Vitality Supreme* (New York: Physical Culture Publishing, 1915), 139.

42. Griffith, *Born Again Bodies.*

43. Albert Edward Wiggam, *The Fruit of the Family Tree* (Indianapolis: Bobbs-Merrill, 1924), 4.

44. On the eugenics movement in the United States, see Edwin Black, *War against the Weak: America's Campaign to Create a Master Race* (New York: Four Walls Eight Windows, 2003); Elof Axel Carlson, *The Unfit: A History of a Bad Idea* (Cold Spring Harbor, NY: Cold Spring Harbor Laboratory Press, 2001); Susan Currell and Christina Cogdell, *Popular Eugenics: National Efficiency and American Mass Culture in the 1930s* (Athens: Ohio University Press, 2006).

45. Currell and Cogdell, *Popular Eugenics.*

46. B. G. Jeffries, *The Science of Eugenics: A Guide to Purity and Physical Manhood* (Naperville, IL: J. L. Nichols, 1920), 6.

47. Quoted in Currell, "Eugenic Decline and Recovery in Self-Improvement Literature of the Thirties," 49.

48. Paul Bowman Popenoe, *Modern Marriage: A Handbook* (New York: Macmillan, 1925).

49. Charles F. Collin, letter to the editor, *Physical Culture* 23 (January 1910): 100.

50. Griffith, *Born Again Bodies,* 117. In formulating this idea, MacFadden took euthenics—a popular alternative to eugenics typically associated with the feminine realm of home economics whose proponents believed in the possibility of racial betterment through education and environmental manipulation—and gave it a macho spin.

51. Woods Hutchinson, "The Color Line in Foods," *American Magazine,* March 1913, 86.

52. Woods Hutchinson, "Some Diet Delusions," *McClure's,* April 1906; "Why Not Eat What You Like?" *Los Angeles Times,* May 6, 1906; "Bread Eaters Lead the World" (advertisement), *Bedford (IA) Free Press,* July 6, 1915.

53. As one man remembered in an interview with the UCLA Oral History Program, "[During the 1920s,] my mother would give me sandwiches made on rye bread. And the kids would make fun of me . . . because they would be eating their sandwiches on white bread, on what we called *kvachehdikeh,* soft white bread. But my mother was a Jewish woman; she would go to the Varshehveh Bakery on Brooklyn Avenue and get good Jewish rye bread. And I remember feeling ashamed, somehow, that I was eating rye bread and the other kids weren't." Interview with Fred Okrand, conducted by Michael S. Balter, February–December 1982, UCLA Oral History Program, http://oralhistory.library.ucla.edu/Browse .do?descCvPk=27430. See also Anzia Yezierska, *Bread Givers, a Novel: A Struggle between a Father of the Old World and a Daughter of the New* (New York: Persea Books, 1975); Anzia Yezierska, *Hungry Hearts* (Boston: Houghton Mifflin, 1920).

54. Woods Hutchinson, "The Joy of Eating," *Good Housekeeping,* May 1913, 668–74.

55. Ibid.

56. Logan Glendening, "Clean Bill of Health Given to White Bread," *Simpson's Daily Leader-Times,* February 10, 1931, 4.

57. Ibid. Statements against white bread are from Louis A. Rumsey, *Resume of Statements against White Bread* (Manhattan, KS: American Institute of Baking, 1927).

58. Rumsey, *Resume of Statements against White Bread.*

59. All quotes from ibid.

60. Philip M. Lovell, "Care of the Body: Thirtieth Anniversary Column," *Los Angeles Times,* January 20, 1929, H24–32.

61. Calculated from United States Department of Commerce, *Biennial Census of Manufacturing.*

62. These cartoons can be viewed at the Ruth Emerson Library of the American Institute of Baking in Manhattan, KS.

63. H. C. Sherman to A. F. Woods and Marked-up Draft of the Statement, April 21, 1930, Records of the Office of the Secretary of Agriculture, General Correspondence, 1906–1976, RG 16, "1930," box 1486, National Archives II, College Park, Md. (hereafter USDA-NA). Except where specifically cited, I have constructed this story based on examination of correspondence, affidavits, drafts of the statement, and marginalia on drafts of the statement found in "1930," box 1486, USDA-NA.

64. E. V. McCollum, "The Real Truth," *Everybody's Health* 15, no. 5 (1930): 12–13.

65. "Bread: A Wholesome Food (Final Draft)," May 1930, "1930," box 1486, USDA-NA.

66. R. Adams Dutcher to A. F. Woods, April 23, 1930, "1930," box 1486, USDA-NA.

67. Henry Stude to A. F. Woods and Enclosed Newspaper Clippings, June 7, 1930, "1930," box 1486, USDA-NA.

68. This specific version of the complaint adapted from http://www.gluten freesociety.org/gluten-free-testimonials/.

CHAPTER 4. VITAMIN BREAD BOOT CAMP

1. Rod Dreher, *Crunchy Cons: The New Conservative Counterculture and Its Return to Roots* (New York: Three Rivers, 2006).

2. Although the title "America's most influential farmer" is widely used in conjunction with Salatin's name in print and on the web, it is difficult to discern the honorific's original source.

3. Michael Pollan, "An Open Letter to the Next Farmer-in-Chief," *New York Times,* October 12, 2008, MM62.

4. Mary MacVean, "Victory Gardens Sprout Up Again," *Los Angeles Times,* January 10, 2009, http://www.latimes.com/features/la-hm-victory10 –2009jan10,0,5210624.story; Eat Local Northwest blog, January 10, 2008, http://eatlocal.wordpress.com/2008/01/10/local-ish-lentils.

5. Charlotte Biltekoff, "The Terror Within: Obesity in Post 9/11 U.S. Life," *American Studies* 48 (2008): 5–30.

6. David F. Smith, "Nutrition Science and the Two World Wars," in *Nutrition in Britain: Science, Scientists, and Politics in the Twentieth Century,* ed. David F. Smith (London: Routledge, 1997).

7. "Draft Officials Reject 380,000," *Los Angeles Times,* May 10, 1941, 10; "How Serious Is Draft Rejection Rate in Waterloo?" *Waterloo (IA) Daily Courier,* April 11, 1941, 4; "Plan to Rebuild 20 Pct. of Men Unfit for Draft," *Chicago Daily Tribune,* October 11, 1941, 8; W.H. Sebrell, "Urgent Problems in Nutrition for National Betterment," *American Journal of Public Health* 32 (1942): 15–20.

8. "Plan to Rebuild 20 Pct. of Men Unfit for Draft"; Sebrell, "Urgent Problems in Nutrition for National Betterment."

9. Margaret G. Reid, *Food for People* (New York: J. Wiley & Sons, 1943); Sebrell, "Urgent Problems in Nutrition for National Betterment"; H.D. Kruse, "The Ocular Manifestations of Avitaminosis A, with Special Consideration of the Detection of Early Changes by Biomicroscopy," *Public Health Reports* 56 (1941): 1301–24.

10. Robert R. Williams Papers, MSS 47241, "Diaries," box 1, "Enriched Foodstuff," box 8, and "Enrichment Promotion," box 11, Library of Congress, Washington, DC (hereafter Williams-LOC).

11. Stanton Meyer, "The Whiter Your Bread, the Sooner You're Dead," *Plans and Pointers,* September 1941, 8–9.

12. "U.S. Army May Eat Bread Enriched with Morale Vitamin," *Science News Letter,* November 2, 1940, 277; "A Bread Revolution," *Science News Letter,* January 11, 1941, 26–27; R.M. Wilder, "Hitler's Secret Weapon Is Depriving People of Vitamins," *Science News Letter,* April 12, 1941, 231.

13. Clive M. McCay, "Bread of the Future," in *Food in War and in Peace: Consolidated Report of the New York State Joint Legislative Committee on Nutrition* (Albany: New York State Legislative Documents, 1944), 180.

14. Along with primary sources cited individually, this section draws on M. Ackerman, "The Nutritional Enrichment of Flour and Bread: Technological Fix of Half-Baked Solution?" in *The Technological Fix: How People Use Technology to Create and Solve Problems,* ed. L. Rosner (London: Routledge, 2004); Youngmee K. Park, Margaret A. McDowell, Eric Hanson, and Elizabeth A. Yetley, "History of Cereal-Grain Product Fortification in the United States," *Nutrition Today* 36, no. 3 (2001); R.C. Sherwood, "Accomplishments in Cereal Fortification," *American*

Journal of Public Health 33, no. 5 (1943): 526–32; R.M. Wilder and Robert R. Williams, *Enrichment of Flour and Bread: A History of the Movement* (Washington, DC: National Research Council, 1944).

15. Extraction rate is the proportion of the whole wheat berry retained in flour after the milling process. True whole wheat has an extraction rate of 100 percent. In the United States, white flour has an extraction rate of around 72 percent. Increasing extraction rates to 80 or 90 percent conserves flour by utilizing more of the bran and germ of the wheat berry, while yielding a flour somewhere between white and whole wheat.

16. "Act of the Parliament of Canada P.C. 489 of January 22, 1942," in MSS 47241, "Enriched Foodstuffs," box 8, Williams-LOC.

17. Extensive discussion of debates between Cornell Bread advocates and enriched white bread backers can be found in Roger William Riis Papers, MSS 75875, box 9, Library of Congress, Washington, DC; Records of the Food and Drug Administration, Division of General Services, RG 88, "General Subject Files, 1951," box 1435–1438, National Archives II, College Park, MD (hereafter FDA-NA); "1952," box 2080, and "1954," box 2580, USDA-NA.

18. "Priority Goes to Energy," *Parent's Magazine*, April 1943, 50; "To Enrich or Not to Enrich: A Symposium," *Journal of Home Economics* 37 (1945): 397–40; "Tenth Anniversary of Bread Enrichment," *What's New in Home Economics* (1951): 526–32; "The Best Bread in History," *Today's Health*, April 1960, 42–43; Robert Froman, "Our Daily Bread," *Collier's*, August 11, 1951, 28–29; Phipard, "Changes in the Bread You Buy"; Sherwood, "Accomplishments in Cereal Fortification."

19. Helen S. Mitchell, "A First Step," *Journal of Home Economics* 37 (1945): 402.

20. A. Thomas, "Future Prospects for the Milling Industry," April 30, 1942, "Enriched Foodstuffs," box 8, Williams-LOC. Although it took several years, the use of enriched flour produced by millers eventually displaced dough-ready enrichment tablets marketed by yeast manufacturers.

21. Correspondence between Robert R. Williams and representatives of the milling and baking industry, found in "Diaries," box 1, "Enriched Foodstuff," box 8, and "Enrichment Promotion," box 11, Williams-LOC.

22. This section draws from Williams's letters and diaries, found in ibid.

23. The following paragraphs draw from correspondence found in "Diaries," box 1, Williams-LOC.

24. B. Stowe, "Mrs. Consumer Looks at Bread," *Northwest Miller*, March 4, 1947, 58–60.

25. "Diaries," box 1, "Enriched Foodstuff," box 8, and "Enrichment Promotion," box 11, Williams-LOC.

26. Amy Bentley, *Eating for Victory: Food Rationing and the Politics of Domesticity* (Urbana: University of Illinois Press, 1998), 67; Mary

Anne Meehan, interviewed by Louise G. Bassett, February 6, 1936, "American Life Histories: Manuscripts from the Federal Writer's Project, 1936–1940," http://memory.loc.gov/ammem/wpaintro/wpahome .html.

27. Thomas Parran, "Bread Fights a Famine," *Better Homes and Gardens,* April 1941, 16.

28. Ibid.; "A Bread Revolution," 26.

29. D. Marsh, "More for Your Money in Enriched Bread and Flour," *Good Housekeeping,* July 1942, 98–99.

30. Town Talk bread advertisement run during 1941.

31. Advertisement run in various editions of the *Syracuse Herald Journal* during 1941.

32. Quoted in "Bakers and Public Backsliding on Use of Enriched Bread," *Science News Letter,* February 7, 1942, 84.

33. "There is a bomb" advertisement from Fleischmann's 1942 enrichment campaign.

34. Mr. Smith of Standard Brands, Inc., "The Synthetic Route to a Successful Enrichment Program," September 16, 1942, "Enriched Foodstuffs," box 8, Williams-LOC.

35. Sherwood, "Accomplishments in Cereal Fortification."

36. James Tobey, "Enriched White Bread: A Greater Sales Asset," *Food Merchants' Advocate,* July 1942; Way and McCoy, *Establishing a Retail Bakery,* 2.

37. Mr. Smith of Standard Brands, Inc., "The Synthetic Route to a Successful Enrichment Program"; "The Best Bread in History."

38. William L. Lawrence, "Chemists Proclaim New Nutrition Era," *New York Times,* April 9, 1941, 28; Sebrell, "Urgent Problems in Nutrition for National Betterment"; Thomas C. Desmond, "Bread—Your New Perfect Food," in *Food in War and in Peace, Consolidated Report of the New York State Joint Legislative Committee on Nutrition,* ed. New York State Joint Legislative Committee on Nutrition (Albany: New York State Legislature, 1944).

39. "The Vital Story of Bread Enrichment," *Journal of Home Economics* 43, no. 9 (1951): 608; Froman, "Our Daily Bread." Local bakeries and bakers' associations around the country reprinted Williams's slogan in newspaper and magazine advertisements celebrating bread enrichment's tenth anniversary in 1951.

40. "Sociologist Looks at an American Community," *Life,* September 12, 1949, 108–19.

41. USDA Agricultural Marketing Service, *Consumers' Preferences among Bakers' White Breads of Different Formulas: A Survey in Rockford, Illinois (Marketing Research Report No. 118)* (Washington, DC: USDA, 1956).

42. Ibid.

43. A few examples of this trend include Lee Anderson, "Busted Staff of Life," *Atlantic Monthly,* December 1947, 112–13; Warren E. Siegmond, "Poisonous Dough for Your Bread Money," *American Mercury,* November 1958, 66–72; Clarence Woodbury, "Our Daily Bread," *Reader's Digest,* May 1945, 49–51.

44. USDA Agricultural Marketing Service, *Consumers' Preferences among Bakers' White Breads of Different Formulas;* Millers' National Federation, *What People Think about "Bread": Summary of Research Studies among Consumers and Nutrition Authorities* (Washington, DC: Millers' National Federation, 1948).

45. Data on consumption patterns in the preceding paragraphs drawn from Burke, "Pounds and Percentages"; Panschar, *Baking in America;* Phipard, "Changes in the Bread You Buy"; "Boost for Bread"; Desmond, "Bread—Your New Perfect Food"; Walsh and Evans, *Economics of Change in Market Structure, Conduct, and Performance;* Wirtz, "Grain, Baking, and Sourdough Bread"; Way and McCoy, *Establishing a Retail Bakery.*

46. USDA Agricultural Marketing Service, *Consumers' Preferences among Bakers' White Breads of Different Formulas.*

47. "Premium-Priced Breads: Are They Worth the Money?" *Consumer Reports,* March 1958, 158–60; W. H. Sebrell, "Recollections of a Career in Nutrition," *Journal of Nutrition* 115, no. 1 (1985): 23–38.

48. Woodbury, "Our Daily Bread."

49. Anderson, "Busted Staff of Life," 112.

50. Woodbury, "Our Daily Bread."

51. Correspondence between Robert R. Williams and representatives of the milling and baking industry, found in "Diaries," box 1, "Enriched Foodstuff," box 8, and "Enrichment Promotion," box 11, Williams-LOC.

52. On the trouble with 1950s nostalgia, see Stephanie Coontz, *The Way We Never Were: American Families and the Nostalgia Trap* (New York: Basic Books, 1992).

53. Steven Mintz, *Huck's Raft: A History of American Childhood* (Cambridge, MA: Belknap Press of Harvard University Press, 2004), 283.

54. K. A. Cuordileone, *Manhood and American Political Culture in the Cold War* (New York: Routledge, 2005); Douglas Field, *American Cold War Culture* (Edinburgh: Edinburgh University Press, 2005); Cynthia Hendershot, *Anti-Communism and Popular Culture in Mid-Century America* (Jefferson, NC: McFarland, 2003); Eugenia Kaledin, *Daily Life in the United States, 1940–1959: Shifting Worlds* (Westport, CT: Greenwood, 2000); Elaine Tyler May, *Homeward Bound: American Families in the Cold War Era* (New York: Basic Books, 2008); Guy Oakes, *The Imaginary War: Civil Defense and American Cold War Culture* (New

York: Oxford University Press, 1994); Lisle Abbott Rose, *The Cold War Comes to Main Street: America in 1950* (Lawrence: University Press of Kansas, 1999); Stephen J. Whitfield, *The Culture of the Cold War* (Baltimore: Johns Hopkins University Press, 1996).

55. Daniel Yergin calls this the genesis of the "national security state"—"the unified pattern of attitudes, policies, and institutions by which [organizing for perpetual confrontation] was to be effected." Daniel Yergin, *Shattered Peace: The Origins of the Cold War* (New York: Penguin Books, 1990), 5. This new and sustained cultural, political, and intuitional commitment to what Dean Acheson called "the long, long pull" is typically associated with Red-baiting, the supercharged military-industrial complex, and foreign entanglements, but it also seeped into the country's domestic culture. It found everyday expression as a culture of civil defense and obsessive concern about the invisible threat of Communist subversion. By 1950, at the latest, "The American people . . . had become exquisitely, constantly aware of communism anywhere and everywhere. Countless polls, editorials, and man-in-the-street interviews supported [this] observation, and there seemed no end to the torment." Rose, *The Cold War Comes to Main Street*, 22.

56. "Bread and Water Diet When A-Bomb Strikes," *Science News Letter,* November 19, 1951, 313; "The London Food Conference: A Summary of Findings," *Public Health Reports* 67, no. 7 (1952): 608–18; "Food in Civil Defense," *Technology Review* 55, no. 4 (1953): 198; Majorie M. Heseltine, "Feeding of Mothers and Children under Emergency Conditions," *Public Health Reports* 67, no. 9 (1952): 872–75.

57. Michael Paul Rogin, *Ronald Reagan, the Movie and Other Episodes in Political Demonology* (Berkeley: University of California Press, 1987), 240–45.

58. Cuordileone, *Manhood and American Political Culture in the Cold War.*

59. Froman, "Our Daily Bread." While marketing study after marketing study indicated that housewives' top two concerns in choosing bread were its softness and flavor, these were virtually indistinguishable across all major brands of standard white bread. Therefore, housewives turned to other distinguishing traits to make their decisions. Advertising of any kind weighed heavily in their choices, studies found, but nutrition seemed particularly important. According to one study, nutrition information was the number one thing housewives wanted to see on bread wrappers, beating out brand name, weight, and baking date. Nabisco, Inc., Market Planning Research Division, "A Survey of Consumers' Reactions to Vital Bread," 1963, Raymond Loewy Papers, MSS 62142, "Nabisco," box 152, Library of Congress, Washington, DC.

60. Siegmond, "Poisonous Dough for Your Bread Money."

61. Horace Reynolds, "Give Us Bread Not Fluff," *Christian Science Monitor,* November 12, 1949, 6.

CHAPTER 5. WHITE BREAD IMPERIALISM

1. This attitude has historical roots that predate the Cold War, of course. For an excellent survey, see Warren Belasco, *Meals to Come: A History of the Future of Food* (Berkeley: University of California Press, 2006).
2. European bread consumption statistics from League of Nations, "Rural Dietaries in Europe. Annex: Report on Bread," August 26, 1939, "France 1950–1954," box 152, FAS-NA. My account of the 1946–48 crisis in this section is drawn from Bentley, *Eating for Victory;* Harry Fornari, *Bread upon the Waters: A History of United States Grain Exports* (Nashville: Aurora, 1973); Thomas J. Knock, "Feeding the World and Thwarting Communists," in *Architects of the American Century,* eds. David Schmitz and T. Christopher Jesperson (Chicago: Imprint, 2000); Dan Morgan, *Merchants of Grain* (New York: Viking, 1979); Robert L. Paarlberg, *Food Trade and Foreign Policy: India, the Soviet Union, and the United States* (Ithaca, NY: Cornell University Press, 1985).
3. Harriman to U.S. Secretary of State, untitled cable, July 19, 1946, "United Kingdom, Breadstuffs, 1946–1949," box 966, FAS-NA.
4. Quoted in Bentley, *Eating for Victory,* 145. See also "Truman's Remarks to Citizen Food Committee," *New York Times,* October 2, 1947, 4.
5. Bentley, *Eating for Victory.*
6. "Bread on the Waters," *Consumers' Guide,* May 6, 1946, 79. See also "How to Do with Less Bread," *Life,* May 6, 1946, 30; "New Dark Bread Is Part of U.S. Contribution to the Grave World Food Crisis," *Life,* March 4, 1946, 79; "Greatest in History," *Time,* June 10, 1946; "Conserve Bread," *Parent's Magazine,* May 1946, 68; "Save Wheat," *American Home,* May 1946, 102. Examples of American skepticism about bread conservation are cited in Paul Mallon, "Overhauling of UNRA by Hoover Expected," Western Newspaper Union Syndication, April 28, 1947.
7. "Bread: It Is the First Concern of a Hungry World. Trouble Looms for the Nations Which Cannot Provide It," *Los Angeles Times,* August 10, 1947, E4; "Guns, Bread, and Butter," *Farm Journal,* September 1953, 24; H. R. Baukhage, "U.S. Farmer Will Beat Communism," Associated Press Syndication, October 2, 1947.
8. FAS Field Office in Paris to U.S. Secretary of State (declassified cable), "French Import Requirements, Food Items," May 12, 1947; FAS Field Office in Paris to U.S. Secretary of State (declassified cable), "Food Situation and Related Political Developments in France," February 20, 1947; FAS Field Office in Paris to U.S. Secretary of State (declassified cable),

"The Breadgrain Situation in France," April 9, 1947; FAS Field Office in Paris to U.S. Secretary of State (declassified cable), June 11, 1946, all in "France, Breadstuffs, 1946–1949," box 9, FAS-NA.

9. "Marshall-Aid Ship Cheered in France," *New York Times*, May 11, 1948, 20; Joseph Alsop and Stewart Alsop, "Food Is Politics," *Los Angeles Times*, May 4, 1946, A4.

10. U.S. Ambassador in Tehran to U.S. Secretary of State (declassified cable), "Irano-Soviet Wheat Agreement," December 3, 1949, "Iran, Breadstuffs, 1946–1949," box 780, FAS-NA.

11. FAS Field Office in Athens to U.S. Secretary of State, August 31, 1948, "Greece, Breadstuffs, 1946–1949," box 724, FAS-NA. See also Yergin, *Shattered Peace.*

12. "Food in Civil Defense." On the effect of the Berlin Airlift on civil defense planners' understanding of bread's role in the Cold War, see also "The London Food Conference: A Summary of Findings"; V. P. Syndenstricker, "Nutrition Conditions under Wartime Conditions," *Bulletin of the New York Academy of Medicine* (1943): 749–65; Heseltine, "Feeding of Mothers and Children under Emergency Conditions."

13. Yergin, *Shattered Peace,* 354.

14. Kaledin, *Daily Life in the United States;* Laura A. Belmonte, *Selling the American Way: U.S. Propaganda and the Cold War* (Philadelphia: University of Pennsylvania Press, 2008).

15. Kaledin, *Daily Life in the United States.* See also Ruth Oldenziel and Karin Zachmann, *Cold War Kitchen: Americanization, Technology, and European Users* (Cambridge, MA: MIT Press, 2009). For a classic expression of the shift in Americans' understanding of what made the country exceptional, see David Morris Potter, *People of Plenty: Economic Abundance and the American Character* (Chicago: University of Chicago Press, 1954).

16. Belmonte, *Selling the American Way.*

17. Records of the U.S. Information Agency, RG 306, American National Exhibition, Moscow, 1957–1959, "Press Clipping File," box 3, USDA-NA.

18. Rudolf Flesch, *Why Johnny Can't Read, and What You Can Do about It* (New York: Harper & Row, 1955); William B. Murphy, "The Challenge of the Future: An Overview," in *Food and Civilization: A Symposium* (Washington, DC: USIA Voice of America Lecture Series, 1966), 6.

19. Oriana Atkinson, "My Life behind the Iron Curtain," *Woman's Home Companion,* October 1946, 30–31; "Russian Works Longer for His Food, ECA Says," *Los Angeles Times,* August 22, 1949, 16; Victoria De Grazia, *Irresistible Empire: America's Advance through Twentieth-Century Europe* (Cambridge, MA: Belknap Press of Harvard University Press, 2005); J. A. Livingston, "U.S. and Soviet Price Systems Far Apart," *Big Spring (TX) Daily Herald,* June 10, 1956, 26.

20. "Some Reds Stand in Bread Lines," *Gastonian*, September 22, 1963, 2-A; "Bread Scarce in Soviet Cupboards," *Lima News*, September 24, 1963, 1.

21. Livingston, "U.S. and Soviet Price Systems Far Apart"; Lauren Soth, "Consumer Goods Scarce," *Corpus Christi Times*, August 30, 1955, 16; Willard Edwards, "Soviet Troops Confused," *Chicago Daily Tribune*, December 19, 1956, A3. Interestingly, some of these articles subtly (and not so subtly) introduce criticisms of U.S. industrial bread. They reverse the binary of good American bread versus bad Soviet bread, while reinforcing the larger architecture of alimentary exceptionalism.

22. Christopher Endy, *Cold War Holidays: American Tourism in France* (Chapel Hill: University of North Carolina Press, 2004); "Bread from France," *New York Times*, May 16, 1962, 37.

23. J.J., "Good Food Again" (letter to the editor), *Los Angeles Times*, June 11, 1948, A4. For an example of concerns about French bread's relation to military defeat during World War II, see McCay, "Bread of the Future."

24. "'Bread of Madness' Infects Town," *Life*, September 10, 1951, 25–27; Murphy, "The Challenge of the Future," 8.

25. Janet Nickerson, "Bread Gets an Airing," *New York Times*, March 13, 1955, SM52.

26. See, for example, Mark Hammond and Jacqueline Ruyak, "The Decline of the Japanese Diet: From MacArthur to McDonalds," *East West*, October 2008, 44–53.

27. On Japan's long struggles over the place of foreign foods in its diet, see Emiko Ohnuki-Tierney, "We Eat Each Other's Food to Nourish Our Body: The Global and the Local and Mutually Constituent Forces," in *Food in Global History*, ed. Raymond Grew (Boulder, CO: Westview, 1999); Katarzyna J. Cwiertka, "Popularizing a Military Diet in Wartime and Postwar Japan," *Asian Anthropology* 1 (2002): 1–30.

28. Yamakazi Baking Company, *From a Corn of Wheat: Yamakazi* (Tokyo: Yamakazi Baking Company, 1996).

29. "Survey of Bread and Flour Utilization by the Japanese People," 1950, Records of the Supreme Commander of the Allies Powers RG 331, Public Opinion and Sociological Research Division, "General Subject Files," National Archives II, College Park, MD (hereafter SCAP-NA).

30. "Supplementary School Lunch Program, Public Health and Welfare Bulletin," June 1948, Civil Affairs Section, Tohoku Civil Affairs Region, "Public Health and Welfare Activities, 1946–1951," box 258, SCAP-NA; "Report on Public Health and Welfare in Japan," c. 1949–1950, Economic and Scientific Section, Price and Distribution Division, "Food Branch, 1946–1951," box 8395, SCAP-NA.

31. "Supplementary School Lunch Program, Public Health and Welfare Bul-

letin"; "Tabulation of Public Opinion of School Lunch," July 25, 1951, Economic and Scientific Section, Price and Distribution Division, "Food Branch, 1946–1951," box 8395, SCAP-NA.

32. On Japanese attempts to connect wheat diets and military strength, which predate the postwar period, see Cwiertka, "Popularizing a Military Diet in Wartime and Postwar Japan."

33. "Survey of Bread and Flour Utilization by the Japanese People."

34. "The Complete School Lunch: Providing Bread and Butter," August 9, 1949, Civil Affairs Section, Hokkaido Civil Affairs Region, "Civil Affairs Files, 1945–1951," box 2534, SCAP-NA; "Instruction from Ministry of Education concerning School Lunch," n.d., Civil Affairs Section, Hokkaido Civil Affairs Region, "Civil Affairs Files, 1945–1951," box 2534, SCAP-NA; Vice Education Minister to Prefectural Governors, "Concerning the Encouragement and Popularization of the School Lunch Program," December 11, 1946, Headquarters Division, "Public Welfare Files, 1945–1951," box 2278, SCAP-NA; "Recent Tendencies of School Lunch Program and Counter Measures," 1949, Civil Information and Education Section, Education Division, Physical Education and Youth Affairs Branch, "Topical Files, 1946–1951," box 5721, SCAP-NA; Chief Manager of School Lunch, Health, and Physical Education Section, Hokkaido Board of Education, to SCAP GHQ, "Nowadays Condition of School Lunch in Hokkaido," c. 1950, Civil Affairs Section, Hokkaido Civil Affairs Region, "Civil Affairs Files, 1945–1951," box 2534, SCAP-NA.

35. "Instruction from Ministry of Education concerning School Lunch."

36. Chief Manager of School Lunch, Health, and Physical Education Section, Hokkaido Board of Education, to SCAP GHQ, "Nowadays Condition of School Lunch in Hokkaido."

37. J.L. Locke, "Suggestions for Improvement of the Health and Attitude of the Japanese People by Supplementing Their Diet with Enriched White Bread," August 3, 1949, Price and Distribution Division, "Food Branch, 1946–1951," box 8395, SCAP-NA; SCAP GHQ to J.L. Locke, September 26, 1949, Price and Distribution Division, "Food Branch, 1946–1951," box 8395, SCAP-NA.

38. General MacArthur to Ambassador Gasciogne, October 6, 1950, Price and Distribution Division, "Food Branch, 1946–1951," box 8395, SCAP-NA.

39. Reprinted in "Feeding the World's Hungry: Cure for Farm Troubles? An Interview with Ezra Taft Benson," *Altoona (PA) Mirror,* March 22, 1958, 15.

40. George E. Sokolsky, "China's Rice," Hearst Newspaper Syndication, January 17, 1953.

41. "Japanese Eat Various Types of Bread, Grow Taller," Associated Press Syndication, December 24, 1957.

42. Yamakazi Baking Company, *From a Corn of Wheat,* 176.

43. Recall that even occupation officials debated whether rice might be a more culturally appropriate bastion of strength. Strains of U.S. popular opinion had also made this argument. For example, a widely reprinted 1951 news piece argued, "The most important thing for the majority of the people of Asia is not Democracy, nor Communism, nor any political ideology—but food, which means life itself. And in most of Asia food is rice." "Who Controls Rice Supply Controls Asiatic Destiny," *Richwood Gazette,* June 22, 1951.

44. I am grateful to Robert Weis for calling this to my attention.

45. Pilcher, *¡Qué Vivan los Tamales!* 38.

46. Ibid., 77–81.

47. Robert Weis, "Por la verdad del Osito Bimbo: Consumo en el Mexico contemporáneo" (master's thesis, Universidad Nacional Autónoma de Mexico, 2001).

48. Pilcher, *¡Qué Vivan los Tamales!*

49. Steven A. Breth, *Principales corrientes de la investigación en el CIMMYT: Una retrospectiva* (Mexico D.F.: CIMMYT, 1986); Ramón Fernández y Fernández, *El trigo en Mexico* (Mexico D.F.: Banco Nacional de Crédito Agrícola, 1939).

50. Fernández y Fernández, *El trigo en Mexico,* 206.

51. Quoted in Enrique Ochoa, *Feeding Mexico: The Political Uses of Food since 1910* (Wilmington, DE: Scholarly Resources, 2000), 92.

52. My account of the Rockefeller Foundation's work in Mexico is drawn from Jonathan Harwood, "Peasant Friendly Plant Breeding and the Early Years of the Green Revolution in Mexico," *Agricultural History* 83, no. 3 (2009): 384–410; John H. Perkins, "The Rockefeller Foundation and the Green Revolution, 1941–1956," *Agriculture and Human Values* 7, no. 3 (1990): 6–18; Breth, *Principales corrientes de la investigación en el CIMMYT;* Joseph Cotter, *Troubled Harvest: Agronomy and Revolution in Mexico, 1880–2002* (Westport, CT: Praeger, 2003); Deborah Fitzgerald, "Exporting American Agriculture: The Rockefeller Foundation in Mexico, 1943–53," *Social Studies of Science* 16, no. 3 (1986): 457–83; Alicia Maria González, " 'El Pan de Cada Día': The Symbols and Expressive Culture of Wheat Bread in Greater Mexico" (PhD diss., University of Texas, Austin, 1986); Cynthia Hewitt de Alcántara, *Modernizing Mexican Agriculture: Socioeconomic Implications of Technological Change, 1940–1970* (Geneva: United Nations Research Institute for Social Development, 1976); Luisa Paré, *El Plan Puebla: Una revolución verde que está muy verde* (Mexico D.F.: United Nations Research Institute for Social Development, 1970); Andrew Chernocke Pearse, *Seeds of Plenty, Seeds of Want: Social and Economic Implications of the Green Revolution* (Oxford, UK: Oxford University Press, 1980); John H. Per-

kins, *Geopolitics and the Green Revolution: Wheat, Genes, and the Cold War* (New York: Oxford University Press, 1997); Pilcher, *¡Qué Vivan los Tamales!;* Edwin J. Wellhausen, "The Agriculture of Mexico," *Scientific American* 235, no. 3 (1976): 129–50; Angus Wright, *The Death of Ramón González: The Modern Agricultural Dilemna* (Austin: University of Texas Press, 1990).

53. These advances were impressive but limited. By the 1970s, for reasons discussed below, Mexico once again had to import wheat to meet its needs. For a more complete discussion, see Ochoa, *Feeding Mexico.*

54. Silvia Cherem, *Al grano: Vida y visión de los fundadores de Bimbo* (Mexico D.F.: Khalida, 2008), 67.

55. Ibid.; González, " 'El Pan de Cada Día,' " 96.

56. Oscar Lewis, *Tepoztlán, Village in Mexico* (New York: Holt, 1960), 11.

57. Aase Lionaes, "Award Ceremony Speech for Norman Borlaug," December 10, 1970, Oslo, http://nobelprize.org/nobel_prizes/peace/laureates/1970/press.html.

58. On the economic policies of the Mexican Miracle, see Héctor Aguilar Camín and Lorenzo Meyer, *In the Shadow of the Mexican Revolution: Contemporary Mexican History, 1910–1989* (Austin: University of Texas Press, 1993); Kevin J. Middlebrook, *The Paradox of Revolution: Labor, the State, and Authoritarianism in Mexico* (Baltimore: Johns Hopkins University Press, 1995); Juan Carlos Moreno-Brid and Jaime Ros, *Development and Growth in the Mexican Economy: A Historical Perspective* (Oxford, UK: Oxford University Press, 2009).

59. Michael Lipton and Richard Longhurst, *New Seeds and Poor People* (Baltimore: Johns Hopkins University Press, 1989).

60. Perkins, "The Rockefeller Foundation and the Green Revolution," 6.

61. Aguilar Camín and Meyer, *In the Shadow of the Mexican Revolution;* Werner Baer, "Import Substitution and Industrialization in Latin Amercia: Experiences and Interpretations," *Latin American Research Review* 7, no. 1 (1972): 95–122; Fitzgerald, "Exporting American Agriculture"; Harwood, "Peasant Friendly Plant Breeding"; Ochoa, *Feeding Mexico;* Paré, *El Plan Puebla;* Perkins, "The Rockefeller Foundation and the Green Revolution."

62. Harwood, "Peasant Friendly Plant Breeding"; Paré, *El Plan Puebla.*

63. Lipton and Longhurst, *New Seeds and Poor People,* 3; Vandana Shiva, *The Violence of the Green Revolution: Third World Agriculture, Ecology, and Politics* (London: Zed Books, 1991).

64. Bernhard Glaeser, *The Green Revolution Revisited: Critique and Alternatives* (London: Allen & Unwin, 1987); Lipton and Longhurst, *New Seeds and Poor People;* Paré, *El Plan Puebla;* Pearse, *Seeds of Plenty, Seeds of Want.*

65. Amartya Kumar Sen and Jean Drèze, *The Amartya Sen and Jean Drèze*

Omnibus (New York: Oxford University Press, 1999). See also Frances Moore Lappé, Joseph Collin, and Peter Rosset, *World Hunger: 12 Myths* (New York: Grove, 1998).

66. Warren Belasco and Eric Ross provide excellent accounts of the enduring appeal of Malthusian crisis narratives. Belasco, *Meals to Come;* Eric B. Ross, *The Malthus Factor: Population, Poverty, and Politics in Capitalist Development* (London: Zed Books, 1998).

67. The history of Grupo Bimbo is drawn from Cherem, *Al grano;* Jaime Crombie, "Man of the Year: Leading Mexico's Global Champion," *Latin Finance,* March 2010; Roberto Servitje, *Bimbo: Estrategia de éxito empresarial* (Mexico D.F.: Pearson Educación, 2003); Weis, "Por la verdad del Osito Bimbo."

68. Cherem, *Al grano,* 319.

69. For example, McWilliams, *Just Food;* Robert Paarlberg, *Starved for Science: How Biotechnology Is Being Kept out of Africa* (Cambridge, MA: Harvard University Press, 2008); Paarlberg, *Food Politics.*

CHAPTER 6. HOW WHITE BREAD BECAME WHITE TRASH

1. Bill Reed, "Redneck Chic: Endearment or Ridicule?" *Colorado Springs Gazette,* May 9, 2006, 1–3.

2. My analysis of white trash parties draws inspiration from a number of sources, including John Hartigan, "Unpopular Culture: The Case of 'White Trash,'" *Cultural Studies* 11, no. 2 (1997): 316–43; Daniel Harris, *Cute, Quaint, Hungry, and Romantic: The Aesthetics of Consumerism* (New York: Basic Books, 2000); George Lipsitz, *The Possessive Investment in Whiteness: How White People Profit from Identity Politics* (Philadelphia: Temple University Press, 2006); Greg Smith and Pamela Wilson, "Country Cookin' and Cross Dressin': Television, Southern White Masculinities, and Hierarchies of Cultural Taste," *Television New Media* 5 (2004): 175–94.

3. Jeff Foxworthy and David Boyd, *You Might Be a Redneck If . . .* (Nashville: Rutledge Hill, 2004).

4. Damian Whitworth, "Gutsy Rednecks Know How to Make a Splash," *Times* (London), July 10, 1999.

5. James Salter, *Dusk and Other Stories* (San Francisco: North Point, 1988).

6. This chapter owes a great debt to Warren Belasco's path-breaking history of counterculture food politics and its legacies, *Appetite for Change.* Other key sources informing this chapter include Peter Braunstein and Michael William Doyle, "Historicizing the American Counterculture of the 1960s and 1970s," in *Imagine Nation: The American Counterculture of the 1960s and '70s,* eds. Peter Braunstein and Michael William

Doyle (New York: Routledge, 2002); Craig Cox, *Storefront Revolution: Food Co-ops and the Counterculture* (New Brunswick, NJ: Rutgers University Press, 1994); Thomas Frank, *The Conquest of Cool: Business Culture, Counterculture, and the Rise of Hip Consumerism* (Chicago: University of Chicago Press, 1997); Stephanie Hartman, "The Political Palate: Reading Commune Cookbooks," *Gastronomica* 3, no. 2 (2003): 29–40; Maria McGrath, "Food for Dissent: A History of Natural Foods and Dietary Health Politics and Culture since the 1960s" (PhD diss., Lehigh University, Bethlehem, PA, 2005); Stephanie A. Slocum-Schaffer, *America in the Seventies* (Syracuse, NY: Syracuse University Press, 2003); David Steigerwald, *The Sixties and the End of Modern America* (New York: St. Martin's Press, 1995).

7. "Consumer Survey of Bread Wrapper Recognition," 1954, Loewy Papers, MSS 62142, "Gordon Baking," box 148; Sister Corita, *Enriched Bread by Corita, Camus, Wonder Bread* (1965).

8. Quoted in Belasco, *Appetite for Change*, 48.

9. Paula Giese, "The White Bread Scandal," *North Country Alternatives* 9 (1973): 6.

10. For example, Jerome Goldstein, "Earl Butz as Wonder Bread," *Clear Creed*, no. 14 (1972): 53–54.

11. Consumers also worried (erroneously) that federal bread regulations would prohibit the marketing of "health breads" containing soy protein and other nonsynthetic enrichment ingredients. Letters, news clippings, and reports related to these and other bread-additive anxieties are found in "General Subject Files, 1951–1953," boxes 1435–1438, 1562, 1711, FDA-NA. See also "Your Bread: How Safe Is It?" *Consumer Reports*, October 1949, 460–61.

12. On 1950s-era bread hearings, see Suzanne Junod, "Chemistry and Controversy: Regulating the Use of Chemicals in Foods, 1883–1959" (PhD diss., Emory University, Atlanta, 1994); "General Subject Files, 1951–1953," boxes 1435–1438, 1562, 1711, FDA-NA.

13. "General Subject Files, 1951," box 1435–1438, FDA-NA.

14. King called for the boycott against Wonder, Coca-Cola, and other food processors discriminating against African Americans in Memphis the night before his assassination. Although this took place in 1968, I consider it an example of the earlier approach to food activism because King's roots lay solidly in the late-1950s and early-1960s civil rights movement.

15. Crescent Dragonwagon, *The Commune Cookbook* (New York: Simon & Schuster, 1972); Beatrice Trum Hunter, *Beatrice Trum Hunter's Baking Sampler* (New Canaan, CT: Keats, 1972), 1. See also McGrath, "Food for Dissent."

16. Braunstein and Doyle, "Historicizing the American Counterculture of the 1960s and 1970s."

17. Edward Espe Brown, *The Tassajara Bread Book* (Berkeley: Shambhala, 1973), 12; "Digger Bread," *Mother Earth News* 1, no. 1 (1970): 1.

18. Brown, *The Tassajara Bread Book,* 12.

19. Mo Willett, *Vegetarian Gothic* (Harrisburg, PA: Stackpole Books, 1975), 87.

20. Dragonwagon, *The Commune Cookbook,* 18–20, passim.

21. Ibid., 128.

22. Ibid., 127.

23. Barbara Hansen, "A Harvest of Goodwill Celebrating Day of Bread," *Los Angeles Times,* October 23, 1969, J1–2.

24. E. J. Pyler, "Uniformity Vs. Conformity," *Baker's Digest,* October 1968, 7.

25. "Whole-Grain Bread Sales Seen Higher," *Los Angeles Times,* October 20, 1977, J14; Rose Lee Cravitz, "Variety Bread Sales Slow after Hot '76," *Supermarketing,* June 1977; Charles A. Stillwell, "A Study on Current Trends of Bread Consumption Prepared for Prof. Dik Twedt, University of Missouri," June 7, 1978, Ruth Emerson Library, American Institute of Baking, Manhattan, KS; "Sharp Gains Seen in Bread Consumption," *Milling and Baking News,* July 12, 1977; Barbara Love, "Variety Bread Sales Gain," *Supermarketing,* September 1976, 63.

26. Fred Robbins and David Ragan, *Richard Pryor: This Cat's Got 9 Lives!* (New York: Delilah Books, 1982).

27. International Multifoods, *Naturally Good Baking* (Minneapolis: International Multifoods, 1970), 1.

28. "Chicago's Bread Shop: A Cooperative Business That Serves the People," *Rising Up Angry,* March 17–April 7, 1974, 10; Ray Wagner, "Little Bread Company: A Socialist Working Collective," *Northwest Passage,* April 1974, 8.

29. Laurel Robertson, Carol Flinders, and Bronwen Godfrey, *Laurel's Kitchen: A Handbook for Vegetarian Cookery and Nutrition* (New York: Bantam Books, 1976), 50.

30. McGrath, "Food for Dissent."

31. Peggy Orenstein, "The Femivore's Dilemma," *New York Times Magazine,* March 11, 2010, 11.

32. Ibid. Critiques of the piece include Laura Flanders, "The Femivore's Real Dilemma," *Nation,* http://www.thenation.com/blog/femivores-real-dilemma; Bonnie Azab Powell, "The 'Femivore': New Breed of Feminist or Frontier Throwback?" *Ethicurean,* http://www.ethicurean.com/2010/03/14/femivore/; Members of WAM! "Femivores in the Henhouse: Feminists Debate the Meaning of 'Chicks with Chicks,'" *In These Times,* http://www.inthesetimes.com/article/5914/femivores_in_the_hen house/.

33. Quoted in McGrath, "Food for Dissent," 151.

34. For more on this shift, see Belasco, *Appetite for Change;* McGrath, "Food for Dissent."

35. Bernard Pacyniak, "White Bread Poised for a Comeback," *Bakery,* August 1985, 88–90.

36. Leonard Sloane, "Baking Industry Is Rising above Its Past Conservatism," *New York Times,* October 9, 1969; Walsh and Evans, *Economics of Change in Market Structure, Conduct, and Performance.*

37. "Control on Food Ads Asked of U.S. Agencies," *Los Angeles Times,* February 16, 1971.

38. Examples include "Digger Bread"; Ed Minteer, "Our Slant: Order Certain to Prevail," *Albuquerque Journal,* November 1, 1970, A4; John Nobel Wilford, "White Bread Diet Starves Rats, Scientist Reports," *New York Times,* October 22, 1970, 32; "White Bread Fatal," *Alternate Society* 3, no. 1 (1971): 1.

39. Jeanne Voltz, "Faddists Do Some Good, Says Expert," *Los Angeles Times,* November 20, 1972, F3.

40. Senate Select Committee on Nutrition and Human Needs, *Dietary Goals for the United States* (Washington, DC: U.S. Government Printing Office, 1977). Under pressure from the cattle, dairy, and other industries, the report's recommendations were revised and tamed later that same year.

41. "Sharp Gains Seen in Bread Consumption"; Cravitz, "Variety Bread Sales Slow after Hot '76"; Love, "Variety Bread Sales Gain"; Patricia Wells, "In U.S. Kitchens Bread Baking Is on the Rise," *New York Times,* April 19, 1978, C1; "Fiber Breads on the Move!" *Bakery Production and Management,* November 1976, 66–72. *Baking Industry* marked the fiber era with a series of articles in its December 1976 issue.

42. This account of Pepperidge Farms draws on "Rudkin of Pepperidge," *Time,* July 14, 1947; "Margaret Rudkin: Champion of the Old-Fashioned," *Time,* March 21, 1960; "Bread Company Notes 25th Year," *New York Times,* September 20, 1962, 37; "Henry Rudkin" (obituary), *New York Times,* April 23, 1966, 31; "Mrs. Margaret Rudkin" (obituary), *New York Times,* June 2, 1967, 41; Jean Hewitt, "New Breads Boast Natural Ingredients," *New York Times,* March 20, 1972, 44; Clarence Woodburn, "Our Daily Bread," *Reader's Digest,* May 1945, 49–51.

43. This account of Arnold Bakers draws on Hewitt, "New Breads Boast Natural Ingredients"; Robert D. McFadden, "Paul Dean Arnold" (obituary), *New York Times,* April 6, 1985, 26; Mimi Sheraton, "If Bread Boredom Sets In, Try an Innovative Slice," *New York Times,* February 22, 1976, 22.

44. Pacyniak, "White Bread Poised for a Comeback." See also Martha Shulman, "The Graining of America," *Texas Monthly,* December 1978, 160–66; Cravitz, "Variety Bread Sales Slow after Hot '76."

45. Mimi Sheraton, "The Good Foods of '76 and Some of the Bad," *New*

York Times, December 27, 1976, 44; "Fiber Breads on the Move!" See also Levenstein, *Paradox of Plenty,* 198.

46. Sheraton, "If Bread Boredom Sets In, Try an Innovative Slice."

47. John L. Hess, " 'Plasticized, Tasteless Breads' Give Rise to a Kitchen Revolt," *New York Times,* October 4, 1973, 52. See also Wells, "In U.S. Kitchens Bread Baking Is on the Rise"; Levenstein, *Paradox of Plenty;* Karen Hess, "Boom . . . in Bread," *Vogue,* April 1979, 272; Craig Clairborn and Pierre Franz, "For the Do-It-Yourself Baker," *New York Times,* August 15, 1982, SM46; "Five Healthy Breads to Make from One Basic Recipe," *Glamour,* January 1979, 41; "Fiber in New Bread Is Wood Pulp, Not Grain, McGovern Says," *Los Angeles Times,* April 1, 1977, A30; Marian Burros, *Pure and Simple: Delicious Recipes for Additive-Free Cooking* (New York: William Morrow, 1978), 24; Donald Davis, "The Wheat in Bread," *Los Angeles Times,* July 14, 1974, J11; Jean Mayer, "Investigating Charge of Adulterated Darker Bread," *Los Angeles Times,* December 5, 1974, K13.

48. Hess, "Boom . . . in Bread."

49. David Harvey, *A Brief History of Neoliberalism* (Oxford, UK: Oxford University Press, 2007), 25.

50. Gary S. Cross, *An All-Consuming Century: Why Commercialism Won in Modern America* (New York: Columbia University Press, 2000); Harvey, *A Brief History of Neoliberalism.* Ronald Butler spoke of the way baking followed this trend toward segmentation and niche marketing in a February 13, 1986, speech, "Trends in the Baking Industry," at the American Institute of Baking, Manhattan, KS. Transcript available at the institute's Ruth Emerson Library.

51. Heather Brown, "Vying to Become the 'Starbucks' of Bread," *Modern Baking,* September 1997, 70–78. See also "The New Multi-Unit Retail Bakeries," *Modern Baking,* August 1995; "Artisan Bread Popularity Creates Challenges for Bakers," *Modern Baking,* June 1997, 32; Margaret Littman, "Bread Rises to the Occasion," *Bakery Production and Marketing,* May 15, 1996, 52–64; "The Rise of Speciality Bread," *Baking Buyer,* August 1997, 26–29.

52. Carol Meres Krosky, "Retailers Sharpen Focus on Specialty Products," *Bakery,* July 1986, 120–32. See also Pacyniak, "White Bread Poised for a Comeback"; Stillwell, "A Study on Current Trends of Bread Consumption."

53. Mimi Sheraton, "A Toast to Ethnic Bakeries," *New York Times,* April 20, 1977, 57.

54. Bernard Pacyniak, "Making the Right Move," *Bakery,* May 1989, 50–51.

55. Nan Ickeringill, "Food: The Flavor of France in Bread," *New York Times,* April 15, 1963, 52.

56. Interview by author at the American Institute of Baking, Manhattan, Kansas, September 26, 2006.

57. Dragonwagon, *The Commune Cookbook,* 17.

58. Greg Beato, "In Our Foodie Culture, White Bread Is Toast," *Washington Post,* August 15, 2010, B3.

59. Ibid.

60. Ernst Matthew Mickler, *White Trash Cooking* (Berkeley, CA: Ten Speed, 1986); Connie McCabe, "KC BBQ," *Saveur,* May 21, 2007.

61. Crimson Spectre, "White Trash Manifesto," lyrics, *S/T* (Fredericksburg, VA: Magic Bullet Records, 2004).

62. Zimmers Hole, "White Trash Momma," lyrics, *Legion of Flames* (West Yorkshire, UK: HevyDevy Records, 2001).

CONCLUSION. BEYOND GOOD BREAD

1. Sandor Katz, *Wild Fermentations: The Flavor, Craft, and Nutrition of Life-Culture Foods* (New York: Chelsea Green, 2003), 32.

2. The original spark for this chapter emerged from a conversation with Melanie DuPuis.

3. Ann Vaughan-Martini and Alessandro Martini, "Facts, Myths, and Legends on the Prime Industrial Microorganism," *Journal of Industrial Microbiology* 14 (1995): 514–22. Organized use of yeasts for bread and fruit-wine production began around 6000 BCE, and what was probably the first "human-initiated" fermentation (the brewing of sickly sweet, slightly fizzy, mildly alcoholic wine from honey and water) may date as far back as 15000 BCE. Katz, *Wild Fermentations;* Isak Pretorius, "Tailoring Wine Yeast for the New Millennium: Novel Approaches to the Ancient Art of Winemaking," *Yeast* 16 (2000): 675–729; Graeme Walker, *Yeast Physiology and Biotechnology* (New York: Wiley & Sons, 1998).

4. Pretorius, "Tailoring Wine Yeast for the New Millennium"; Vaughan-Martini and Martini, "Facts, Myths, and Legends on the Prime Industrial Microorganism."

5. This operates through numerous pathways, but yeast's importance in animal nutrition plays a key role. *Drosophila melanogaster,* for example, a fruit fly indigenous to even the cleanest winery, consumes prodigious quantities of yeast, blending *Saccharomyces* DNA in its digestive tract and spreading mutated yeast spores through the environment via its feces. Sandra Rainieri, Carlo Zambonelli, and Yoshinobu Kaneko, "Saccharomyces Sensu Stricto: Systematics, Genetic Diversity, and Evolution," *Journal of Bioscience and Bioengineering* 96, no. 1 (2003).

6. M. de Barros Lopes, J. R. Bellon, N. J. Shirley, and P. F. Ganter, "Evidence for Multiple Interspecific Hybridisation in Saccharomyces Sensu Stricto Species," *FEMS Yeast Research* 1 (2002): 323–31.

7. Dominique Fournier, "A Gift from the Gods," *Slow: The International Herald of Taste*, July–September 2001.

8. On companion species, see Donna Jeanne Haraway, *The Companion Species Manifesto: Dogs, People, and Significant Otherness* (Chicago: Prickly Paradigm, 2003).

9. On the biopolitics of fermentation, see Heather Paxson, "Post-Pasteurian Cultures: The Micropolitics of Raw-Milk Cheese in the United States," *Cultural Anthropology* 23, no. 1 (2008): 15–47.

INDEX